Rome's De...
to Greece

Current and forthcoming titles in the Bristol Classical Paperbacks series:

ROME'S DEBT
TO GREECE

Alan Wardman

First published in 1976 by Paul Elek Ltd
This edition published in 2002 by
Bristol Classical Press
an imprint of
Gerald Duckworth & Co. Ltd
61 Frith Street
London W1D 3JL
e-mail: inquiries@duckworth-publishers.co.uk
Website: www.ducknet.co.uk

A catalogue record for this book is available
from the British Library

ISBN 1-85399-630-0

Printed in Great Britain by
Booksprint

CONTENTS

PREFACE

The aim of this book is to offer a brief outline of Roman opinion about the Greeks and Greek thought. There are two separable but related questions: first, what did Romans think of earlier and contemporary Greeks, and, secondly, how did they adapt Greek ideas and discoveries to suit their own purposes? In modern times interpretations of Greece and Greek ideas have had an important influence on European thinking, and I hope that an outline of the Roman view will be useful, if only by way of contrast. I am therefore concerned with defining philhellenism in its Roman variant and with exploring the nature of Rome's intellectual debt to Greece.

Most of my evidence comes from the so-called golden and silver ages of Latin literature, from the time of Cicero to the middle of the second century A.D. There were powerful Hellenic influences both earlier and later, but this was the great period of classical Latin when many writers achieved a kind of mature dependence on their Greek models. Within this period I have drawn mainly on the historians and reflective writers on oratory and philosophy, as they were usually the most explicit about their relationship with Greek thought. The sources for a study such as this are very unequal, and there is a risk of treating a phrase or epigram as seriously as a longer work; I have tried to avoid this pitfall, and have sought, for example, to let Cicero's voice be heard above the rest of the chorus.

Romans first began to formulate their ideas about Greece in the course of their eastward expansion in the second century, and this historical background is discussed briefly in the introduction. The first chapter analyzes some of the stereotypes which underlie Roman descriptions of Greek character, and chapter two considers whether Romans were motivated by philhellenism in their political relationships and in their attitudes to Greek language and art. The remaining chapters illustrate Roman criticisms of Greek tradition and theory in particular areas: the value of

Homeric poetry, the significance to Rome of Greek history and Greek historians; the nature of rhetoric; and the transference of Greek philosophy into Latin. The sequence of these chapters is meant to reflect the ancient educational order, and is not an order of literary merit. I have endeavoured to indicate what the Romans knew and how they used their knowledge.

The contrast between Romans and Greeks should not lead us to think that there was a permanent division between a ruling power (Rome) and a larger world of subjects (e.g. Greeks). The Roman empire can be regarded as a successor to the Hellenistic kingdoms; just as Greeks had been important in Ptolemaic Egypt, so too at Rome they came to wield power and influence, whether or not they had acquired the citizenship or senatorial rank. Men like Appian and Arrian thought of themselves as Romans. What I have in view is the attitude and sensibility of those Romans whose primary allegiance was to Latin and to traditional ideas associated with the past greatness of Rome; many of them were consciously striving to make a literature that would equal or surpass the Greek on which they drew.

It is a pleasure to acknowledge the advice and encouragement I have received from Tessa Rajak, F. Robertson and R. D. Williams, of Reading University; J. B. Trapp of the Warburg Institute; and my wife, Judith Wardman. To all of them and to Doreen Janes, the secretary of the Classics Department at Reading, I express my warmest thanks.

INTRODUCTION

Horace's well-known phrase, 'captured Greece took her fierce victor captive and brought the arts into rustic Latium', is a reminder that Roman literary taste was developed by study of the Greek classics. In the same poem (*Epistles* 2.1) Horace also shows us that the Greek influence affected Roman life as well as Roman literature. He draws a striking contrast between the practical 'pre-Greek' Roman and his latter-day equivalent, no longer innocent of Greek or Greek ways. The former delighted in expounding the law, lending money on strict security, listening to his elders and giving sound (financial) advice to his juniors; the new Romans, however, are said to be solemn devotees of scribbling and the relaxed life. Horace's light irony points to the fact that the Roman experience of Greece did more than set new standards in literary taste. It caused profound changes in Roman society as a whole and modified Roman values. Since many of these changes seemed regrettable to the writers of the late republic and early empire, their attitudes will be more readily understood if we consider the effects of Rome's expansion into the Greek world in the second century B.C. Even though Rome had been exposed to some sort of Greek influence from an early date in her history, this part of the age of expansion was a decisive period.

Many of the details about earlier Roman history are uncertain, but there is enough information to enable us to follow the main outline of events and to estimate the character of society. Between the end of Etruscan dominance (which for Romans was dramatized in the expulsion of the last Tarquin in 509 B.C.) and the early third century, Rome engaged in a series of wars until she came to control much of the Italian peninsula. Her victories were won by a citizen-army and by political leaders who had much in common with the soldiers they led. Both groups were made up of farmers who fought to defend their land or acquire more; there was probably little difference of scale between the land-holding of the general and that of the more prosperous soldiers. Agriculture, in the form of subsistence farming, and war, which was a defence of agricultural interests, helped to unify society and give it a common aim. The values of this society were stern and practical. Since defence and victory were all-important, men admired successful generals who won glory for themselves by their service to the state; wealth was not highly prized and it was seldom found among people who worked the land in order to support a family, rather than to make a profit. Both greater and lesser Romans were attached to one another by the ties of good faith (*fides*); the more important were obliged to requite the services of their dependants. It was a conservative society, with great respect for ancestral custom (*mos maiorum*). The political structure was oligarchical in spirit, as the power of the leading magistrates was limited by short tenure of office and by regard for the experienced men who formed the Roman senate. This early Rome was a somewhat dour and narrow city-state, which fought hard to survive, but it was unlike other city-states in one important respect, since it was more generous with grants of full or partial citizenship to other places in Italy. This political generosity, whatever its origin, played a large part in making Rome a great power.

There was, however, a darker side to this picture of the Romans in the fifth and fourth centuries B.C. Some political leaders were arrogant or tried to keep power beyond the lawful term. The story of Coriolanus shows that a general's pride in martial exploits could be divisive. Above all, society was torn by a long-continuing struggle between patricians and plebeians. Through a conflict that lasted some two hundred years the latter gradually secured the right to hold the offices which had at first been monopolized by the patricians. But Rome still remained an oligarchy, in which the holding of high office determined a man's position in society. The true beneficiaries of the long conflict between these groups were a relatively few plebeian families who now associated with surviving patrician lines on terms of equality; pride in patrician lineage did not die out, but what mattered most was whether a family had reached high office over several generations. In this way a broader but still hereditary oligarchy was maintained.

Peninsular Rome had demonstrated her military and political superiority over the other powers in Italy by 208 B.C. Economically, however, she was not as advanced as the Greek city-states of the south: her trade was less developed and she did not establish her coinage until about 269 B.C. Her agricultural economy was viable as long as her peasant-soldiers had time to farm as well as to fight, but once the armies became involved in longer campaigns or wars outside Italy, the strain on this class was to be intolerable.

Between 264 and 148 B.C. Rome became a great power, the dominant force in international politics. For much of the third century she was engaged in a 'double war' against Carthage; these Punic wars, especially the second, Hannibalic war, were the most serious military threat ever faced by Rome. Victory over Carthage gave Rome two large spheres of influence in the western Mediterranean, Spain and Sicily, though the conquest of Spain was not to be completed until the Augustan age. In the second century, Rome continued her expansion into the eastern Mediterranean, where the dominant powers were the Hellenistic kingdoms, Macedonia, Syria and Egypt. Roman policy was probably motivated by a kind of defensive imperialism, the desire to prevent any one power from constituting a threat to her own security; annexation of territory was to follow later. Philip V of Macedonia was defeated in 197, Antiochus of Syria in 190 and Perseus of Macedonia in 168 B.C.; and the Macedonians' last feeble attempt to remain an independent power was defeated in the brief war of 149–148 B.C. Rome had by now overpowered the armies of the most advanced states in the known world. In one sense the second-century wars in the Greek world should be seen as part of a lengthy process, the overseas expansion of Rome; but the consequences of these same wars were unique in that they brought about a continuing interpenetration of Greek and Roman ways.

The foreign wars of this whole period enriched Rome and Italy. Defeated states were obliged to pay war-indemnities, and ambitious generals plundered tribes and towns. Although the senate was no friend of indiscriminate plundering, taking war- booty of this sort was regarded as legitimate if the Roman state was engaged in a 'just war' against the victims. To a certain extent the Roman state benefited as a whole; after the campaigns of Manlius Vulso in 187 B.C. the treasury was able to pay off the war-loans raised during the Hannibalic war, and later on the tribute was abolished. But much of the wealth stayed in the possession of the eminent senatorial politicians who led Rome's armies to victory. The new riches won from the Greek world, in the form of money and servile manpower, changed the nature of the Roman agricultural economy and altered the quality of political life. Rome also began to develop a new business-class, which became wealthy through the profits on trade and state-contracts.

The safe, traditional investment was in land; hence one obvious outlet for money was to add to the size of one's land-holdings. The means were now available and so was the opportunity, since the nature of foreign wars made it difficult, if not impossible, for Rome's peasant-soldiers to serve abroad and still attend to their farms. Although the peasant-farmer did not become extinct, larger holdings tended to increase. On some estates cheap slave-labour and acquaintance with foreign techniques enabled the owners to develop a type of farming which was new in Italy. From mixed farming for subsistence they could turn to cattle-ranching for profit. Foreigners supplied the gangs of slaves (it has been estimated that a quarter of a million slaves came to Italy between 200 and 150 B.C.); from abroad too came the knowledge of the transhumance system of pasturage, which exploited the higher land in summer and brought the cattle down to the lowlands for winter. On such farms there was no place for the small farmer who had fought and was still fighting in Rome's legions. This change was fraught with serious consequences. Tiberius Gracchus, who introduced land reform in 133 B.C., was concerned about the decline in the number of peasant-farmers. At the end of the second century the property qualification for military service was removed. Men who served in the armies began to look increasingly to their generals to distribute land to them after victory as the reward for their loyal service.

Disposable wealth also caused changes in political life. It was still true that military glory was highly valued and the great conquerors, men like Flamininus, the Scipios and Aemilius Paulus, deserved their prestige. The wealth procured by victory could be spent on acquiring popularity. The conquerors erected triumphal arches and had new temples built, temples which did honour to a god and also helped to keep a politician's family in the public eye. Those who sought office could and did spend large sums on the promotion of games and festivals, of which there were an increasing number. The important Romans now had many more dependants (*clientes*) than their forebears could have maintained. And some, like Flamininus, had contacts in the Greek world which added to their political weight. When overseas communities sent presents of corn to Rome, they were often bearing witness to the visible power of a politician who by custom looked after their interests. Thus wealth gradually produced a gap between the few who sought office and the mass of the people, whereas in the past, before the second-century expansion, the leading men had not been so differentiated by their possessions.

Aemilius Paulus, who is said to have died a poor man, was still wealthy by the standards of the austere Roman past.

Money and slaves were two principal forms of wealth. Another was the artistic treasures which many of the victorious generals brought from the Greek world to adorn the city of Rome. Marcellus, it seems, was the first to bring back art-trophies, after his capture of Syracuse in 211 B.C. Both then and later, Romans debated about the ethics of making such acquisitions. They were seldom bothered about the rights of the owners who had been deprived, but some were concerned about the possible adverse effect on the Roman people as a whole, who had long been accustomed to plainer, less artistic monuments of victory. Critics felt that the new Rome was becoming more beautiful but less true to itself than in the past. The Greek Polybius, much though he admired Rome's achievement, agreed with these critics, on the grounds that the public display of Greek art stood for a departure from the traditional education in martial valour.

There is no doubt that foreign wealth, much of it from Greek sources, had far-reaching effects on Roman life. Romans of the late republic showed a keen, if disapproving, interest in the phenomenon. Sallust gave a late date to this invasion of wealth and held that Sulla's return from the province of Asia in 83 B.C. brought corruption in its train. Livy, however, blamed the earlier commander Manlius Vulso whose army had acquired a liking for art-objects and expensive furniture in its campaigns in Asia (187 B.C). The reasons for this difference of opinion about the exact date of Rome's decline through wealth need not detain us here. Both historians rightly agree on the essential fact that Roman ways and standards had been altered by the accumulated riches of the Greek east; though Roman valour and virtue had proved its right to dispose of this wealth as a result of victory in war, the new prosperity changed the old Roman character for the worse.

Increased contact with the Greek world also introduced a taste for alien modes of behaviour. Though Romans, as far as we know, did not play the Spaniard or the Carthaginian, they certainly sought to ape and emulate the Greek. Scipio Africanus, when he was in Sicily before his invasion of North Africa, enjoyed visiting the *palaestra* and even wore Greek clothes, with a view, perhaps, to making himself acceptable to the local Greeks. The compliment to the Sicilians was treated as a mark of unRoman behaviour by his political enemies in Rome. In the Greek world some pursuits, such as dancing and music, were socially acceptable, whereas it was thought to be unbecoming for a serious Roman to demean himself by such activities. To some extent complaints about Romans indulging in these Greek practices were merely another weapon in the armoury of Roman abuse directed at political opponents; nonetheless it seems clear that many upper-class Romans had developed a taste for spending money on hedonistic behaviour which showed itself in Greek forms. Polybius confirms the Roman sense of a moral decline; he says (31.25) that Romans had picked up easy-going Greek ways in the war against Perseus and that Roman nobles were now spending large sums on drink, handsome slaves and rare foods.

Men also began to think that Greek duplicity was contaminating the conduct of Roman politics and preparations for war. The senate was displeased when it listened to the report of its representatives at the start of the third Macedonian war (171 B.C.). The envoys had acted with too much guile and indirectness, and their manoeuvres smacked of 'Greek cunning'. Roman tradition looked back with pride to the austere Fabricius, the third-century hero who had fought against King Pyrrhus: he had refused a diplomatic present and had honourably informed the king of a secret proposal made by his own doctor to poison him for a bribe. It should be added that bribery, according to Polybius, was prevalent in Greece. That was why the Aetolians found it impossible to believe that Flamininus had agreed to discuss terms with Philip V without some inducement. Though some Romans remained loyal to their old ways, others adapted themselves to the expectations of the Greeks.

Religion too was subject to influences from the Greek world, though in this field the second century was a relatively late stage in the Hellenization of Rome. The gods of early Roman society had been functional powers, related to the needs of an agricultural community. The Roman state religion of the fifth and fourth centuries had imported and accepted certain Hellenic practices; the gods were represented in human form, they were housed in temples and sometimes feasts were held in their honour in which they were deemed to participate (*lectisternia*). The object of the state religion was to make sure that the 'peace of the gods' was intact; if Rome lost a battle or unnatural events occurred, it was necessary to carry out the right ritual so that the peace could be restored. It was not a religion which would provide emotional satisfaction for the individual. The religions of the Hellenistic world were eventually to provide the citizens of Rome with beliefs and rituals that helped to satisfy the individual's sense of mystery. But in the second century the senate tried to guard against the orgiastic side of new religions from abroad. It was discovered in 186 B.C. that the worship of Bacchus was so wide-spread in Italy that it was felt to be a conspiracy against public order and morals. The senate did not proscribe the cult but it laid down strict conditions to be observed by those who could justify their worship of this god.

The inadequacy of the state religion might also be exposed by the influence of Greek philosophy. Epicureanism, which denied that the gods are concerned with human affairs, was obnoxious to traditionally minded Romans, and Epicureans were banned from the city in 173 and 161 B.C. Some Pythagorean books were burned as a public danger. The scepticism of the New Academy, the practice, that is, of arguing both for and against a case, could well be used to shake men's trust in the gods and traditional morality. But much philosophy, we should remember, was deistic and could coexist with the state religion like the mystery religions from the Hellenistic east. Besides, no Roman aristocrat needed to take lessons in doubt from the Greeks in order to realize that the state religion could be manipulated. Roman wilfulness and' pride had already practised this art.

These Greek influences helped to create a different society at Rome, with other values than those which had once prevailed. The Roman of the second century was beginning to inhabit a new world. One more example will serve to indicate the scale of change. The slave-immigrants to Italy included many Greeks or men with Greek skills—doctors, teachers, cooks, secretaries and so on. Such men, unlike the slaves condemned to a short life of ranching, were sometimes well rewarded and were often manu-mitted. This class of freedmen therefore continued to grow in numbers and influence, as they knew arts which their employers needed and could afford even if they disdained to practise them. The freedmen constituted a fresh outside element in Roman society; clientship bound them to their patrons, but they were strangers to much of the Roman tradition.

So far we have examined changes in conduct and life-style which can be attributed to the interaction with Greeks in the second century. In this period too the Romans began to form a good opinion of themselves and to take an adverse view of the Greeks. They based their opinions on their own success in war and politics. In the wars against Macedonia and Syria between 214 and 148 B.C., Rome's victories did not always come quickly but they were relatively easy; the heavy losses of Perseus' army, defeated at Pydna in 168 B.C., showed that the Romans (helped to an extent by their Greek allies) had a clear margin of superiority. Romans had justifiable grounds for supposing that their legions surpassed 'in courage and technical expertise' the phalanx of their Macedonian adversaries. The legionary formation was shown to be more flexible than the phalanx when a veteran tribune outmanoeuvred the army of Philip V at the battle of Cynoscephalae (197 B.C.). Some Romans, like the elder Cato, covered ground which was already consecrated in Greek history. Cato took part in a manoeuvre which helped to turn the position of Antiochus' army at Thermopylae, and he could think that the recent exploits of Roman armies deserved even more praise than the unsuccessful resistance of Leonidas against the Persians. Roman pride in the army helped to create a feeling that Romans had won because of their sterling military character, that all they lacked was a brilliant historian to set them above the fame of the Greeks of history.

Roman self-congratulation was echoed by the praise of Polybius, who devoted a lengthy digression to a study of the Romans at war. He admired Roman military discipline, believing that the Roman system of rewards and punishments contributed to good order and eventual success. The Romans, according to him, were adept at taking good ideas from others and putting them to even better use. Thus Roman soldierly competence was increased by the use of the Spanish sword. When the Romans pitched camp, they sought to overcome the difficulties of a given site in order to adhere to certain fixed principles. Greeks, however, were lazier; they were less prepared for hard work and would do their utmost to fit their camp to the terrain instead of seeking to alter the lay-out of the land in order to suit the prime requirements of military security.

The pro-Roman Greek Polybius agreed with his Roman aristocratic friends that the Roman was better at war. It was a superiority based on courage, discipline and adaptability; the well-organized effort of Rome did not find it difficult to overcome Macedonians and Greeks. Roman opinion did not respect contemporary Greeks and Macedonians as soldiers and generals. Carthage had been far more serious as a military threat, and survived as a war-bogey in Roman rhetoric as well as in the *Aeneid*. The legendary reputation of the Greeks and Macedonians as warriors seemed insignificant when compared with recent events like Hannibal's defeat of Roman armies in their homeland and his long occupation of Italy. It should also be remembered that Rome met with no major set-backs in her wars in Greece in the second century B.C., whereas campaigns in the Spanish peninsula were lengthy, less rewarding and sometimes discreditable. The memory of Carthage and the never-ending wars in Spain reinforced the idea that the Greek world was no match for Roman military prowess.

In politics and administration, as in war, Roman self-esteem was enhanced through experience of the Greek east in the second century. The world of Hellenistic politics was dominated by the great powers, Macedonia, Syria and Egypt; the federations called the Achaean and Aetolian leagues, Rhodes and Pergamum were powers of the second rank but still important. Independent city-states no longer flourished as they had in the classic age of the fifth century. But the speeches of contemporary Greek politicians continually stirred their audiences with reminders of their past freedom and equality. In the Roman view these pretensions seemed to be at variance not only with the past glories of Greece but also with present capabilities. Athens, for example, could not call on many battalions to fight for her cause against the misdemeanors of Philip V. Roman policy in mainland Greece increasingly favoured those politicians who stood for law and order and for the protection of men with property and land. Roman statesmen, as landed aristocrats themselves, were naturally inclined to support those whose position resembled their own, men whose interest was against internal revolution.

We have already noticed that Roman politicians built up systems of patronage in the Greek world. In Rome and Italy the importance of a politician was measured by the number of his dependants; he was as great as the client-system of his family group. The Greeks found little difficulty in accommodating themselves to this practice as they had been used to seeking the influential support of Hellenistic kings. They turned now to court the Romans. When Flamininus, who had proclaimed the freedom of Greece in 195 B.C., was appointed as a special envoy to assist Acilius Glabrio, it was because he had political connections in Greece. Similarly the father of the Gracchi had a *clientela* in parts of Macedonia and Greece. The system only developed because it was familiar to Greeks and Romans alike. But the practice merely heightened the Roman's sense of his own grandeur, as a politician who could make or break the obsequious Greeks who needed his support.

If the politicians of Greece (except perhaps for Philopoemen the Achaean, who was called 'the last of the Greeks') met with little respect, the kings and potentates of the Greek east fared no better. The Macedonian rulers Philip V and Perseus seemed to the Romans to fall short of what they expected from the successors of Alexander the Great. Philip made too many jokes and was too hot-tempered for his office; Perseus was blamed for unworthy behaviour after his defeat by Aemilius Paulus. The elder Cato sneered at Antiochus the Great 'for making war by post, for doing battle with pen and ink'; the ruler of Syria was thereby brought down to the level of the Athenians who were accused of fighting for their grievances with words instead of actions. The Roman senate had earlier been styled by Cineas, the envoy of Pyrrhus, as an assembly of kings, but the second-century senators, whether as a group or as individuals, did not treat their royal Greek contemporaries as equals. The envoy Popillius drew a circle round Antiochus Epiphanes and unceremoniously insisted that the king should answer his demands before he moved outside those limits. It is possible that Romans were swayed by their own anti-regal traditions, which dated back to the expulsion of the last Tarquin; but certainly conscious pride in their own political ability made them feel superior to the kings with whom they fought or negotiated. On the other hand there was one feature of Hellenistic kingdoms which appealed to some Romans. It had long been the custom for these rulers to be hailed as benefactors and present gods, and this adulation or gratitude was now redirected towards the Romans as the effective new rulers. In the long run the accumulation of such titles by individuals would prove to be incompatible with the oligarchical spirit, which allowed men to rise but did not want them to ascend to the heavens. Thus, even though the Romans showed little respect for their royal counterparts, they indulged in a kingly practice which eventually helped to undermine the republic as they knew it— the elevation of an individual above his peers.

The Greek influence was most beneficial in the field of literature. Romans became self-conscious about their lack of a literature and they recognized that here Greece was supreme. Some took back books to Rome and enjoyed the company of the Greek learned men who could expound these works and educate Roman children. The prime need, however, was to create a national literature in Latin that would do justice to Roman achievements and be attractive to read. Livius Andronicus began the process by translating Homer into Latin; Plautus adapted and translated Greek comedies, making use of the Greek background as a scene of greater licence which the Roman audience could enjoy and disdain at one and the same time; and Ennius wrote tragedies as well as his grand epic on Roman history. Between 240 and about 160 B.C., when Terence wrote, Latin poetry seemed to make an auspicious start. The writing of history was more cautious; Fabius Pictor wrote about Rome in Greek. Cato's *Origines* was the first major history of the Roman world in Latin but he too was indebted to Greek ideas since the model for his book came from Greek historiography, learned works on the founding of cities.

Some of these early Latin writers were not always acceptable to the more critical writers of a later age. Cicero objected to the tragedies of Livius, and Horace found fault with Plautus for his lack of polish. There was a sense in which the pioneers of Latin seemed to be lacking in refinement and art. But they were always valued for their antique dignity and vigour. Hence Gellius, in the second century A.D., delighted in the Roman ancients and studied their language, which seemed to him to have the true flavour of an archaic and better Rome.

Rome's involvement with the Greek world in the second century created a sense of pride in Roman achievements and a feeling that they deserved a lasting monument in Latin. In this same period, however, as we saw earlier, Greek wealth and Greek manners were effecting radical changes in the old Roman way of life. The ruling oligarchy was aware of some of the dangers; it sought to domesticate foreign religion and it tried unsuccessfully to curb conspicuous extravagance by sumptuary laws. The better men were critical of those who took to the path of self-indulgence which was scornfully labelled Greek leisure (*otium*). But the oligarchy was less sensitive to the dangers inherent in the decline of the peasant-farmer class and to the wealth and power acquired by its own most successful members. A later age admired most those heroes of the second century who had lived a full Roman public life and had made a prudent, Roman use of leisure by conversing with educated Greeks. Scipio Aemilianus, the destroyer of Carthage, was distinguished as an active Roman and as the friend of serious Greeks—the historian Polybius and the philosopher Panaetius.

Hellenic influences, in the broad sense of the word, brought corruption as well as civilization in their wake. This accounts for what has been aptly called 'the curiously ambivalent attitude of Romans to things Greek' (Donald Earl, *The Moral and Political Tradition of Rome*). The causes of this ambivalence are to be found in the second century; the more complex and more articulate expressions of this attitude in later writers are the subject of this book.

I

THE GREEK CHARACTER

Romans believed that their political and military successes were founded on moral superiority; other peoples, divided broadly into Greeks and barbarians, were tarnished with faults and imperfections which could even be a threat to Roman uprightness and virtue. In the first part of this chapter, I indicate the various defects which were attributed to Greeks: lack of good faith, lying, flattery, talkativeness and inept behaviour; even their learning was sometimes presented as a defect, if it was learning in the wrong area or if it could be made to look like useless knowledge.

Though Romans, in speeches and other forms of literature, gave Greeks a bad character, it is difficult to say whether they actually lived by their prejudices in their dealings with Greeks. There are indications that Roman governors treated Greek provincials as their inferiors and were advised to be on their guard against Greek opportunism. But many Greeks or men with Greek training were a necessary part of the political and domestic way of life. Romans needed Greek men of letters and such specialists as doctors, who enjoyed positions of trust, intimacy and power; they could hardly have done so if the character-prejudice expressed in literature had made a deep mark on the relationships of real life.

COMMONPLACES

Latin accounts of character are usually concerned with presenting general traits, hardly, if at all, with the personal quirks and eccentricities that can be relished by an intent observer. Individuals are given the virtues or defects of the class or people to which they belong. Quintilian has in mind this importance of the general type when he is discussing the kinds of proof that are related to the persons in a legal case and says that each nationality has its own peculiar character (*mores*).[1] He goes on to make the point that we apply different standards in judging the behaviour of barbarians, Greeks and Romans. Thus characterization of this kind often implies a contrast or comparison with the traits of other peoples, and many of the qualities which Romans ascribed to Greeks can be interpreted correctly only if at some stage we consider whether these are typically Roman or not. Here I shall discuss some presuppositions of Roman character-drawing and indicate the main features of the Greek character as portrayed by Romans.

Character-descriptions were of great interest to orators and rhetorical theorists. A full account of a character, as in a panegyric, would satisfy the formulae of rhetoric only if it included material on the birthplace or home-country of the subject. We might say that praise of his country would be the proper introduction to the subsequent encomium of a famous individual; the qualities of Rome would reflect credit on the virtues of her sons. We may, then, begin this enquiry into character by comparing Roman accounts of Italy with those of Greece. It is true that Roman writers found time to applaud Greece; thus the elder Pliny introduces the Peloponnese with the compliment that it is a country second to none for distinction.[2] Greek place-names were employed as familiar symbols of beauty by Roman poets, and some politicians gave Greek names to parts of their estates. But though Greece was admired, Romans were more enthusiastic about Italy. Virgil's encomium of the Italian countryside in the *Georgics* offers an earlier, poetic treatment of a theme that was developed by the elder Pliny. Pliny leaves us in no doubt that his preference is for Italy.[3] 'It is a country which is at one and the same time the nursling and mother of all lands. It has been appointed by the gods to make heaven itself more glorious, to unite separate empires and combine the jarring tongues of many peoples so that they can converse, to bestow civilization (*humanitas*), and to become the one fatherland of all peoples in the world.' This is not just a glorification of Italy as the parent of Roman history; Pliny also has in mind the beautiful landscape and country, the Campanian coast and Italy's agricultural wealth. Even her excrescences are beneficial: her promontories are said to dash eagerly into the waters in order to help mankind. The Greeks themselves admit that Italy is superior; they are fond of marvelling at their own land, as Pliny observes when he mentions the thousand-foot bridge in Thesprotia; but though they sing their own praises they have themselves given a mere part of Italy the significant name Magna Graecia or Great Greece. Pliny

ingeniously exploits the name of this rich area as an argument
that even the Greeks are voices on the side of Italy.

Pliny's rhetoric is far less persuasive than Virgil's poetry, but
both writers can help us to realize that a Roman would not
readily prefer Greece, whether we think of the climate or the
country. Later philhellenes from northern Europe have delighted
in the Aegean both as a climatic haven and as a homeland of
ideas. But Romans were not affected by the sense of geographical
difference in this form, as Italy provided a like climate with an
even richer variety of lands and rivers. A Roman character-
sketch of Greece would not naturally give the country precedence
over Italy.

Any character-sketch of other peoples, crude though it may
appear to the outsider, is an attempt to make sense of the apparent
divisions among mankind. The Roman scheme of character does
little more than amplify the Greek distinction between Hellenes
and barbarians.[4] In its basic form this is a contrast between those
whose speech can be understood and those whose language is
incomprehensible. But other ideas of cultural superiority are often
present, as when Herodotus remarks that Hellenes can be distinguished from barbarians because they are cleverer. A more
sophisticated version of the idea (though the term barbarian is
not found) appears in Aristotle, who distinguishes between northern peoples, easterners and Greeks. Differences of character are
here correlated with climatic differences. Northerners, who live in
cold places, are compensated by a hot temperament which makes
them reluctant to accept political order and discipline; easterners
have more talent but are made servile and submissive by the
heat; Greeks, however, are in the temperate zone and enjoy the
mean between anarchy and autocracy. A similar theory is
advanced by Vitruvius, except that for him it is no more than a
philosophical ornament in a preface, and he, as we might expect,
makes Italy the favoured zone of climate and character.[5]

The antithesis between Hellene and barbarian is a poor relation
of the theories in Aristotle and Vitruvius; it opposes Greeks to all
others, whatever their cultural level, though it is true that in the
fifth and fourth centuries B.C. the most important barbarians
from the Greek point of view were the Persians. Eratosthenes[6] the
geographer, writing in the third century, thought it would be
better to distinguish between men on the basis of virtue; good
men, presumably, would be Hellenes, whether or not they
spoke Greek, and bad men similarly would be barbarians. But the
simpler idea, that superior beings were those who spoke Greek

and lived for the most part in city-states, kept its hold. Livy shows us a Macedonian delegate at a meeting just before the second Macedonian war, who warns the Greeks against inviting the Romans to intervene in their quarrels. 'Aetolians, Acarnanians and Macedonians have a common language; our disputes and alliances arise over those trifling matters which occur from time to time. But between all Greeks and barbarians there is and will be a state of everlasting war. They are our enemies by nature, not for reasons which can vary from day to day.'[7] The elder Cato complained about the Greek habit of dubbing Romans *barbari* and *Opici* (a pejorative term for the Oscans, who were supposed to be uncouth).[8] Philip V observed that the barbarians from the west were remarkable for their military organization. Such faint praise was gradually replaced by acceptance of Rome as a civilized power, since Greeks were impressed by Roman victories and by the well-advertised policies of men like Flamininus, who proclaimed the freedom of Greece in 195 B.C.[9] Though Greek critics of Rome did not become extinct, there were other Greeks who gave Rome the highest commendation they could find. Thus Dionysius, writing in the Augustan age, rejects the view held by some Greeks that Romans were a barbarian people, and traces their origins to Arcadia.[10]

For Dionysius the Romans were Hellenes not only by origin but in character, men whose achievement was founded on justice and piety. Romans may have been gratified by such compliments, but they chose, understandably enough, to speak in terms of three groups: Romans, Greeks and barbarians. The ultimate praise is comprised in the word Roman. As value-words Greek and barbarian sometimes approximate to each other, insofar as both refer to what is non-Roman, while at other times barbarian denotes the lowest stage of civilized values. But it is not the case that Romans had nothing but disparagement for Greeks and barbarians; at times they found themselves admiring both. It may be useful to preface a study of Greek characteristics with a brief account of Roman ambivalence towards barbarians.

The same objection can be brought against the Roman use of 'barbarian' as against the Greek; it is a term applied to many peoples at very different stages of civilization, merely because they exhibit qualities which Romans have a reason for disliking or thinking inferior. It is counted barbarous to practise human sacrifice in one's religion, as the Suebi do; the Jewish religion is also dismissed as barbarous by Cicero and Tacitus, though they probably knew converts to Judaism.[11] It is common to find that 'barbarian' is used of peoples who are less well organized or disciplined than Romans are. Gauls and others are sometimes described in language which suggests they are closer to wild beasts than to mankind.[12] Their appearance and battle-cries are strange and wild; though they fight with great verve, they are often incapable of stomaching a reverse or outlasting the tenacious discipline of the Roman legions. Romans liked stories which show that barbarians have to be persuaded by different techniques from those employed in dealing with Greeks. When Gracchus[13] (in Spain, 179 B.C.) was visited by representatives of the Celtiberi, Romans were amazed at their behaviour. Their first request was for a drink: 'when they had finished that they asked for another, to the great amusement of the bystanders on seeing people who were so uncouth and ignorant of all custom'. Gracchus told these envoys that his confidence in making war on them was based on his army, and he impressed them by getting his troops to put on a display of manoeuvres. With barbarians, seeing was believing. We may compare the tale in Velleius, where a German ancient asks for permission to come within sight of Tiberius, so that he can admire the Roman commander's majestic expression.[14] Had the Celtiberi been Greeks we may suspect that they would have been treated to a speech; at a meeting with Greeks in 197 B.C., Flamininus delivered a speech which made much of 'Roman good faith' and said little about Roman military resources. It was right to conceal from Greeks the armed fist which would impress barbarians.

However, some barbarians behave in unexpectedly admirable ways. Valerius Maximus includes in his collection of moral examples stories of *barbari*, which, like the Greek stories, are an appendage to his largely Roman tale. Livy praises the Ligurians for their energy in war, which provides the legions with an adequate challenge for Roman courage and virtue. Masinissa the Numidian was admired by his contemporary Scipio and by Livy as one who showed the loyalty and good faith that are expected of Romans, not of lesser breeds. There is a tendency to speak of such people, as Livy writes of a certain Timasitheus, as men who resemble Romans more than their own.[15] The well-behaved foreigner is made an honorary Roman. Tacitus' *Germania* is perhaps a more complex treatment of barbarians, in that he allows them to retain their faults along with the virtues for which he admires them. The chastity of their women and the loyalty of the men to their leaders make them the moral superiors of contemporary Romans. Even their ignorance is turned into a contrast with Roman knowledge; thus the Suebi collect amber on the sea-shore, even though they do not understand its nature or how it is produced; it was part of the debris thrown up by the sea until 'our luxury gave it a name'.[16] But in Tacitus too barbarian innocence is not examined for its own sake; it is a reminder to the Romans of qualities which they once had but have lost through over-sophistication.

If *barbari* usually behave in an inferior way, how do some of them rise above their circumstances and behave like true Romans? Valerius tells how the Scythians retreated before Darius, announcing to him that he would discover their fighting qualities only when they reached the site of their ancestors' tombs; then they would turn and resist. Valerius sees in this incident a proof of Scythian piety: 'by this one pious speech an uncivilized and barbarous people has redeemed itself against all charges of being savage'. The credit (so Valerius goes on) must be given to nature, which can teach men virtues such as piety without the help of books; indeed, in this passage nature is contrasted with learning (*doctrina*), which is said to make men more polished, not to improve them. Here the rhetorician in Valerius carries him into an attack on learning at the expense of nature. But another passage shows that learning too can make men virtuous. In his account of high seriousness (*gravitas*), Valerius first praises some Spaniards who refused to buy off an avaricious Roman commander and prepared to fight for their freedom to the death. 'They were led into the paths of seriousness by nature.' But he then quotes Socrates as an instance of this seriousness, because he declined the offer of a persuasive speech composed by Lysias, and in *his* case the virtue must be ascribed to the operation of learning. Which, then, is more effective, nature or learning? Cicero, in his defence of Archias, gives the preference to nature. 'I admit that many men have attained self-control and seriousness by themselves, through the almost divine force of nature itself, and I also add that nature without learning has often been more productive of glorious virtue than learning without nature.' By invoking nature Romans could think they had explained the virtue sometimes found among barbarians and the more sustained grandeur of their own forebears.[17]

It is doubtful whether a writer like Valerius could have explained more clearly what he meant by nature. But a remark of Cicero may throw some light on the topic: virtue, he says, is nothing else but nature made perfect.[18] He means that all human beings differ from lower creatures in that they have a natural tendency towards virtue and that completed nature in this sense enables man to draw closer to the gods. It will not be surprising if some men are better endowed by nature than others. Perhaps, too, we should bear in mind that Romans were not very interested in the theoretical answers that might be given to such questions as those put by Meno to Socrates: 'Is virtue taught? Or acquired by training? Or does it come about by nature?' They believed that their ancestors (or most of them) had been men with great virtues; how else could Rome have become victorious? They could not say that earlier Romans had learning, at least not until 'the arts from overseas'[19] became more familiar in the second century B.C. They had, then, little choice but to praise nature or the customs and training of earlier Rome. Since the customs of barbarians were usually thought to be less admirable than those of Rome, nature was left as the principal explanation of whatever seemed great among the barbarians.

The Greeks, on the other hand, according to the stock Roman portrait, were creatures of a civilization that had gone wrong;[20] they seemed to be men with faults and vices that made Romans feel conscious of their own superiority. The main charges against them were fickleness, idleness, telling lies and foolish or inappropriate behaviour.

'Fickleness' here is offered as a convenient version of the word *levitas*, though it should be said that in Gellius' view this sense was an innovation;[21] he quotes passages from Cicero which seem to him to show that in the Ciceronian age the word described men who were no good or of no account. But the idea of fickle change certainly seems to be uppermost in many passages in Cicero. He complains of Athenian *levitas* on the grounds that Athens had exiled many of her best politicians, whom she first admired and then came to hate. He probably has the same political failing in mind when he tells a Roman audience of the bad effect that can be produced by an address to a meeting of the people: 'you must remember the rashness of their popular assemblies, the fickleness which is the characteristic of Greeks'.[22] Roman prejudice here attributes this moral defect to the excessive power of popular assemblies in some Greek states. It was felt that such Greek audiences were too easily swayed by shallow rhetoric of the demagogic kind. Greeks had a passion for talking and for listening to orators which was held to have caused their volatile behaviour.

The charge of irresponsibility was not confined to Greeks in their political activities but was also levelled at some Greek philosophers. Cicero refers to the *levitas* of Greeks who utter personal abuse against thinkers with whose views they happen to disagree. He makes a similar complaint against Dionysius of Heraclea on the grounds that he was inconsistent: he professed Stoicism but renounced Zeno's doctrine—that pain is not an evil—when he was himself struck down with pain in the kidneys. Inconsistency, fickleness, lack of moral weight, such are the qualities which Romans had in mind when they spoke of Greek *levitas*. Roman disapproval is most strongly voiced by Cicero in his defence of Flaccus against Greek witnesses; he asks the judges not to let a true good citizen be the victim of men who are 'Greek in their fickleness and barbarians for their cruelty'.[23]

Romans liked to contrast with this one of their own favourite virtues—seriousness (*gravitas*). A serious Roman is one who has the true measure of what is important in life, is not easily ruffled, and keeps his dignity. The elder Pliny speaks of applying Roman seriousness to the large number of Greek works on administering wine to the sick; a prudent selection will avoid the pedantry of the medical writers and yet provide the reader with useful practical advice for keeping in health. He says too that medicine is the only Greek art as yet untried by Roman seriousness; he means that nearly all doctors are still Greek or write in Greek on the subject; and, he rather implies, so much the worse for medicine.[24] As Romans felt they were more serious, more worthy, than their Greek contemporaries, they tended to look to their past as the fount of authoritative instances. Thus Cicero comments that a discussion on an important subject like friendship gains in seriousness when the speakers are earlier Romans of distinction in public life; and Gellius describes a legal decision from long ago as characterized by 'antique seriousness'. Seriousness in the Roman sense stands for an attachment to moral principle, with what seems a philistine intolerance of anything that is irrelevant.[25]

Romans also complained about Greek indolence (*otium*); Greeks could be seen as men who went in for interminable discussions but had no part to play in important public affairs. Hence there was some dislike of philosophy, which was considered a form of activity remote from the serious business of life; Cicero indicates that his own affection for philosophy could expose him to the charge that he was busy with irrelevancies. Philosophers, however, were not the only supposed idlers among the Greeks. It was a generalized indictment, as Cicero shows when he assures his audience in the *Verrines* that the Sicilians are not like other Greeks; they are hard-working, free from the usual Greek sloth and self-indulgence. Drinking-parties were another aspect of Greek leisure; thus Cicero seeks to damage the credibility of a Roman witness by alleging that he chose to spend his inheritance not at Rome but on drinking-parties in the Greek east. [26]

Untruthfulness was yet another bad habit among the Greeks, though it should be said that Romans liked to bring the same accusation against several other peoples as well. [27] Greek historians, as we shall see later, were particularly suspect. They made Greek achievements seem larger than life and invented stories about marvels in distant lands. Juvenal sums up Roman scorn for this aspect of Greek intellectual life in the phrase 'everything that Greece, the land of liars, dare say in history'. The average Greek was also stigmatized as a liar. Virgil exploits the theme of Greek mendacity when he portrays the wiles of Sinon, persuading the Trojans to take the wooden horse inside the walls of Troy. [28] Falsehood was alleged to be a common Greek failing; a Roman orator, faced with hostile Greek witnesses, would seek to belittle their evidence by reminding the judges that Greeks were uncertain friends of truth.

Fickle, idle and untruthful, these are terms of an indictment which embraces ordinary Greeks as well as Greek intellectuals. The latter were exposed to the even more serious charge that they were tactless or irrelevant (*inepti*). Crassus, speaking in the *de oratore*, has some regrets at having made a lengthy speech, even though his audience is delighted with his discussion of oratory 'in the Greek fashion as though it were a school'. He feels he has been led astray, merely because the younger Romans wished to hear him talk, into the sort of discussion he would never have touched upon even as a young man; he has forgotten his position as a Roman grandee of mature or advanced years. He then gives his definition of folly or irrelevance, saying that the word *ineptum* is one of the most powerful Latin words. 'We call a man *ineptus* when he does not see what the occasion calls for; or says more than is necessary; or draws attention to himself; or does not take account of the rank or convenience of his companions; anyone, in short, who strikes a discordant note or overdoes things.' This, he alleges, is a particular fault of the Greeks with all their learning, and he adds that they have no word to describe this fault because they do not see how important it is. And, for Crassus, the worst ineptitude is to indulge in lengthy discussions in any company on subjects which are either extremely difficult or unnecessary. [29]

Crassus speaks with the assurance of a Roman who has in fact made great speeches (he modestly bows to *this* opinion of his contemporaries) and does not believe that rhetorical theory by itself can make men succeed as orators. His is not the only case of Roman intellectual embarrassment and distaste for talking theory. Messalla, in Tacitus' *Dialogus*, ends a speech on the decline of oratory with the remark that critics will say he has been 'applauding his own irrelevancies'.[30] It was only natural that rhetorical theory would seem irrelevant to Roman orators, for whom success in the courts far outweighed any amount of Greek advice. But a similar criticism was made of Greek philosophers. Seneca, though himself a Stoic, complains that Chrysippus has introduced into his book on benefits irrelevant and fanciful ideas about the three Graces and their names.[31] Such stories should be left to poets, who aim to please men, not to make them better. Romans thought that Greek intellectuals put too much extraneous matter round the central truth which (they believed) was all that was required. Greeks are men who are looking for work; hence they write separate treatises on individual topics when a single survey would provide what is relevant.[32]

Some of these faults were in part confessed by Greeks themselves: Cretans were proverbial liars, and Strabo complains of that Greek addiction to talk and chatter which is in Crassus' mind when he condemns Greeks for their ineptitude.[33] Nor are they faults specific to Greeks alone; Romans said that barbarians too were fickle and false; and if Greeks were indolent so were Germans, at any rate in the intervals between campaigns.[34] Greek and barbarian faults were therefore alike when compared with virtues such as good faith and seriousness, on which Romans congratulated themselves. But there were striking differences. Cicero comments that some barbarians fight with great energy but cannot bear sickness with manly fortitude; whereas Greeks, who are lacking in spirit but have a sufficiency of wisdom, are the opposite. Though they are unable to face up to an enemy in open war, they can endure disease and sickness in a patient, civilized way.[35] Perhaps we should infer that only Romans can fight on both fronts. But civilian fortitude was not the greatest Greek distinction. The quality or excellence by which Romans marked off Greeks from barbarians and themselves was learning (*doctrina*). Romans freely recognized that for a long time Greek rhetoric and philosophy had been unfamiliar lore. In the Ciceronian age and later, 'learned' was a polite compliment among poets. Cicero's review of Roman oratory draws attention to those earlier Roman speakers who had in fact shown more than just native wit and had been acquainted with the Greek learning. Among Greek philosophers Socrates and Plato were admired as great, good men whose character was the moral correlate of their *doctrina*. Romans of Cicero's time perhaps tended to exaggerate the learning of their own second-century predecessors in the Scipionic circle; with more reason on his side Aulus Gellius looked back on the Ciceronian age as a time of learning, and used Varro and Nigidius Figulus to prove his point.[36]

However, Roman criticism did not leave even Greek learning unscathed. Some learning seemed objectionable on the grounds that it would lead to undesirable behaviour. Romans thoroughly enjoyed the story of their primitive heroes who were astonished to hear about Epicurean ethical theory from Cineas,[37] the ambassador of Pyrrhus; M' Curius hoped that all Rome's enemies would be converted to this theory, as they would then be easier to defeat in war. Cicero repeats Plato's criticism of the poets, saying that they show us brave men in tears, a bad example to the audience; 'yet we,' he observes ironically, 'since we have been so taught by Greece, read and learn their works from childhood on, and we say it is knowledge and learning worthy of a free man'.[38] Another objection was founded on the idea that cleverness with ideas does not necessarily make one a better man. Some anecdotes were designed to show that Athenians, who had plenty of opportunity to know better, were less well behaved than Spartans.[39] And Tacitus remarks about a freedman who acted as an agent for Nero in despoiling Greece, 'he was well versed in Greek learning, but his knowledge was word-deep only; his mind and attitude were not permeated by good arts'.[40] It seems, then, that one might be learned in the wrong subject, or that learning could make one accomplished without improving the character.

For convenience I have here described the faults of Greece as so many separate traits of character. They are, as it were, fictional ideas which might help a writer to encapsulate a Greek character or explain an action. I shall end with a short study of two speeches in which we can see how Cicero uses some or all of these ideas in talking about Greeks.

In his defence of Flaccus (59 B.C.), Cicero had to contend with witnesses from cities in Asia which his client was said to have misgoverned. He first undermines their credibility by assassinating their character. Who are these witnesses? Why, Greeks. Cicero says he is not the only Roman to impugn the good faith of Greeks, though he is himself a friend of Greeks. He points out that there are good and bad Greeks, though those present in court include only 'the brazen, the unlettered and the fickle'. But even if one makes this necessary distinction, it still has to be said that Greeks in general make unscrupulous witnesses. They do not answer the questions put by defence counsel, whereas they go out of their way to give more than helpful answers to the prosecution. The reason is that they have no respect for the oath, and they do not confine themselves to the facts; they seek to harm the defendant, unlike the Romans, who would not allow injured feelings to alter their strict regard for the truth.

Furthermore Greeks are treacherous and have an upside-down view of human relationships. There was a rumour in Asia that Pompey, as a political enemy of Flaccus, had asked his own friend Laelius to prosecute. And this (so Cicero continues) seemed all the more likely to Greeks because shortly before they had seen Laelius on good terms with Flaccus in the province. Being Greeks, he means, they ascribed to Laelius a duplicity in his friendly dealings with Flaccus; *they* would naturally feign friendship while premeditating an injurious prosecution.

Though all Greeks have some faults, there is a distinction to be made between the more solid Greeks of Europe and the west and the Asiatic Greeks. Flaccus is supported by the testimony of Athens, Sparta and Massilia, states which once held power and won glory in war. Against them are pitted the Asiatic Greeks, the hostile witnesses in the case. These are inferior Greeks, so Cicero argues, on the evidence of their own proverbial sayings; Phrygians, Mysians, Lydians and Carians are written off as men charac- terized by fickleness, changing purpose and greed.

Individual Greeks also are exposed to Ciceronian ridicule. Heracleides of Temnos is said to be 'tactless (*ineptus*) and talkative': in his own eyes he is learned and professes to teach the art of eloquence, though he is that ludicrous object, a teacher of rhetoric who has been defeated in courts of law.[41]

In this case Cicero portrays many of the alleged Greek faults. He takes a different view in the prosecution of Verres, when the Greek witnesses from Sicily are on his side. Thus he makes a general comparison between these Sicilians and the Romans of an earlier age—both are hard-working and frugal. The Sicilians are unlike other Greeks and have a great affection for their Roman rulers. Throughout the *Verrines* Cicero takes discreet pains to emphasize what one might call the Roman qualities of his witnesses—their respect for truth and their scrupulous regard for religious objects handed down in the family. Philodamus, who refused quite properly to bring his daughter into a drinking-party, is described as a man of great seriousness (*gravitas*).[42] Cicero repeatedly asserts that decrees from Sicilian towns condemning Verres were passed by respectable Greeks at meetings in their local senates. It should be noticed that in the Flaccus case he pours scorn on decrees hostile to his client, on the grounds that they were passed in public meetings of assemblies where mob-orators could arouse the passions of the fickle, volatile crowd.

It was relatively easy to run down the Greek character, whereas one would seek to commend a Greek, if at all, for qualities and actions which might be presented as Roman or close to Roman. We have been examining stereotypes which were specially useful to orators. However, disparagement of Greeks and the Greek character is a frequent motif in all Latin writers, even though few are as vehement as Juvenal with his hatred for 'Rome gone Greek'.[43] Whether Romans actually lived out their contempt for the Greek character in real life is a question to be considered next.

ROMANS AND GREEKS

The Greek character, as we have seen, was contemptible compared with those qualities which Romans felt to be typical of themselves; and even if the Greeks were distinguished from the barbarians by learning (*doctrina*), it was often alleged against them that this learning had not been applied to its proper end, the improvement of character. But it may well be that the portrait was exaggerated by those Romans who had a special interest in denigrating Greeks. Lawyers, for example, would understandably exploit Roman prejudice in an attempt to make Greek witnesses look untrustworthy: Cicero displays writer's animus against Greeks in the *de oratore*, where he contrasts the interminable irrelevance of theory with solid Roman experience. Similarly, Juvenal is obliged by his theme to paint Greek flattery in lurid colours in his famous third satire on Rome. Hostility to Greeks in these cases was partly determined by forensic motives and literary purposes.

It is impossible to judge how other Romans responded to these descriptions. But we can attempt to find out whether Romans in fact treated Greeks as severely as their character would seem to have deserved. I shall examine the Roman government of Greeks in their provinces and then consider some relationships between Romans and individual Greeks.

In the late republic, Roman governors were faced with a task of administration for which they were unqualified. They were often ignorant of local conditions and were obliged to satisfy the conflicting interests of different pressure-groups. On the one hand there were the local Greek communities, which depended on the governor as a judge and asked for his influence to be used in their favour in financial matters; on the other hand the Roman tax-collectors and businessmen also looked to the governor for help. He could not afford to offend either group, since unpopularity might lead to prosecution at Rome on his return. Cicero says it is the governor's job to bring about harmony between the two sides.[44] But in general the governor was more likely to be influenced by his fellow-Romans, who could send adverse reports on his conduct to political enemies at Rome. In the *Verrines*, for example, Cicero is careful to point out that Verres is barred from a line of defence which must have been common: he cannot say that he has looked after the interests of Roman citizens at the expense of the Sicilians. Cicero gives convincing evidence that Verres had abused Greeks and provincial Romans alike. But, clearly, a defence based on real services to Romans would induce men to turn a blind eye on injuries to Greeks.[45]

Most of the demands made by Romans worked to the financial disadvantage of the Greek provincials. Resident businessmen and tax-collectors expected the governor to assist them and to see that cities paid their taxes and a good rate of interest on loans. In some cases the governor appointed Romans with financial interests to the position of prefect[46] and allowed them to have an escort of troops; the show of force was intended to ensure that Greeks complied with the Roman order. The governor's own staff could be another problem for him, as his officers expected to gain from their period of service.[47] They could take a percentage of bribes or gifts, and hoped to have a share if part of the governor's allowance was unspent, though this would deprive the Roman treasury rather than the funds of the provincials. The governor was often asked by his political friends to supply wild animals for games at Rome (the so-called aedile tax), and the recruitment and expenses of the hunters were another burden on the cities. Cicero's refusal to supply animals was probably exceptional.[48]

However well or ill the provincials had been governed, they were expected to send deputations to Rome to present their official thanks to the senate for the governor's administration. These were so numerous that they became a diplomatic cliché and the senate did not always have time to hear them. But they were yet another expense for the provincials, since they had to be done in style. Emperors certainly tried to make this aspect of provincial rule less wearisome for themselves and cheaper for their subjects. In A.D. 62 Thrasea Paetus complained of a Cretan who boasted that his influence could determine whether or not such a deputation would be sent. Thrasea was annoyed by what he considered to be a piece of upstart Greek behaviour—he resented the fact that praise due to Romans should be at the whim of such impertinence—though he also pointed out that the practice of expecting official deputations tended to corrupt. He meant that a governor's conduct would deteriorate near the end of his term, as he would then seek to make friends among the local men of influence. But in general the practice was obviously welcome to upper-class Romans; thus the upright Pliny declares that the ruler of a province should be able to add the honorific decrees of colonies and cities to the commendations of his own Roman friends.[49]

The governor's office, even if it was prolonged beyond a year, was no more than an interlude in a man's political career. If he had to grant or parry the requests of other Romans, he also intended to advance his own interests. His need for money and prestige was satisfied at the expense of those he administered. The more unscrupulous, like Verres, accumulated art-treasures and received presents of money. Some deigned to accept the honorific award of statues and temples. And in many cases the governor did not wish to give offence to the tax-collectors by reducing their demands on the provincials, since his political future might then be at risk. Cicero was greatly relieved that the tax-contracts had already·been settled before he started his term in Cilicia (51–50 B.C.); he would not therefore be drawn into haggling which might force him to take sides either with Greeks or with tax-collectors. Cicero's own desire for prestige and a good reputation was based on ideas of administration that were superior to those of most Romans. But though he wanted to give an exhibition of just rule, he certainly did not wish to stay longer in his province than was absolutely necessary. The people in his province were to have good government, because he thought that both right and prestigious for himself. But he meant to enjoy the benefit as soon as possible by returning to Rome, and he would have been appalled if he had had to stay longer than a year on the grounds that his justice would then be even more beneficial to Greeks.[50]

The provincials, on their side, were not without means of persuading the governor to act in their interest. They had connections with other Romans, who might be political enemies of a governor whom they wished to prosecute for extortion. But help from the law came after the event and was uncertain, at any rate in the republic; there was a better chance of redress under the empire. It is, however, somewhat misleading to think of Roman interests as completely opposed to those of the provincials. Bad governors like Verres were aided and abetted by willing Greeks who made a living for themselves at the expense of their fellow-Greeks.[51] The wealthier Greeks were closer in outlook and sympathies to the ruling Romans, and would have had much to lose if a disturbance like a slave-war broke out.[52] Respectable Greeks of this type accepted the onus of giving hospitality[53] to the more important Romans, but they drew the line when lesser officials looked for better quarters than their position seemed to warrant.·

It is clear that fair administration of the provinces was hard to come by in the late Roman republic. In the light of these general remarks we should consider how Romans dealt with their provincial Greek subjects, to see whether their attitude betrays a prejudice against the Greek character.

Verres, not surprisingly, showed his contempt. When he was anxious that his Roman advisers should be absent so that he could judge a case as he wanted, he observed to one of them that he could manage by himself: ' ... *if* you think me a fit man to pass judgment on one who is both a Sicilian and a Greekling'. Verres, of course, was notorious even by the standards of his time. Cicero, both as governor himself and as adviser to his brother Quintus, was more sympathetic to Greeks, and prided himself on being easily approachable in his province—evidently something of a novelty. But he too showed something like contempt on occasions. He tells Atticus that the Greeks in Cilicia are delighted because they are being allowed their preference in allocating judges for law-suits involving Greeks.[54] Atticus, he imagines, may well suppose they are men of no substance to think this so important. 'But what does it matter? They think they have got their independence.' Greek satisfaction with this limited local autonomy seemed a trifling matter to Cicero. He tells his brother to be very careful about admitting Greeks to intimate acquaintance, except those who are 'worthy of Greece in the past'. The Greeks, he adds, are deceitful, fickle, servile and given to flattery, and he gives them much the same character here as in his speech for Flaccus. The friendship of Greeks is unreliable; the reason is that they do not dare to oppose the wishes of Romans, and they are jealous not only of Romans but of other Greeks. In a later letter he tells Quintus that he has tried to get on good terms with those

Greeks who had been offended by Quintus' governorship in Asia. They have to be placated because they have a talent for deception. Cicero says his reason for being conciliatory is not because the particular Greeks concerned or the people as a whole give him any pleasure. 'I am tired of their fickleness and flattery, the fact that they change with circumstances and are not loyal to their duties.'[55]

Cicero would not have been as arrogant as Verres in a judicial capacity, but his general attitude to Greeks is here seen to be nearly as scornful. On the other hand, his first letter to Quintus reveals a gentler disposition. He suggests that it would be Quintus' duty, even if he were ruling over barbarians like Spaniards and Gauls, to give evidence of his civilization (*humanitas*) by looking after their interests and advantages. Such a policy is even more necessary as he is ruling Greeks; they are the people who have given civilization to mankind, and Romans should show that they too have this quality. According to this passage the Greeks have a higher claim on Roman administrators than do their barbarian inferiors. Cicero anticipates that his efforts to conciliate some offended Greeks will be dismissed by his brother as just another indication of his tenderness for that people; he stresses that his motive is political and says he has tried to win over his brother's Roman enemies as well. Evidently he had a reputation for liking Greeks which would lead Quintus to expect him to show a partiality for them.[56]

Was Cicero, styled 'philhellene' by both himself and others, no gentler than Verres in his attitude, except that he took care to hide his real views under a mask of devotion to Greeks? It has to be remembered that he was also suspicious of many Romans. He spoke disparagingly of provincial Roman businessmen, finding it impossible to understand how they could bear to be parted from Rome. As a 'new man' of merit in Roman politics he scorned and feared the presumption of birthright aristocrats like his predecessor in Cilicia, Appius Claudius Pulcher.[57] His feelings about Greeks and Romans have to be interpreted in the light of his general approach to politics. Political careers, in his view, are at the mercy of slanderous tongues. The governor of a Greek province should not give his enemies grounds for attack. If he is too close to Greeks he may be manipulated by them, which could easily be misrepresented to Romans; and if he has offended some of the Greeks they in turn must be soothed in case they abuse him to important Romans. His advice to Quintus is based on the assumption that the governor must make sure of a good name.

It is this concern with fame and reputation that marks the important political difference between himself and Verres.

As a politician Cicero valued good relationships with Greeks for the effect they might have on his career or that of Quintus. He also gives his view on the position of Greeks within the empire as a whole. He admits that Greeks are bound to feel bitterness at having to pay taxes, but says that they have gained more than they have lost through association with Rome. They paid taxes to great powers even before Rome intervened; taxes are a necessary contribution to Roman rule, in the absence of which the Greeks would be exposed, without defence, to the risk of war. Rome, then, is a guarantor of peace. The Greeks should not complain about the activities of the tax-collectors, as they need their presence in order to pay the taxes imposed by Sulla; and Greeks in the past had been no gentler than the tax-collectors in exacting their dues (and, perhaps, offering loans). Since the work of the tax-collectors is justifiable and good, the function of Greeks is to help Roman politicians keep on good terms with the tax-collectors. Greeks, Cicero means, by behaving as loyal subjects, can play a part in establishing his ideal of a harmony between the leading Roman classes—the politicians of the senatorial order and the financiers of the equestrian order. Such a view does not give the Greeks a special or privileged position within the Roman empire. But it does suggest that a governor should try to please both tax-collectors and Greeks. As a governor himself, Cicero tried to ensure that tax-collectors received fair sums and that Greek cities were not burdened by debts. Thus the harmony of Greeks and Roman businessmen would not only help the individual politician but would also add to the welfare of the whole empire. Whether we consider Cicero as a self-interested politician or as a theorist of empire, he does not think much of Greeks; their moral failings must be checked by the governor's wariness and their administrative incompetence needs to be supervised by Rome.[58]

Finally, in connection with Cicero's attitude to Greeks, we should consider his ideas on the part played by nature and learning in the governor's role. We saw above that Greek learning (*doctrina*), though often admired, was sometimes thought to be a fussy irrelevance. But Cicero did not think that Greek learning was ineffectual in Roman politics; he expected it to assist and improve the natural talents of the Roman character. He claimed that his own achievement in politics was based on Greek learning, and held up his governorship as the living proof of the theories described in his *Republic*, which was an adaptation of Greek ideas to Roman experience. His letters to Quintus are more revealing still. Quintus' nature, he says, is such that even without assistance from learning he would make a good ruler, practising moderation; but in fact Quintus' (Greek) learning is considerable and would repair the faults of the worst possible nature. Cicero here refers to the 'good rulers' extolled as models in Greek literature, the Cyrus and Agesilaus admired by Xenophon. He believes that the *Cyropaedeia* was constantly read by Scipio Africanus, the great Roman politician and general of the second century.[59] Works that influenced the great Scipio should also improve the lesser Romans of the present; eventually he reproaches Quintus, who is informed about Cyrus and Agesilaus, for being a worse governor than Romans in nearby provinces who were ignorant of these Greek exemplars. It is apparently true that Quintus was severe and irascible, almost to the point of eccentricity; and it is therefore possible that Cicero merely invoked Greek learning as a means of persuading Quintus to make good the deficiencies of nature from the resources of his education. Even if that is so, Cicero clearly believed that Greek learning could have a good practical effect on Roman rulers, though he is convinced that such learning must be relevant and useful, drawn from the moral and political wisdom of the Greek classics. However, even if he thinks that Greek learning can or should improve the Roman nature, it is far from certain that he would be optimistic about its having the same effect on the Greeks themselves.

But were all Greeks as bad as one another? We have seen that according to a passage in the *pro Flacco* the inhabitants of mainland Greece were preferable to the more easterly Greeks, such as those in the province of Asia. Juvenal, describing the Greek invasion of Rome, implies that the 'scum of Achaea' is not so depraved as the Greeks from further afield.[60] Can we then decide whether Romans did make this distinction in practice, apart from special pleading in rhetoric and literature? Verres, it seems, did not discriminate; he abused a Greek official at Sicyon just as he misbehaved to Greeks elsewhere.[61] Cicero, in writing to Quintus, speaks with two voices: he praises the Greeks of Asia who are to be administered by Quintus as 'most civilized', but he also remarks that the province of Asia is extremely corrupting. The younger Pliny[62] echoes the preference for Achaea when he writes to a friend who has already held office in Bithynia and is about to undertake a special mission in mainland Greece: he must remember that he is about to enter that 'true, unadulterated Greece', the fount of

civilization and literature. He should respect the antiquity of
Greece, its great history, even its fictitious stories. A Roman
governor should also be gentle in handling Greek faults, such as
boastfulness. Pliny is conscious of the fact that mainland Greece
is nearer to Rome, and implies that a good reputation won in
Achaea will be more important for his friend's future than his
previous achievement in 'distant' Bithynia. But though his
observations are partly concerned with the governor's fame, his
picture of past Greece is dominated by the prestige of Athens and
Sparta; he gives no acknowledgment to the culture of the Ionian
cities in the sixth and fifth centuries B.C. He seems to think that
there will be less servility in Greece proper than in the more
eastern Greek provinces.

Roman emperors, however, were mostly unaffected by this
sentimental preference for Achaea. Both Achaea and Asia were
(for the most part) safe provinces, administered by the senate.
Nero, admittedly, believed that Achaea deserved special favour
as the home of games and artistic competitions. But in general
emperors sought to maintain the prosperity and welfare of Greek
cities wherever they were. Pliny himself was sent by Trajan on a
special mission to Bithynia, to set in order the finances of the
cities; neither Pliny nor Trajan[63] gives any sign that these Greeks
are to be treated differently from, say, Greeks in Athens. The
main problem for the imperial administration was to prevent
Greeks overspending on amenities like theatres, aqueducts and
gymnasia. And though Hadrian had a high regard for Athens he
did not neglect other Greek cities.

In a sense, Roman governors saw Greeks at their worst; they
were harassed by their demands and bound to feel that the
provincials would try to take advantage of them. Longer-term
Roman residents in the Greek world were in a different position
from their fellow-Romans with official posts, who often stayed no
longer than a year. Cicero's friend Atticus must be regarded as
one of the most generous and likeable of Roman businessmen. He
was popular at Athens, where he resided, since he made interest-
free loans and occasionally paid for distributions of corn. Many
Roman magistrates honoured him with the rank of prefect, but
he did not take advantage of this in order to press his business
interests. Atticus could not have been generous to Athens if he
had not made money out of Greeks elsewhere. But it should not
be thought that as a benefactor he was self-seeking like Appius
Claudius, who dedicated a propylon at Eleusis. Atticus did not
seek fame like the ex-governor of Cilicia; he refused Athenian

citizenship and tried to prevent the Athenians from erecting a statue to him, though they did finally succeed when he was away from the city.[64]

Well-educated Romans of high standing were reluctant to pull rank in Greek lands. When Tiberius stayed at Rhodes for some six years (2 B.C.–A.D. 4), he lived in a modest house, frequented the gymnasium and exchanged visits with the 'Greeklings, almost on equal terms'. Once he announced that he wished to visit all the invalids in the community. His kind intentions were misinterpreted in accordance with Greek cleverness and flattery, and he was embarrassed to find that the patients had been arranged according to types of illness. Yet here too he was polite; the aristocrat apologized to all, even the humblest, for the trouble they had been caused. On another occasion, however, he reacted like a true Roman politician of the old school. He was present at a dispute between some teachers on the island when one of them insulted him on the grounds that he was too sympathetic to one side in the argument. This was the only time he made use of his tribunician power to invoke the law, and the offender was put into prison. Aristocrats might condescend but Greeks had to be careful not to go too far.[65]

Greek communities were open to the charge that they were too ready to flatter, whether they were greeting a governor in the province or acclaiming his services by means of a deputation at Rome. Financial interests led them to employ forms of polite ceremonial address that could easily look like insincere deference. These courtesies helped to confirm Roman suspicions of Greek 'faith', talkativeness and unreliability. But if, as Cicero maintained, Greek tribute was essential to the workings of Roman rule, the services of individual Greeks were no less important to the Roman statesmen who managed the late republic and the empire. Poets, philosophers and rhetoricians were respected not only as intellectuals but also as diplomats. The Romans acknowledged their dependence on such men more graciously than they did their debt to the Greek provinces. I shall take a few examples which will show how various Romans discussed the relevance of Greek learning in other spheres of life apart from politics, as we have already taken note of Cicero's views on the value of knowing about Greek rulers like Agesilaus.

Like his contemporary Crassus, the orator Antonius in the *de oratore* makes a sharp contrast between learning as shown by Greek teachers of rhetoric, and experience as an orator in the Roman school of life. All Greek teachers, he says, think that

Romans fail to understand the first thing about oratory. Antonius' attitude to them is based on confidence in himself as a real-life orator. He does not find the theorists of rhetoric a nuisance— either they make points of which he approves or they make him feel no regrets at his ignorance of doctrine. But though he says their theory is laughable- he is careful not to give offence. He sends them off without insulting them, even though this makes more trouble for him later on; evidently the Greeks did not take a hint very quickly but were pleased to lecture the Roman man of affairs.[66]

Antonius is perhaps made to overstate the case for Roman experience. But even he observes a rule of politeness in his behaviour towards Greek professors, though their knowledge is said to be useless and his tolerance causes him inconvenience. Cicero himself, to judge by his account, was more grateful to his rhetorical masters than Antonius had been. He has a special word of praise for Apollonius Molon, who not only taught rhetoric but was himself an experienced and successful speaker.[67] Though Cicero gave most of the credit for his own achievement to philosophy, he was clearly indebted to his Greek teachers of rhetoric and was warned against studying the subject with Latin teachers. Roman literature on rhetoric began with fierce words against this Greek irrelevance but came later to speak more generously, as we see from Quintilian.

There was a similar prejudice against philosophy. Just as Romans asserted that men had made effective speeches before theory was invented, so too they believed that their ancestors had been good men before Greek moral philosophy was known at Rome. But though philosophers were expelled at various times, respectable Greek philosophers were welcomed into Roman houses and lived on good terms with their hosts. The younger Cato made a special journey in order to persuade Athenodorus the Stoic, an independent figure who had refused many invitations, to come and live with him. At first, Romans were mainly interested in philosophy as a medicine of the soul. But they came to be more tolerant of other parts of philosophy; thus Gellius in the second century A.D. records how the Platonist Calvisius Taurus gave a justification for certain verbal puzzles, which the company thought were pointless and insane.[68] The demand that philosophy should be obviously relevant became less imperious.

I am suggesting that there was something of a gradual change in the attitude of Romans to the products of Greek theory (to leave on one side entirely the fact that Greek men of letters were diplomatists as well as intellectuals). Men became more receptive to activities of the Greek mind which Crassus or Cicero might have condemned as irrelevant. The second century A.D. was an age of revival in Greek rhetoric, when the professors of the second sophistic delighted Greek citizens and Roman emperors with their oratorical prowess.[69] A desire for sophisticated entertainment made men enjoy speeches which to an earlier age would have seemed a florid irrelevance.

Many Greek rhetors and philosophers were free men, persons of substance, whose reputation and position gave them some independence of Romans. Even more Greeks were influential as freedmen in the service of important Romans, though it is not always easy to be certain whether a particular freedman was Greek: a Greek name is no guarantee that the freedman was of Greek origin.[70] Now it is undeniable that there was a continuing prejudice against freedmen as a class, especially against those who were employed by the great men of the day. The younger Cato, as he approached Antioch, was astonished to find that the people of the town were waiting outside, marshalled in anticipation.[71] In fact they were not there to honour Cato but to welcome Demetrius, Pompey's influential freedman. Cato thought little of Antioch for this gesture, though he was able to laugh at the incident later on. Both Cicero and Tacitus express their disapproval of upstart freedmen with too much influence. Cicero tried to tell his brother Quintus that his freedman Statius made a bad impression because he appeared to be able to make Quintus do what he liked. Cicero believed that freedmen should be subordinate, and in a better, more truly Roman, age, had been kept in their place. Tacitus was exasperated by the wealth and political power exercised by the freedmen of Claudius and Nero.[72] Though it was natural for emperors to use their own freedmen in a way which brought them great influence, it is understandable that such freedmen were feared by aristocrats as usurpers of their own rightful place. But though freedmen are criticized, there are few signs of animus against Greek freedmen in particular. Cicero provides one example of this form of antipathy. At first he approved of M. Pomponius Dionysius, a freedman of Atticus, as one who was learned, responsible in his duties and an enthusiast for Cicero's fame. But later, at the start of the civil war, Dionysius was not ready to do what Cicero wished. Cicero says, by way of complaint: 'I know what a learned man and a friend should have done, but I don't expect such things very much from Greeks'.[73] But this seems an isolated expression of anti-Greek

sentiment directed at freedmen; adverse judgments usually en-
compass the class as a whole.

We have been considering the difficult question whether
prejudice against the Greek character is apparent in the Roman
treatment of Greeks. It seems that in the late republic, cities and
communities in Greek lands were often badly treated by governors,
who were mostly interested in making money for themselves and
assisting the tax-collectors. Some Roman aristocrats did not need
the excuse of prejudice against Greeks; they had more than
enough confidence in themselves. But it is clear from Cicero that
governors should be on their guard against Greek faults and vices.
Under the empire the provincial subjects of Rome were better
off; we might suppose that governors would then be more likely
to act with prudence towards the emperor's agents rather than
be suspicious of the alleged vices of Greeks.

Eminent Greek individuals were less exposed to this prejudice.
The need for doctors[74] prevailed over the strictures of the elder
Cato and Pliny. Men of talent—architects, rhetoricians and
philosophers—were often on close terms with their patrons and
employers. Entertainers too were socially acceptable, though
Greek philosophy and traditional Roman values disapproved of
them. The best Greeks were men who satisfied Roman norms and
earned the sort of praise that Cicero bestowed on Dionysius when
he was still in favour—responsible in his duties, modest in his way
of life, concerned with his Roman friend's fame.

The idea of Greek inferiority[75] was a product of the Romans'
pride in their own history. Since Romans were the imperial people,
who owed their success to virtue, defeated peoples must be
morally worse. If this idea was engendered by experience, it was
fostered by the competitive spirit which characterized the making
of Roman literature. Romans sought to show that their literary
achievements were as fine as their conquests; the polemical
energy of the writer comes from the same family as the forensic
hostility of the orator. These are noticeable features of the
Ciceronian age. But tolerance of Greeks increased as their abilities
became more and more necessary in politics and administration,
and gradually the sense of an achievement in Latin literature
caused writers to be less aggressive on the subject of Greek
irrelevance. Some would even allow that Greek was the superior
literature, though at the same time they were conscious that
Latin was very close behind.

2

PHILHELLENISM

This chapter sets out to discuss some of the features which are peculiar to philhellenism at Rome.

The first part is concerned with political relationships between Greeks and Romans in the late Roman republic and early empire. In the first century B.C., the Roman civil wars brought distress and hardship to some of the Greek cities which were sometimes involved in the power-struggle; but after Augustus' victory at Actium (31 B.C.) the cities in general benefited from the imperial peace. In the early part of the period especially, Roman statesmen were seldom swayed by appeals to Greek history or by reminders that Greek states had rendered distinguished services to Rome; they usually pursued their own, often self-seeking, political and military objectives. In the more settled conditions of the empire, however, arguments that a Greek city had a special, historical claim were given a more tolerant hearing. The appeal to the past was perhaps most effective when Romans felt that matters of high policy were not involved.

In the second part, I examine various Roman opinions about the Greek language and Greek art. Though many Romans knew Greek (in the sense that they had read Greek authors, spoke the language well and composed in it) they often had reservations about the different genius of the language and were conscious of a need to protect and develop Latin. Nor did they give an uncritical welcome to the numerous paintings and statues which were part of the spoils from Rome's wars in the eastern Mediterranean; there was a strong feeling that Greek art, even if legally Roman by right of conquest, might corrupt the austere Roman character, and the private collector was thought to be less excusable than the public benefactor who dedicated his magnificent plunder in a temple.

POLITICAL RELATIONS WITH GREEKS

The history of Roman thought and sentiment about Greek culture is largely a matter of discovering the views of the articulate few whose works have survived. We know most about the men who made Latin literature, from Cicero to Gellius, much less about the businessman or ordinary Roman. But any attempt to show how opinion changed or persisted needs to be set against the background of public events; the philhellenism of Romans can be seen at work in politics as well as in literature.

Towards the end of the Roman republic, foreign wars and conflicts between eminent Romans inflicted great hardship on cities in the Greek world. War with Mithridates brought Roman armies into the east, and the decisive battles of the civil wars were fought in Greece, at Pharsalus, Philippi and Actium. It was a time when many events that occurred in the Greek world were politically important to the Roman world as a whole. With the advent of an imperial system there was a change. The Greek east was relatively unmolested by the adverse effects of high politics; the civil wars of A.D. 68–69, for example, were decided in Italy, though support for Vespasian's army did impose some burdens on Greek cities. The Greeks, like other peoples, gained from the imperial peace; they had difficulties over finance, but when they appealed to Rome for help they knew they were addressing administrators who would listen sympathetically.

The interdependence of Greek and Roman is clearly shown by the growing number of associations between important Romans and Greek intellectuals. The latter often served Rome well and were rewarded by individual grants of citizenship or privileges for their cities, and Roman citizenship was merely the start of a process which led to Greeks entering the Roman senate.[1] There is an understandable element of self-interest about the Greeks' liking for or dependence on Rome. The Roman attitude to Greeks is perhaps more elusive, on the political side at least. We can gain some insight, however, by analyzing the policies of particular Romans; from the late republic various degrees of sympathy for Greeks are exemplified in the careers of Sulla, Lucullus, Brutus and Cassius, while during the empire we can observe important aspects of philhellenism in the policies of Nero and Hadrian. In several cases we can examine the arguments advanced by Greek envoys and see how Romans were affected by them.

The first Mithridatic war (89–84 B.C.), though nominally a war between the king of Pontus and Rome, inflicted most damage on the cities in European Greece and the Roman province of Asia. Many Greeks welcomed Mithridates (who laid claim to philhellenic ancestry) and were not slow to carry out his order to put to death all resident Romans and Italians; probably 80,000 lost their lives because the exploitation by tax-collectors and moneylenders had caused widespread resentment. Although Greek support for Mithridates waned, the memory of the massacre hardened the mood of the Roman soldiers, who wanted revenge as well as plunder.

When Sulla came out as the Roman general, enemy forces had advanced and occupied parts of mainland Greece; his first task was to drive the enemy garrisons from Athens and the Peiraeus. To a large extent his attitude to the Greeks was determined by his need for ready money. The temple-treasuries at Olympia, Epidaurus and Delphi were asked to part with their funds; they were assured that Sulla would give them better protection or return the like amount at the end of the war. The temples were reluctant to obey: Delphi objected that Apollo's lyre had been heard striking a note, but Sulla, who could play the diplomatic game with grim humour, insisted that the sound was a note of relief, not of sorrow at the departing treasures. But his actions were remembered against him; thus Plutarch draws a contrast between Sulla, obliged to find favour with his undisciplined troops, and the Roman heroes of the past who defeated the enemies of Greece and added to the endowments of the temples. Some Greek hostility is understandable as Sulla was not remarkable for his philhellenism; but he was perhaps fairer than Plutarch allows, since he did allocate some Theban land to Delphi in compensation. Yet even this looked questionable, as Thebes had quickly returned to the Roman fold, and it was felt by some Greeks that he had merely vented his anger, behaving in a way that was foreign to the best Roman character in its dealings with Greece.

At the siege of Athens and the Peiraeus Sulla was visited by a deputation from the garrison. The members were probably Athenian hangers-on of the ruler Aristion, for they started to rehearse the old story about Theseus, Eumolpus and the Persian Wars. Sulla did not wish to hear about Athens' glorious past and merely said that he had come to drive out the rebels.[2] Greeks were constantly tempted to give untimely reminders of their history, as Plutarch shows when he advises the budding politician to leave such eulogies to the sophists. Perhaps Sulla's blunt rejection betrays the practical Roman more than the adversary of Greece.

However, his destruction of the Peiraeus and the capture of
Athens were held against him. Plutarch says that the streets were
flowing with blood and adds that Sulla did not stop the carnage
until he was persuaded to do so by some Athenians and Roman
senators. Then he remarked, 'I will spare the few (the men of the
present) for the sake of the many (the glorious dead)'. At best
this suggests little more than a grudging respect for Athens' past.
Lucullus later admired Sulla's good fortune in saving Athens
from fire, but he can hardly be called a philhellene; his policy was
mostly governed by the need to allow his troops some plunder
and by his sense of outrage at the disloyalty of Athens. He could
not have sympathized with the more generous view expressed
later by the epitomist Velleius Paterculus; 'if anyone blames
Athens for this defection, he is ignorant of truth and history. The
loyalty of Athens was so reliable that the Romans said of any
actions performed in genuine good faith that it was done with
Attic faith'.[3]

A later incident is also revealing. Sulla was given a present of
fish by some men from Halae, one of the towns destroyed after the
battle of Orchomenus. He expressed his astonishment that there
could be any survivors from the place, but told the fishermen
they had brought persuasive advocates and need not be alarmed.
The men felt sufficiently heartened to go back to their ruined
town.[4] This humorous sarcasm did not impress Plutarch, who
probably felt that Sulla's taste for low company and the pleasures
of the table made it impossible for him to sympathize with things
Hellenic.

Is it fair to dismiss Sulla as a barbarian who captured Athens
even though he did not destroy the Parthenon? For all his heavy
humour at the expense of Greeks he was less vindictive than his
rival Fimbria. When the town of Ilium was besieged by Fimbria,
the townspeople were instructed by Sulla to say it was under his
protection; Fimbria then told Ilium that it could therefore admit
him as a Roman friend, since the people of Ilium boasted of their
Trojan connection with Rome, the new Ilium in the west.[5] This
was sheer malice, as once he was admitted he killed the inhabitants
and burnt the place. After the war was over Sulla imposed on the
defeated Greeks of Asia taxes and fines which seemed (and were)
harsh. But he is supposed to have said that whereas the atrocities
committed by Greeks against Romans were barbaric, his actions
were motivated by 'mercy for the Greek people and the Greek
name, the fame of Asia and a concern for the good reputation of
Rome.'

It is not easy to be sure about Sulla's attitude to the Greeks, since much of the evidence is late, even if some of it is ultimately derived from his memoirs. As a commander he had many problems; he was aware that the government in Rome was run by his enemies, he was short of money, and he felt that Rome had been wronged by the murder of her citizens in Asia. Mithridates had to be expelled from Roman spheres of influence. It is, then, not surprising that he was impatient with Greek arguments and excuses that seemed to him to be so many academic obstacles put in the way of what had to be done. He seems to have believed that Greeks had violated their obligations to the recent past and did not wish to have his time wasted by arguments from legends and long ago. He was certainly blind to the long-term interests of the Greek provincials, but he was exasperated; it was not much of a compliment to things Greek if he did say that only regard for the Greek name held him back from retaliating their assassinations in kind.

If Sulla's memory was detested by many Greeks, his treatment of Romans and Italians was no better. 'Sullan cruelty' was a tag applied to the proscriptions in Italy and was long remembered against him. But his friend Lucullus, who led the Roman armies throughout most of the second Mithridatic war, seems to have deserved the name philhellene. His merciful nature helped to ease the burden of Sulla's fines and taxes imposed on the Greek cities of Asia. When his troops, who were less particular than their general, wanted to sack the Greek towns, Sinope and Amisus, Lucullus did not allow it. His zeal for the Greeks was shown in other ways at Amisus; the town had been originally an Athenian settlement and had sheltered refugees from Athens in Sulla's war. Lucullus supplied the Athenian survivors there with clothes and money, and sent them back to Athens. The same policy of returning Greek refugees to their homes was followed after the defeat of Tigranes, king of Armenia. Lucullus was acclaimed as a benefactor and founder, and his popularity was confirmed by a festival named in his honour.[6]

Lucullus' kind treatment of the Greeks was probably dictated by a realistic sense that the cities had suffered much and should not be exploited by the army or by Roman financiers. Also, this Mithridatic war was unlike the first; fewer parts of the Greek world were occupied by the enemy, and the general's ambition urged him to carry the war into Mithridates' kingdom. His conduct is in marked contrast with the ruthlessness of his colleague Cotta, who sacked the town of Heraclea, carried off works of art

and, on his return to Rome, was at first honoured with the name
Ponticus. But this glory was short-lived, and a delegate from
Heraclea put some persuasive arguments against him: Heraclea,[7]
because of her recent services to Rome, should not have been
maltreated once the enemy garrison had left; the Greek citizens'
actions against Rome could be excused on the grounds of compulsion; and, lastly, Cotta had committed sacrilege against
temples. Although an appeal to recent Greco-Roman relations
carried more weight than a recital of past glories, it is unlikely
that the Romans were swayed by the Heracleot case on its own.
They probably reflected that Cotta's war-service included a
discreditable failure at Chalcedon, and when Cotta was deprived
of his senatorial rank his misconduct at Heraclea was no more
than part of the Roman case against him.

Lucullus' name as a true friend of Greece depends mainly on
Plutarch's eulogy. Plutarch's own idea of Hellenic values would
not have been approved by all Greeks, but it is worth noticing
that he makes some criticisms of the Roman hero. He does not
have much sympathy for Lucullus the art-collector and owner of
grand villas; in his eyes such expenditure is a display of wealth,
it is ostentation rather than taste. Lucullus' hospitality was too
lavish for some visitors who 'had true Hellenic feelings' and were
embarrassed; he replied that receiving on the grand scale was not
only a tribute to Greeks but satisfied his sense of what was owing
to Lucullus. On the other hand Plutarch acknowledges that he
was also a *serious* Hellenist; he had a good library and often joined
in the discussions held by Greeks in his porticoes. 'His house was a
Greek hearth and home.' The encomium seems justified, even
though we should allow for the fact that Plutarch was grateful to
Lucullus as a friend of his own city, since his evidence had saved
Chaeronea against a charge of murder.[8] But Lucullus' philhellenism was more important in Greek sentiment than in Roman
politics. He was replaced as general because the tax-collectors
resented his interference and were able to exploit Roman feeling
that Lucullus had had too long a period in command without
finally ending the war.

The Roman civil wars put a strain more on the financial
resources of the Greek cities than on their manpower. There were
enough Roman legionaries, but there was not always sufficient
money to make sure of their allegiance. This was apparent in the
campaigns of Brutus and Cassius against Xanthus and Rhodes,
though it is also true that they did not wish to leave for Greece
without having neutralized the Rhodian naval base and fleet.

Cassius, who was given the task of taking Rhodes, was embarrassed by the resistance of a city to which he owed some of his education. The Rhodians were more sympathetic to the side of Antony and Octavian; there was also some difference of opinion among the classes, since the better-off did not want to risk open conflict with a Roman force, whereas the lower classes were carried away by the memory of their past glories. Popular leaders inspired them by mentioning Rhodian opposition to Mithridates and by reminding them of events earlier still, in the time of Demetrius the Besieger. Their chief delegate, Archelaus, had taught Cassius during his stay at Rhodes and had some claim on his respect; Appian attributes to him a speech which begins with the words, 'Do not destroy a Greek city, you who are a philhellene'. The speech is not genuine but shows what Appian, a Greek devoted to Rome, believed to be the plausible arguments put forward on this occasion. These included the past glories of Rhodes and her services to Rome, a reminder that there was a treaty of friendship between Rhodes and Rome, and a plea that the matter should be referred to the senate. None of these arguments was likely to have much effect on a Roman politician and general who was looking for cash to distribute to Roman soldiers. Rhodes was soon defeated and Cassius imposed his own terms; the Rhodians were compelled to contribute sums of money, and much of the temple-treasure also was taken. But although Cassius showed that he was treating Rhodes as captured territory he did not allow his troops to plunder the city.[9]

Dio and Plutarch are in disagreement about Cassius' conduct. Dio says that he treated Rhodes leniently, because he had been educated there; Plutarch, however, is prejudiced against Cassius on the grounds that he took a larger sum of money from Rhodes than Brutus took from Patara. The apparent severity of Cassius, in Plutarch's view, was not consistent with his republican answer to those who called him king: 'I am neither king nor lord, but the executioner sent to punish the king and lord'.[10] It is not possible to adjudicate between these opinions, though they are of interest as a record of Greek judgments on Cassius. It is clear, however, that Brutus and Cassius did not wish to waste a lot of time on the cities in this part of the Greek world, but nor did they want to get a bad name by sacking cities, as demanding money was already a sure way to unpopularity. The Greeks, apart from Xanthus which was destroyed by its own obstinacy, were prepared to pay rather than lose their lives. But it would be wrong to think that the Romans were only concerned with the economic motive.

Brutus, at least, wanted to punish a Roman officer because of a charge brought by the people of Sardeis;[11] in this he showed a concern for good administration that could conflict with the narrow factional interest in gaining Roman adherents at any cost. Greeks, too, were coming to recognize that their feeling for the glorious past was offensive or indifferent to a Roman. Romans were willing to listen to a historical sketch of Rhodes when they were there on a visit or for educational purposes, but they were not impressed when it was used as a diplomatic counter.

In these wars it was difficult for a Greek city to say no to whichever Roman general was near and pressing, even if it could foresee that someone else was going to win. There were severe financial·penalties for having been on the defeated side. After Philippi and the death of the liberators, Antony, in an address to Greek delegations from Roman Asia, declared that Asia was better off under the Romans than under the Attalids, since Rome took a fixed percentage of the harvest and would therefore get less revenue in a bad year. He did not point out that the Romans would do correspondingly better when the crop was abundant. Asia deserved to be punished heavily for having joined the liberators but would instead be required to pay ten years' tribute in a year. When the Greeks protested, the demand was reduced to nine years' tribute, to be paid within two years. Places like Rhodes were rewarded because they had not complied willingly with the requests of Cassius; Antony, then, distinguished between Greeks on the basis of recent services to Rome. His main aim was to provide money for the Roman forces, and the Greeks who had supported the losing side were the obvious people to look to for supplies. Antony was flattered by the Greeks; at Ephesus he was greeted as the new Dionysus and at Athens later he was told that Athena was betrothed to him. But Greek adulation did not deflect him from his Roman objectives; he accepted the Athenians' match-making and asked for a large dowry. When he relaxed at Athens and Alexandria and made the polite gesture of wearing Greek clothes, he was still a Roman general enjoying a holiday.[12]

A slight change in the pattern is apparent after Augustus' victory at Actium; he did not exact money, and even returned some works of art which Antony had taken. But he rewarded friendly communities and punished cities which had committed offences against Roman citizens. He emphasized the victory of Rome by founding a city near Actium, and at Pergamum and Nicomedia he allowed temples in honour of Rome and himself. Greeks were ready to honour the man who had brought peace while Augustus himself wished to make the name of Rome the principal object of attention.

Our judgment of this period is that Romans did not on the whole think that Greek cities deserved special treatment just because they were Greek or because some Romans admired Greek literature. Romans were guided by what was important at Rome. There was now more glory in saving a Greek city from total destruction than in letting it burn, since the cities were often in a Roman province or allied to Rome. Romans were inured to reminders of the Greek past; but when they listened they often acted according to their political sense of what Rome required. A record of recent services to Rome was more likely to make an impression, but even this would be overlooked when money was short. This is not surprising as the cities had wealth available or valuable objects that could be realized. Initiation,[13] as at Athens, was welcome; but though the Romans were often grateful for these marks of respect and flattery, they also felt that they had given proof of their condescension.

The eastern Greek world looked very different by the end of the first century B.C. More territory was incorporated in the form of Roman provinces whereas a century earlier only Macedonia and Asia were organized in this way. Many of the cities had obtained or gradually acquired various privileges, though in general their freedoms were insignificant compared with the paternalist rule of governors and emperors. The Greek cities recovered financially from the extra tax-burdens which some of them had suffered during various phases of the civil wars; and in the early empire the problems facing Roman rulers were often concerned with the rivalries of Greek cities that were now safer and prosperous. But, politically, these were of local significance only; looked at through Roman eyes they were no more than a part of the government's wide task of administration. One thing, however, seemed to change very little under the empire. Greek envoys continued to support their claims by appeals to Greek legend, Greek history and their relationship with Rome. A Greek city would appeal to the past as a plea that it deserved special treatment or honour compared with other Greek cities.

There are some interesting examples of this in Tacitus. In A.D. 22 the government thought it should take some action because too many Greek cities in Asia claimed that they had temples with the right of asylum. There was social disorder as a result because numbers of slaves, debtors and dangerous criminals took refuge in the temples. Local pride obviously felt that the prestige of a god, who could offer this degree of protection, extended also to the city; but there was a danger that too many such places would make it difficult to bring the guilty to justice. Tiberius therefore instructed the senate to hear the claims of envoys from the cities concerned and to decide which should be allowed. Tacitus' account of this episode is ironical. It was, he says, a 'reflection of the old times', that the emperor should require the senate to adjudicate the demands of the provinces; but he sets off this apparent recovery of past senatorial freedom by stating that in his view 'Tiberius was making the power of the principate more secure'. He means to suggest that real power rested with the emperor while the senate was being asked to handle matters of no importance.

The senators had to listen to various arguments. It was fortunate for Tacitus' ironical purpose that the first speakers were from Ephesus; they based their claim to have a temple-refuge on the alleged fact that Diana and Apollo had been born not at Delos but at Ephesus. They invoked other mythology as well and ended with confirmation from history: Persian, Macedonian and Roman had all apparently respected this asylum with its divine origin. Tacitus takes advantage of these 'proofs' from the remote past to underline his conviction that the senate was asked to waste its time on something trivial to Romans. Other delegates produced a similar blend of ancient and recent history until the senators were exhausted by their rhetoric and referred the whole subject to the consuls. Some of the refuges were confirmed but others were rejected on the grounds that the claim rested on 'obscure origins'.[14]

We can only guess at senatorial reaction to these arguments from the Greek past. The opposite extremes, politeness and antipathy, are clearly illustrated in the behaviour of Germanicus and Piso at Athens. Germanicus paid Athens the compliment of appearing there with only one lictor, though as a holder of imperium he was entitled to more. The Athenians replied by granting him extravagant honours; they also spoke about their glorious past as a way of showing their belief that Germanicus deserved as much as had been awarded to the great men of Athenian history. There was agreeable flattery on both sides. Germanicus was soon followed by Piso, who interpreted his appointment as governor of Syria to mean a watching brief on his superior. Piso at once showed a different Roman reading of Athenian history; he made it plain that he saw in Athens the ally of Mithridates against Sulla, the friend of Antony against Augustus. Earlier Athenian history also was reinterpreted: Athens' defeat by Macedonia and her victimization of great Athenians were major points of the indictment. Piso wanted to take a different line from Germanicus; but he was also annoyed because Athens had not been merciful to a protégé of his who had just been convicted of forgery. For personal and political reasons Piso denied Athenian grandiloquence about the past and belittled Athens as the mere relic of her glory.[15]

In A.D. 23 the Greek cities of Asia asked for permission to dedicate a temple to Tiberius, his mother and the senate. Once their prayer was allowed, the next task was to decide which city should have the honour; there were eleven claimants, all with much the same enthusiasm, though they were not all equal to the expense. There was little to choose between the different arguments based on antiquity of lineage and services to Rome in the Macedonian wars against Perseus and Aristonicus. First of all the senate eliminated the cities which would not be able to meet the expense; thus Ilium was made to drop out because she had in her favour no better claim than that she was the mother-city of Rome. Once the initial sifting was over, historical arguments were given more scope. Smyrna won because her services to Rome were put in a good light; she had acknowledged Rome at a time when there were other major powers and she had volunteered to help Sulla in Rome's hour of need. As often, Romans were persuaded that it was right to honour the city whose contributions to Roman history could be placed in the most favourable light.[16]

The importance of current or recent services can also be detected somewhat later, in Claudius' plea that Cos should be granted immunity from taxation. Claudius began his case with the usual arguments based on antiquity; but his decisive point was that Xenophon, his own doctor, came from the Cos school of medicine, and he asked that Cos should be favoured because of her distinguished citizen. The city of Byzantium had a good case too, if one only looked at historical arguments; but she had no Xenophon on whom to rest her case and so only received exemption for five years.[17]

But, although Roman philhellenism was most likely to have some practical effects when it was a response to past or recent Greek services to Rome, this does not mean that Greek cities as such were preferred to others. After the cities of Asia had been allowed to build a temple to Tiberius, his mother and the senate, the province of further Spain made the same request.[18] It was disallowed by Tiberius, not because of any general preference for Hellenic places, but because he thought that once was enough.

The tribute to an emperor would become empty and meaningless if all the provinces were granted that form of worship; and as a moderate Julio-Claudian emperor Tiberius tried to follow a religious policy which would not raise him too high above the level of all his subjects.

Greek cities had had a long tradition of honouring Hellenistic rulers and it was natural to offer a similar cult to important Romans both in the republic and under the empire. Romans often disparaged Greek flattery but at the same time they expected and received such offerings. They granted favours and benefits because a city was thought to deserve or need them, not just because it was Greek. Nero's philhellenism, however, was of a different order, because he wished to excel not merely as a ruler or politician but as a public performer in Greek games. The official Roman self-portrait showed a general, an administrator or an orator; aesthetic talents had usually been indulged at leisure as a private hobby; but Nero, through seeking acclaim for his performances, tried to make the artist an acceptable public figure.

He wanted to take part in chariot-races and to appear as a singer and a player on the lyre. His political advisers hoped that he would be satisfied with private performances as a chariot-driver; but his need for an audience made him invite the Roman people to admire the show. In A.D. 59 a special festival was held, the Juvenalia, in which Nero himself appeared on the stage, played on the lyre and was supported by his own claque. In A.D. 60 and 65 there were more contests 'in the style of Greek games', the Neronia; these were modelled on the Greek and included competitions in music, athletics and driving chariots. Finally Nero could not be content with the applause of Rome. He decided, late in A.D. 66, to visit Greece itself and to complete his aesthetic triumph in the homeland of these contests. The time-table of the games was rearranged so that they could be held within one year. There is no doubt that Nero took his art seriously; he practised hard and went through the conventional routine of showing signs of nervousness before the judges; but the judges knew what was expected of them and proclaimed him the victor in all the major games.[19]

In a sense there was nothing untoward about holding Greek festivals of this type, even at Rome; they provoked nothing like the hostility of Jewish opinion to the games celebrated by Herod the Great. Tacitus himself, a severe critic, indicates that there was a popular demand for these entertainments, as might be expected if only because there were now more Greeks in the city. Augustus himself had patronized Greek games at Actium, to celebrate his victory, and again at Naples in A.D. 2. After Nero, in A.D. 86, Domitian instituted the Capitoline games, which were popular and were repeated on several occasions. Furthermore, there was some attempt in Nero's time to justify the games and give them a Roman setting. Nero declared that song was sacred to Apollo, whose image had musical accoutrements both in Greece and in Rome. The Juvenalia was a festival intended to honour a Roman god, Juventas, and to commemorate a Roman custom, the first shaving of the emperor's beard. The Neronian festival was to be held at five-yearly intervals, not (in the Greek style) after four years. The religious traditions of Rome were honoured by inviting the Vestal virgins to attend; their presence was to be the Roman parallel to the Greek custom at Olympia, where the games were witnessed by the priestesses of Olympia.[20]

Tacitus, however, outlines a number of arguments against the games, at least one of which appears to be specifically anti-Greek. There was a strong Roman sentiment against the Greek liking for gymnasia, on the grounds that they provided a training for athletes not soldiers. The younger Pliny reflects this feeling when he writes approvingly of an official who put a stop to an athletic contest at Vienne; and Pliny suggests that the disease has spread from the head (Rome) to other parts of the body politic.[21] Some conservative patriots would therefore have objected to Nero's games as another Greek intrusion, especially as Nero built a new gymnasium in the Campus Martius. The gymnasia were also objected to on the grounds that they led to a cult of homosexuality.[22] Cicero had declared that in his opinion 'this habit seems to have originated in the gymnasia of the Greeks'. It was believed that Roman morals had been affected for the worse by taking from Greece the custom of allowing men of different ages to bathe together. These ideas conveniently enabled Rome to look on homosexuality as a Greek habit, another instance of moral deterioration introduced from the outside into the purer world of Rome.

Although conservative moralists complained about Greek games, it is obvious, from the imperial precedent set by Augustus, that they were in themselves inoffensive. The literary prejudice against gymnasia did not stop Trajan from allowing a guild of athletes to have its own buildings, including a gymnasium, at Rome. The Romans of real life did object, however, to the fact that Nero himself took part as a performer and compelled

Roman nobles to do the same, though some, it seems, were not
unwilling. The objection was based on the commonsense feeling
that the competitive aesthetic of the artist-performer did not
become the ruler of the world. The crowns awarded by judges
had only the name in common with the crowns decreed by cities
from a sense of gratitude to the emperor. It seemed extraordinary
that the man who was the judge of mankind should submit to the
judgment of others. The soldier who tried to release Nero, when he
appeared in gold chains as the role prescribed, was making an
elementary mistake about art; but though ignorant of art he
knew how an emperor should act.[23]

Nero himself was serious about his aesthetic philhellenism, even
though it was resented by officers as well as ordinary soldiers. Yet
he did not let this Greek enthusiasm conflict with his interest. The
Greeks were privileged to admire him, but he did not shrink from
taking away their pictures and statues; and the crowns and prizes
were worth money as well as fame.[24] In return he conferred on
Greece freedom and tax-exemption. But the inscription which
records this shows the true Roman side of his philhellenism; he
announced that Greeks had not enjoyed immunity from taxation
even in earlier times, since then 'they were the slaves of others or
themselves'. Nero, in fact, was asserting that Rome had improved
the state of Greece whether one looked at past or present; his
generosity was not conceived as merely a restoration of the Greek
past. But the Greek recipients, in acknowledging the gift, explicitly
connected it with the indigenous freedom of which they had been
deprived. Thus, even though Nero was an aesthetic philhellene,
this record of his favour shows the contrast between Roman disparagement of Greek history and the Greek sense of what was
owing to their past. His action ensured Nero a better name among
Greeks; but they did not benefit for very long, since Vespasian
rescinded Nero's decree, observing that Greece had unlearnt the
ways of freedom long ago.[25]

In the second century A.D. there was something of a Greek
revival; Roman officials and emperors improved city-administra-
tion and gave new buildings, and the cities could afford the
expense of professional sophists. Among the second-century
emperors the most remarkable for his philhellenism was Hadrian.
Though he travelled all over the empire he had a special regard
for Athens, which he visited three times; he was always delighted
to have a reason for conferring a benefit on Athens or individual
Athenians. He completed the building of the temple to Zeus
Olympius and added to Athenian prestige by making the city the

centre of a new organization, the Panhellenion. Its members were Greeks and, among other matters, they discussed what qualified a state to belong. Also the range of Hadrian's interests shows that he was versatile in the arts derived from Greece; in his case (unlike Nero's) the taste of the aesthete seems to complement the work of the public benefactor. When the temple of Zeus was inaugurated the occasion was marked by a speech from Polemon the sophist; the art of the Greek orator was here used to thank the admiring Roman for his services to Greece.[26]

Yet the Panhellenion[27] can hardly be called a political body. Its deliberations, as far as we can judge, were very tedious, concerned, for example, with receiving decrees of thanks to Hadrian from member-states, confirming them and thanking the delegates in their turn for their good work. It had no real power over events, since important decisions were taken by Roman officials. Yet the idea was itself an honour to Greece and Athens in particular; it shows that Hadrian had a genuine regard for Greece (not shared to the same degree by all Romans) and believed that Greek pride in the past was still usable in the wider context of the Roman empire. But even at Athens there was a reminder that the emperor, however courteous a friend, was the ruler of other peoples too. The Pantheon contained a list of the places, both Greek and barbarian, that had been helped by the munificence of Hadrian. This form of philhellenism did not hesitate to state the full record of the imperial bounty in a temple of the favoured people. Hadrian seems exceptional among ruling Romans for two reasons; his gifts to Greece were on the grand scale, and he showed a respect for the Greek past which is far removed from the contempt of a Piso or the gruff realism of Vespasian.

In general, though Rome often protected the Greeks and earned the name philhellene, she also consulted the interests of other peoples; Jews, for instance, were given practical help when Greek communities in Asia passed anti-Jewish measures, such as imposing fines for observing the Sabbath. In the modern, post-Renaissance world political philhellenism has been more complex. Perhaps the important constituents are admiration for the political and aesthetic achievement of the Greek past, and the belief that contemporary Greece is oppressed either by autocrats from within or by an occupying power. Non-Greeks have fought or intrigued for political change in Greece because they have felt that the Hellenic present was in decline from the high standards of a meritorious past. It is, of course, undeniable that the champions of Greece have sometimes pursued their own advantage, but their attachment to Greece has often made them look convincing idealists, in the eyes of others as well as in their own. But ideology and sentiment did not affect the Roman view of Greece in this way. There was no foreign power like the Turk to convince men that occupation and tyranny were an affront to a great history. Roman regard for the political achievements of Greece was uttered with faint praise; Greek 'freedom', whether this refers to autonomy or democratic government, was less valued, partly because it seemed anarchic and undisciplined; and the Romans felt that for them to praise Greek history would be to deny the more legitimate claims of their own success. Similarly, the masterpieces of Greek literature were not always valued for their own sake or because they were evidence of the Greek mind; the Romans experienced these works as a challenge to themselves, to create a literature that would be equal or even superior.

Roman philhellenism was therefore less ideological than its modern variants. Although the Greeks and their cities were important to the Roman empire, their requests were often treated piecemeal rather than in the light of a general theory of Hellenic values. The Greek world was only part of a large empire; and there was as yet no military threat to Greece compared with the German menace to the provinces near the Rhine and Danube. Tacitus felt that Germans like Arminius had not received their commemorative due, because Greeks 'only admire what is theirs' and Romans choose to dwell on the glories of the republic.[28] The emperors and their advisers were not affected by this escapism into the past, understandable though it is, and they did not neglect the north and west to the benefit of the Greek east. Aesthetically, too, Roman philhellenism was not over-generous in thanking Greece for what she had given; the Greek language and Greek art were often criticized, as we shall see, on the grounds that they were uncongenial or ill-suited to the Roman character.

GREEK LANGUAGE AND GREEK ART

Although the Romans were indebted to Greece for most of their models in literature and thought, they did not concede that dependence or imitation meant inferiority. They liked to feel that they had improved the inheritance; thus Cicero says that where the Romans had been original they had been wiser than the Greeks, and that when they had borrowed they had changed

things for the better. He adds that Romans knew how to extract
what really mattered from their Greek sources.[29] It would not be
right to dismiss this claim as so much Ciceronian pride in creating
clear, expository prose. Quintilian, though he is more generous
to the Greeks, assumes that the two literatures are at least comparable; and even Gellius, who often shows a sense of deference
to Greek, delights in expounding and justifying what are for him
the Latin classics. If Cicero's assertion was at too high a pitch,
later Romans acquiesced in a note of equality.

The Romans could only have adapted Greek forms to enshrine
their own experience if they felt some degree of kinship with
the Greeks. On the other hand the size of the Greek loan often
led the borrowers to assert their independence, since it can be
humiliating to be too precise about this kind of debt. Romans
often sought to emphasize, not their likeness to, but their difference
from Greeks, since they were proud of their own creations whether
the model was openly acknowledged or not. Although there are
many ways in which cultural difference can be felt or shown, two
subjects seem to be particularly important for the historian of
Roman attitudes to Greece. One is language. It is instructive to
see what the conquerors thought about the difference between
the two languages and to ask why they spoke or quoted Greek.
The other is Greek art, which, like language, affected the
Romans with a sense of the Greek aesthetic achievement. But
there was an important difference between art and language: art
was plunder, an ornament of conquest, and could be shipped off
to Rome. The captured statues and paintings were therefore
less dispensable than the Greek tongue, which was acquired by
many but not always used, since Latin was an emergent rival. A
Roman who read and admired the masterpieces of Greek oratory
could always find satisfaction in the thought that the important
issues of his time were debated in the Latin language, in the
courts or senate at Rome. The Roman spectator of Greek art had
to wait longer for such consolation, and Romans did not honour
their artists as much as their writers and poets. Thus the objects
of Greek art seemed matchless (except to those purists who
admired the earthenware vessels of earlier Rome and saw in them
an image of frugality); but the Latin language seemed quite as
good as Greek even if the literary monuments were not yet as
polished. Yet there is a common element in the Roman reactions
to Greek art and Greek language; in both cases there is evidence
to suggest that the Romans did not admire the Greek achievement
without reservations.

We may introduce the first subject—Romans' knowledge and use of Greek—by considering some passages which compare the nature of the two languages. Cicero stands out as an aggressive exponent of the view that Latin is the superior language. We have to take into account that his ideas on the subject are mostly expressed in his philosophical works, though this is not to say that he only came to hold them late in life. How this view affected his translations and imitations of Greek thinkers is a subject that can be left till the discussion of Roman philosophy. At this stage it should be enough to refer to his main contention, which he repeats in several works: that Latin is a richer language than Greek and has a greater supply or abundance of words (*copia verborum*).[30] When Cicero wrote in this way he knew that many Romans were convinced of the relative poverty of Latin compared with Greek, at least for philosophical purposes; and his thesis seems therefore to be inspired by the polemics of the creative translator.

Seneca's remarks on the subject are of more interest because they are not tied to the particular difficulties of the translator or imitator. In discussing the relative speed at which one should speak, he maintains that different characteristics suit different peoples. Speed of discourse is a 'freedom' (*licentia*) that one will allow to Greeks; but Latin is different, since Romans, even when they are writing, separate their words, and Seneca implies that the pauses or gaps will be even more noticeable when an audience is addressed. His particular proof is Cicero himself; though Roman oratory leaped forward because of his speeches, he himself spoke at a steady pace. 'Roman discourse is more inclined to weigh itself and to offer something weighty.' This contrast between Greek quickness and Roman deliberation is expressed in terms which have moral overtones; Seneca means that Greek freedom or licence is a reflection of the Greek moral and political character, whereas the more measured Roman delivery speaks for the greater discipline of the ruling power. Seneca's main concern here is to establish that the philosopher's manner of speaking should be weighty and deliberate, the audible sign of his inner seriousness. Yet it is clear that the Latin-speaking philosopher, so idealized, will simply be a higher version of the natural Roman character. Valerius Maximus, writing under Tiberius, and the younger Pliny also draw attention to the rapidity of Greek speakers, and they say—or imply—that this quality is less admirable than the more careful delivery of Romans; there is more than a suspicion that Greek speed is intended to secure an unfair advantage.[31]

The most important discussion of this topic occurs in a difficult passage in Quintilian. The question here is whether Latin is capable of achieving a particular form of excellence in oratory, the clear, persuasive exposition of an ordinary or unimportant subject, which would deserve the name 'Atticist'; in the context this would refer to a pleasing economy in the treatment, measured both by diction and by the manner of delivery. Quintilian first makes the point that it is difficult to vie with the Greeks in manner of delivery, because the Latin language has a harder sound than Greek. Some Latin letters, for instance, are objectionable to the ear; he gives 'f' as an example and adds that Latin words suffer because they often have to end in 'moaning m', a final sound unknown in Greek. In short, Greek is more euphonious than Latin, which is why Latin poets seek to embellish their poems with Greek names or words. Greek is richer not only in words but also in the number of reputable dialects which make up the whole called Greek.[32]

At this point Quintilian's capitulation to Greek seems complete; we could only be Attic in Latin, he says, if we were allowed the pleasing sounds and wealth of vocabulary that are present in Greek. But the Latin writer must still try the seemingly impossible; if the language is recalcitrant he must try to discover more facts and ideas to help his argument. Again, the strengths of Latin diction are power, weight and, surprisingly, abundance (perhaps he means here that Latin has a wealth of looser synonyms); the Greek qualities of delicacy, subtlety and preciseness of diction do not have their equivalents in Latin, but Latin can still approach their *effects* by a judicious use of arguments and the natural virtues of its words. Latin, we might say, is bound to be more at sea than Greek in dealing persuasively with a humdrum topic, but that is partly because Latin is a grander vessel anyway and finds it more difficult to keep to shallow waters.

Although Quintilian begins by allowing that Greek is more pleasant to hear, he ends by putting the emphasis on certain virtues of Roman diction which are probably to be understood as the language equivalents of character. Power and weight of diction are the seemly expression of Roman moral dignity. The inadequacy of Latin is both surmountable and limited; the defects which create problems in treating a plain theme will in turn contribute to grandeur when the subject is important. We may infer that Latin will not find it so difficult to do justice to a case of treason or a panegyric on a meritorious emperor. These are the topics which provide the real test of true oratory, since the power to sway the emotions is often regarded as the hallmark of eloquence. Quintilian's admission of the weakness in Latin is therefore connected with an appreciation of its strength; because it is suited (at least since Cicero) to the grand themes of deliberative and epideictic oratory, it is less able to cope with the duller sort of forensic disputes.

These general considerations on the merits of Latin were prompted by different reasons: Cicero was thinking of translation or imitation, Seneca of the speech appropriate to good, philosophical character, while Quintilian was discussing whether Atticism of a certain type is feasible in Latin. Interests in philosophy and rhetoric determined the comparisons of the two languages. Yet all three writers express a sense of satisfaction with the language. It is different from Greek, but is equal or even superior to it, and some of the remarks point to the feeling that Latin can or should be spoken in such a way as to reflect the dignity or majesty of the Roman character. Quintilian's orator, for example, is to be truly Roman, and the qualities of the language correspond to a valued stateliness of mind and morals.[33]

As theorists found so much to praise, it is not surprising that Latin was defended as the proper medium of public affairs, whether in Rome or in the provinces. The right language for a Roman was Latin; so Cato made fun of Albinus, who wrote in Greek and apologized for any solecisms, and the notorious philhellene Albucius was teased by Romans who addressed him in Greek.[34] There are signs that official visitors to the senate were at first required to speak Latin or to use a translator; the Greek philosophers who visited Rome in 155 B.C. were heard in the senate through an interpreter. The custom was justified by Valerius Maximus, who commends, rather vaguely, the practice of earlier Roman officials; they would never deliver their judgments to Greeks except in Latin, and the Greeks themselves were deprived of 'that rapidity of speech which is their main resource' and were obliged to put their case through a translator. The object was to make sure that respect for Latin would spread among all peoples. Valerius draws a contrast between the sturdy past, which upheld Latin, and the more lax customs of the present, 'when the ears of the senate are deafened through hearing cases in Greek'.[35] It is true that he does not speak of the positive virtues of Latin, but he does think of Greek rapidity as a cheating device, the correlate of reprehensible moral traits.

Yet, if there was a tradition of this sort, it was probably fading early in the first century B.C.; the rhetorician Apollonius Molon was allowed to put his case to the senate in Greek, and when

Cicero says that 'there is always someone in the senate who asks for a translator',[36] he gives the impression that the veto on Greek was no longer so strict. The emperor Tiberius, in spite of having a fluent command of Greek, attempted to keep up what we may call the official position. 'He refrained from speaking Greek, especially in the senate.' He apologized for introducing the word 'monopoly' on the grounds that it was foreign; similarly he objected to using a convenient Greek term for a clause inserted in a decree and considered that it should be replaced by a Latin word or a periphrasis, also in Latin. Clearly, the advantages of Greek could be resisted only by a show of pedantry; it looks as though Tiberius' insistence on Latin was felt to be old-fashioned and unrealistic. But the philhellenic pedantry of Claudius also seemed odd; whereas Tiberius was unbending, Claudius was willing to go too far, because of his enthusiasm for Greek. In the senate he often delivered whole speeches in Greek to envoys, and he even quoted Homer when he was officiating in the law-courts. It appears then that Greek did enter the senate in spite of protests from the pure Latinists, as we might call them.[37]

A prejudice in favour of Latin seems to have applied to the conduct of officials or governors in Greek-speaking areas. It is true that P. Crassus (about 131 B.C.) had a fluent command of five Greek dialects, but this appears to have been remembered as an exception. He is said to have been popular with the allies because of this accomplishment, but another story about him shows that he acted harshly against a Greek who disobeyed his orders in the interests of efficiency.[38] He was perhaps a philhellene of the tongue only. On the other hand governors were often accompanied by translators (*interpretes*), though these acted as general intermediaries as well. While Cicero was proud of addressing the Syracusan senate in Greek, Verres sneered at him on both counts: for speaking in a Greek senate and (worse) for speaking to his audience in Greek; and Verres may well have been more representative of traditional Roman attitudes.[39] Perhaps we may express the matter in this way: the advocate of Latin for official purposes could always appeal to the standards of dignity expected from a true Roman; but the man who used the language of the natives in governing them could not justify this as acceptable to the aristocratic code or as befitting the 'togaed people'. Considerations of polite behaviour to a civilized people did apply when Romans visited Athens, but perhaps mattered less elsewhere; we should remember too, as the Crassus story shows, that Greek was several languages.

We know very little about the *interpretes*. It is at first sight surprising to find that Cicero had one on his staff in Cilicia, but the complexities of local government could well have made a translator indispensable, even for a linguist like Cicero. It is likely that contempt for speaking Greek on official matters in the provinces declined under the empire. The emperors did insist that a citizen should know Latin, but it was also important that an emperor should have Greek; hence the young Nero was required to make an address in Greek before Claudius as consul, on behalf of Rhodes and Ilium. As an imperial accomplishment Greek became prestigious, whereas Cicero had at times been ridiculed for his attachment to things Greek. But oratorical competence in the second language was still a mark of distinction. Tacitus says that Mucianus, who addressed the citizens of Antioch in A.D. 69, was a good orator in Greek as well as in Latin. It is odd that Tacitus should pay such a compliment if Mucianus' success in Greek were commonplace.[40]

Speaking to Greeks in their own language was a new source of fame. The realization that it could occasion Greek flattery, as well as being more convenient, helped to weaken the prejudice in favour of Latin only. But the practice of speaking Greek and quoting Greek among Romans, whether in conversation or letters, is perhaps more complex still.

In quoting from Greek and using Greek words Romans were in general adding to the resources of their own language. Homeric lines and phrases, especially, were one way of bestowing authority on great events or arguments. Scipio, at the sack of Carthage, seems to have felt pity for the defeated city and to have experienced a sense of foreboding that Rome might suffer the same fate; and he quoted Hector's lines to Andromache in which the Trojan hero foretells the sack of Troy.[41] Augustus, in asserting his position as Caesar's heir, announced that he was even more devoted to Caesar than Achilles to Patroclus.[42] Caligula gave alarming emphasis to his sense of absolutism by calling on the line, 'It is not good for there to be many rulers, let there be one'.[43] The epic seriousness of Homer seemed relevant to the Roman feeling for great or grandiose events. But though Homer was useful 'straight', it was also tempting to quote him out of context, as a kind of illustrative joke.[44] Perhaps the reason for this is that the foreign classic, however much admired, tends to invite debasement, even though that debasement may well be affectionate rather than denigratory. Cicero makes a fairly simple mock-epic use of the invocation to the Muses when he is embarking on an account of Roman politics for Atticus. But Favonius' abuse of Homer was jocularity with a serious purpose, since Cassius and Brutus were quarrelling vehemently and he wished to put a stop to the argument. He forced his way in, put on a voice and uttered Nestor's famous words of peace: 'Come, take my advice, for you are both younger than I am.' Nestor, of course, did not speak to raise a laugh, but Favonius' jesting use seems to have brought about an end to the dispute, though only Cassius was disposed to smile.[45]

Favonius had a name for this sort of clowning. There is a far more sophisticated example of this use of Homer in a Cicero letter, written to Caesar in 45 B.C. to recommend a man called Precilius. Cicero himself observes that it is a novel form of recommendation by letter, and it is in fact adorned with six quotations, five of which are Homeric. The qualities of Precilius are supported by praise of his father, who had urged Cicero to accept Caesar's invitation to join him. ' "But he did not persuade my heart." (*Od.* 7.258). I listened to the call of our nobles:

> "Be firm, that those who come later may praise you.
> So he spoke, but a dark cloud of sorrow covered the other."
> (*Il.* 1.302 and 24.315).

Yet these same people are still consoling me. I have been burnt but they still want to fire me with vainglory. So they now say:

> "Let me not die without effort and fame, but only
> after performing a great action for posterity to hear of."
> (*Il.* 22.304–5).

So I am now leaving Homeric grandeur for the realism of Euripides:

> "I hate a wise man whose wisdom does not help himself."

Precilius' father praises this line and says that the same man can "look before and behind" and yet still

> "Be foremost and above other men." ' (*Il.* 6.208).

Cicero, in short, is excusing his imprudence by suggesting that he is not capable of the heroic qualities which are measured by Homer's lofty utterance, and he has therefore sunk to Euripides.

He has a serious purpose but sets out to achieve it through a
playful adaptation of Homer. The second quotation is particularly
apt, since it consists of two lines from opposite ends of the *Iliad*;
the deft coupling describes his heroic endeavour (on the advice
of others) and is also an admission that he is sorry. [46]

I have suggested that the second language can evoke a sense of
play, an attempt to show mastery by humorous as well as literal
use. It also provides a way of speaking in code—to conceal thought
from those who do not know the language, and, by extension,
as a means of cryptic utterance among those who do. Two of
Cicero's letters, described later by him as composed in riddles,
illustrate the first point. They use Greek at greater length than
is usual in the letters, presumably because Cicero, writing from
Cilicia, is afraid that they may not reach Atticus. The meaning
will be clear to him but may baffle or delay anyone who intercepts
the letters without authority. Thus he uses expressions in Greek
like 'my wife's freedman' (without the name), refers to the
politician Milo as the 'tyrannicide from Croton' and writes of 'the
seven-hilled city', meaning Rome. One may well wonder whether
the Greek periphrases would have delayed the inquisitive for very
long. [47] Cryptic quotation may be regarded as a more sophisticated
form of simple coding. When Tiberius was pestered with complaints from Agrippina, he quoted a Greek line to this effect: 'Do
you think you are injured just because you do not rule?' [48] Of
course Agrippina would have taken the point fairly quickly, we
may assume. But the effect of using Greek rather than Latin is to
give some distance to the thought, to make the truth less blunt and
unpleasant. The second language can therefore increase the
possibilities for euphemism. Some of Augustus' Greek in a letter
about Claudius is relevant here; the disabilities of Claudius are
explicitly mentioned, but the use of Greek softens the shock to the
reader, even though the recipient, Livia, knows the facts well.
Perhaps, too, it seemed less shocking when Caesar quoted
Euripides' lines on committing wrong in order to hold absolute
power than if he had said the same thing in Latin. [49]

It may be said that it is easy to exaggerate what I have called
the play element in the use of Greek, even though this does not
exclude a serious purpose. It is true that many Greek words were
used because they were felt to be better than the Latin equivalents,
or to fill a gap. Cicero's support for Latin and Tiberius' pedantry
were against the tide. Quintilian not infrequently comments on
the superior literal aptness of Greek terms. [50] This literal, matter-
of-fact quality is also shown by the many references to Greek

proverbs, which are valued because they impart truth or good advice succinctly. But even with isolated words or short phrases the play element is noticeable. Sometimes, for instance, a Greek word is used where a Latin one would have done as well, just to add variety. Some Romans had a taste for using Greek compounds, partly because of their satisfying brevity, partly because they look long and complicated; thus Cicero writes to Atticus that 'all *unite in promoting* my good name', where the italics render one Greek word (*sumphilodoxousin*). Caligula's taste was perhaps too exotic here; he spoke of a foreigner as 'worthy to be led in a triumph' (*axiothriambeutos*) and used the word 'immoveability' (*adiatrepsia*), rather than the plain Latin for shamelessness, to describe his tolerance for cruelty. A remark in Quintilian's account of compounds may explain the habit; he says that the whole business of compounds suits the Greeks, whereas it does not work out so well in Latin. 'I do not think this comes about by nature, but because we look with favour on foreign words; and so, when we have marvelled at the word "with curved neck" (in Greek—*kurtauchen*) we can hardly take the word *incurvicervicum* seriously.'[51] Quintilian is saying here that it is taste, not any essential difference in the nature of the two languages, which makes Latin compounds seem awkward and unacceptable.

Greek was used and quoted not only for the sake of precision but also from exuberance. It is noticeable that Cicero's exile letters to Atticus have no Greek[52] at all; he was probably too depressed and worried to employ the resources of Greek for entertainment or as an epistolary grace. Works with pretensions to full literary status in Latin tend to exclude Greek or reduce it to a minimum. In this sense Cicero's letters are pre-literary and are studded with Greek; but the younger Pliny, who is using the letter as a careful literary form, uses Greek much less often. Greek must be present here because the letter is an account of the everyday concerns and habits of an educated Roman; but since the writer's purpose is to leave a monument in his own language, Greek has become an occasional grace, reduced to allow more scope to the perfect Latin. One might have expected more Greek in Seneca's letters to Lucilius, because the subject is philosophy, but here too the claims of Latin are respected. Seneca quotes Cleanthes in a Latin verse translation, acknowledging the precedent set by Cicero in his philosophical dialogues.[53]

In general, it seems that the advantages offered by Greek outweighed the desire to uphold the exclusive majesty of Latin. For many Romans, Greek was an administrative convenience and a sign of polite, leisured interests. Besides, once Latin had its own established classics, by the end of Augustus' rule, Romans felt that these were now the equals of Greek literature. It was possible to make comparisons more objectively, without the competitive note that sometimes jars upon the reader of Cicero. The world described by Gellius in the second century A.D. bears the mark of some critical maturity; though Greek originals are often compared favourably with Latin translations, Gellius and his friends also comment with pride on Roman works of literature. Praise of Greek no longer implies the denigration of Latin.

There is also some discrepancy between theory and practice in the Roman reaction to Greek art. Moralists looked upon Greek art as a foreign intruder in spite of the fact that Rome's temples and the rich villas of Italy were well-stocked with aesthetic trophies. The Romans introduced many statues, paintings and precious objects which were believed to be ancient rather than contemporary and either were or were thought to be of Greek provenance. These acquisitions were often obtained through force—most obviously after victory in war—but purchase and gift were also marked by an element of compulsion. Even Romans who bought paid less than the true price, or manipulated sellers who were unwilling, and gifts made to Rome were a token of submission on the part of client-states or dependent rulers.

The great age of acquisition began towards the end of the third century B.C., during the war against Hannibal. When important Greek cities in southern Italy and Sicily were recovered by the Romans, they were plundered and deprived of their treasures. Marcellus, for example, who captured Syracuse (211 B.C.), took away many of the statues and dedicated them in *his* temple of Honos and Virtus. Syracuse, Capua and Tarentum were the most unfortunate victims. In the second century B.C. the process continued because Rome was now engaged in fighting wars in mainland Greece and the near east. Many generals returned from their campaigns to exhibit their war-booty, which often included statues and paintings. The great victors of the period—especially Flamininus, Fulvius Nobilior, Aemilius Paulus and Lucius Mummius—contributed money to the treasury and art to the temples. The flow of objects did not stop when Rome finally settled the Macedonian wars and brought order into mainland Greece. After the wars at Pergamum (131 B.C.) and the conquests of Sulla and Pompey, the eastern parts of the Greek world were made to contribute their share. In the first century B.C., a quiet province like Sicily had to endure the pillage and compulsory purchases made by Verres. It seems that with the Augustan peace the Greeks could be more confident of keeping their possessions. But Tiberius, we are told, who went off to Rhodes as a private person, obliged the Parians to sell him a statue of Vesta which was to be placed in the temple of Concord at Rome. The 'violence of Nero', as Pliny styles it, caused many famous works to be brought and a home was found for them when Vespasian put them in his new temple of Peace.[54]

We should not exaggerate the numbers of these objects or their importance. In the second century B.C. the amount of gold and silver collected was more significant in assessing the value and prestige of war-booty. It is clear, too, that annexation slowed under the empire, when wars against Greek communities had stopped and Greek provinces were no longer the arena for Roman civil war. But there is reason to believe that Rome as a city suffered from over-crowding by statues. A statue of Heracles is known to have been moved three times, and on one occasion this was because there were too many such objects near the Rostra.[55]

Though Rome became, to an extent, a city of Greek art, there were numerous criticisms of the change. Plutarch, it is true, says that the people were pleased with the objects brought by Marcellus from Syracuse, and he implies that 'Hellenic grace' could humanize men whose previous trophies were instruments of war.[56] But he also points out that there were adversaries who believed that the Romans would become a people of gallery-goers instead of devoting their time to work and war. More thorough criticisms were voiced much earlier by Polybius, who was also prompted to digress on the subject of Marcellus' plunder. He believes that the forcible acquisition was wrong on two counts. In the first place it would entail a change in education; he means that the political and military success of the Romans could not be attributed to art, since they had none; the Romans, therefore, by importing art, were being inconsistent with their own moral foundations. Secondly, to deprive others in this way of their artistic possessions is to make Rome an object of hatred and envy among peoples who have been made to surrender some of their pleasures as well as their liberty.

It is perhaps not surprising that Romans said little or nothing about the second point; they were more concerned with the adverse effects on themselves than with the consequences for their subjects. Livy deplores the action of Marcellus, even though he concedes that the spoils were enemy property and lawfully Roman by the right of war. 'This was when people began marvelling at the products of Greek arts; it marks the outbreak of an excessive freedom in despoiling sacred and non-sacred things indiscriminately.' He sees it as ironical that Marcellus' own temple, dedicated by the first great despoiler of Greek art, had itself been plundered; by Livy's own time few of the Marcellan ornaments were still in position. Livy's main point here is that Greek art has been responsible for a decline in the regard for religion which characterized his early Romans; he would prefer the time of ignorance to that age of increasing connoisseurship which was inaugurated by Marcellus. He makes a similar complaint about the luxury articles from Greek Asia, which were brought back by the army of Manlius Vulso (187 B.C.): Roman discipline was corrupted by a taste for foreign delights.[57] Other writers selected different dates; thus Velleius complains that the Romans have developed too deep an understanding of Corinthian bronzes, a taste which was thought to have become fashionable after Mummius had sacked Corinth.[58] The elder Pliny's history of art is charged with thoughts on the moral decline occasioned by Greek art. The legacy of Pergamum, bequeathed to Rome by Attalus III, was more damaging than the conquest of Asia by Scipio Asiaticus. Pliny's comments on silver are particularly revealing; he complains that in his time the rewards of valour are fabricated out of luxury materials, with the paradoxical result that virtues can only be commemorated because Romans have the wherewithal to be vicious.[59]

It is tempting to suppose, because Cicero and the younger Pliny provide us with so much evidence for their own views, that Romans rather disliked sculpture and painting. In the *Verrines* Cicero speaks of the liking for art as characteristically Greek rather than Roman. Though he is here exaggerating somewhat (since convention requires him to play up to the court), his letters show that he came to grudge spending money on statuary which had been ordered for one of his houses. 'I would never have put so high a value on [the statues of] those Muses, and I would have been supported by all the Muses (i.e. the Muses are ideal and do not care for this incarnation) . . .'[60] The younger Pliny writes of Silius Italicus as one who liked buying, even to a fault; he says, too, that he (Pliny) has acquired a piece 'which even I can understand'.[61] Convention demanded that he should not seem too expert in such matters. For these men certain poems, speeches and works on philosophy were valuable because they represented learning (*doctrina*), the articulated wisdom which can help self-improvement; they did not attribute any such moral purpose to works of art. Besides, ancient books, however carefully produced, were obviously not items of luxury, whereas statues and paintings were the symbols of conspicuous wealth. A prejudice against seeming to be rich, wealthy though these men were, reinforced the higher intellectual status of the written word and made the painting or statue seem a vulgar image. It is also true that many Romans are known to have relaxed by writing Greek poetry or by conversing with Greek philosophers; few, we may suppose, indulged in painting or sculpture for their recreation. Indeed Cicero sneers at Verres for supervising the craftsmen who were adapting his ill-gotten treasures to suit his taste.[62] But it is likely that many more Romans were untroubled by this choice between literature and art; villas were furnished with mosaics and paintings as well as libraries, and men like Lucullus, Tiberius and Hadrian clearly felt no awkwardness about combining literary interests with a taste for collecting.

We might expect to find that the adversaries of Greek art would blame the generals who had brought the sculptures and paintings to Rome. A reasonable view of the matter would suggest that the agents and transmitters of decadence were as much at fault as the objects themselves. The elder Pliny implies some such stricture on a general when he speaks disapprovingly of Pompey's triumph (61 B.C.) as a defeat for Roman simplicity (*severitas*).[63] But on the whole, criticism of the generals is rarer than praise. The great conquerors of the earlier period especially, from Marcellus to the middle of the second century B.C., were admired for not enriching themselves. Marcellus, it was believed, had taken only one object for himself from the siege of Syracuse, a celestial sphere, which was not as fine as the one he placed in the temple of Honos.[64] Aemilius Paulus, Scipio Africanus Minor and L. Mummius were praised in similar terms for filling the treasury. There was a tradition that Mummius, who sacked Corinth, had left no dowry for his daughter. There was another story about Mummius—that he told the men who were in charge of the transport that they would have to make good any losses by replacing old masters with new. The alleged ignorance of the second-century Roman seemed quaint to the sophisticated taste of a later age; it was amused but still impressed by a man whose bluntness seemed to denote the true Roman virtue of the past.[65]

There is some inconsistency here. But there would have been a greater inconsistency if these generals had been criticized, since this would detract from the true (that is, martial) Roman virtue which they had demonstrated by defeating the lesser Greeks and

Macedonians. The more qualities they had, the sharper the contrast between their behaviour and the predatory self-seeking of a Verres.

The critics, it must be said, from Cicero to Pliny, wrote later than the events. Their attitude to Greek art exhibits what has been called 'a nostalgic puritanism',[66] a yearning for the hard primitivism of an earlier Rome. A wealthy man could infer all sorts of grand moral qualities about Scipio when he admired the great man's villa, without forgoing the increased amenities of his own.[67] But this later moralizing over Greek art is only part of the story; we can understand Roman attitudes more fully if we examine the political questions which were argued at the time and try to grasp what motives made the conquerors seek to decorate Rome. The contemporary arguments (contemporary with the first period of acquisition) discussed other questions than those raised by the later moralists.

The actions of Marcellus were resented by all Syracusans and some Romans. The Greeks of Syracuse complained that the enforced loss of their art-treasures was a poor return for the faithful services of Hiero (died 215 B.C.) to Rome. Roman critics of Marcellus believed that Greek art was corrupting (they resemble the moralists in this respect) and they said that it was an offence against religion to treat statues of the gods like prisoners of war.[68] Roman traditionalists contrasted Marcellus' behaviour with the actions of Fabius Cunctator, who recovered Tarentum for Rome (209 B.C.). Fabius took a statue of Heracles to Rome but left others behind, including a huge statue of Zeus. It was probably too big to move, but religion, not convenience, was alleged to be his reason for sparing the treasures of Tarentum. He became famous as the Roman who declared that Tarentum should be allowed to keep her angry gods (angry because they had shown their disapproval by allowing their worshippers to be defeated).[69] Such were the talking-points *against* the acquisition of Greek art. There were, however, various counter-arguments. If war had been justly declared, the property of a defeated enemy could be lawfully disposed of by Rome as the victor. The 'religious scruple' was settled by the practice of putting the statues of gods in temples at Rome; they were therefore still dedicated objects. Greek protests were answered by the claim (made, apparently, by Marcellus) that Greek art would become more widely acclaimed if it were domiciled at Rome. Perhaps the most telling argument was not the easiest to avow; men like Marcellus intended to use the spoils of war to build themselves a monument as a way of ensuring permanent fame for themselves and their family. Marcellus' temple to Honos and Virtus was ostensibly an act of respect and deference towards the divine powers who had helped the Roman side; but the temple-goer or spectator would be in no doubt that the tribute to the gods was the achievement of a victorious Roman general. Even Fabius put up a statue of himself by the side of the Heracles which he took from Tarentum and had erected on the Capitol as an offering to Jupiter Capitolinus.

Fabius' laconic comment on the gods of Tarentum was a particular version of the religious argument, as I have called it. This affected political debate in various ways. The college of priests was sometimes required to decide which parts of enemy plunder were sacred and which 'profane'. The elder Cato protested not only against an admiration for the works of sculptors and painters (the finest image of a good citizen, he believed, was in his soul), but also against the sacrilege of turning the statue of a god into a private possession; a dedicated object should continue to be the property of the whole community, re-dedicated in a temple at Rome.[70] But placing an artistic trophy in a temple was not of itself a guarantee that the act of pillage would be acceptable to the senate. A certain Lucretius returned from Chalcis with paintings which he presented to a shrine of Aesculapius. The people of Chalcis complained officially that they had been loyal allies but that Lucretius had treated them as hostile subjects; his action in robbing their temples was therefore an act of sacrilege. As the senate agreed with the claims made by Chalcis, Lucretius was fined; and another commander in Greece was also criticized and ordered to restore what he had taken. A general's ambition to build his monument in a temple would be tolerable only if his loot came from a state at war with Rome, not from an ally. The depredations of Fulvius Flaccus were another case in point; he wanted his temple of Fortuna Equestris to be the most magnificent in Rome and decided to roof it with marble tiles from the temple of Hera Lacinia near Croton. As censor he was able to arrange for ships to transport the tiles to Rome, but he could not conceal their provenance. He was criticized for insulting the most venerable temple of a friendly ally; it was improper for a censor to destroy temples when a particular task of his office was to maintain the fabric of public buildings; it would be an offence against religion if the Romans were to use materials from other temples to build their own. There was a unanimous decision to return the tiles, but unfortunately they could not be replaced as no craftsman had the skill to carry out the work.[71]

Ambition encouraged the generals to deport statues and paintings; but policy and a sense of rectitude imposed limits, since the senate disapproved of those who plundered allies, and was ready to recognize the merit of Greek states that had served Rome well. The treasures of Greece were admissible if they came from states at war and were then housed in Roman temples. Thus the spoils brought by Aemilius Paulus were legitimate since they were the fruits of defeating Macedonia, the formal enemy of Rome. Yet there were some apparent exceptions; not all Romans sought personal fame by dedicating the works of Greek art in the public temples. When Scipio sacked Carthage (146 B.C.) he rewarded various towns in Sicily by returning some of the treasures·which had been taken from them in the earlier wars between Carthage and Sicily; Segesta, Himera, Thermum, Gela and Agrigentum were favoured by Scipio's magnanimity. His motives were probably mixed. In his triumph he would wish to exhibit trophies from Carthage rather than objects which Carthage had taken from states that were now the friends and allies of Rome. The people of Agrigentum might reflect, as they looked at the famous bull of their former tyrant Phalaris, that Roman rule was tempered with mercy and was preferable to the autocratic régime of their independent past. In one sense therefore Scipio was reconciling the Greeks of Sicily to government by Rome. But he was also concerned with his own political standing. His generosity ensured that many Sicilian Greeks would become his political dependants or clients. He was not an anonymous bene-factor but sought to make his fame permanent by inscribing his own name on the pedestal of the statue of Diana which was restored to Segesta.[72] According to Cicero, the people of Segesta used Scipio's name as one of their reasons for refusing to give the the statue to Verres; they maintained it was the property of Scipio and the Roman people. The victor was self-regarding as well as generous; Cicero emphasizes the latter quality as a foil to the cupidity of Verres, who tried to make his acquisitions at the expense of allies.

Much later the emperor Augustus treated the Greek cities of the east with similar courtesy, and quietly boasted of the fact on his own monument. 'After my victory I replaced in all the temples of the cities of Asia the treasures of which they had been robbed and which my enemy had kept as his own private possession.' It is said that Augustus restored the famous Myron-Apollo to Ephesus; the statue had been taken from the city by Antony, to whom Augustus is referring in the above passage from the *Res Gestae*. Pliny

attributes the return of the Apollo to a warning sent to Augustus
in a dream, but as other places were well treated we may think
that policy was more significant than divine prompting.[73] An
Athena and a Heracles were also returned to Ephesus, and an
inscription from Cyme in Asia confirms the statement in the *Res
Gestae*: '. . . if any [offerings] have been removed or bought or
received as gifts, whoever is in charge of the province is to provide
for their restoration to the public or sacred places of the city . . .'[74]
Augustus was a realist in acknowledging that purchase and dona-
tion were as much tarred with compulsion as was removing a
statue by force.

It is likely that Augustus saw the incident as an illustration of
his piety; he wished to remind men that he had shown respect for
religion whereas Antony had been selfish and irreverent. But there
were also obvious political advantages in undoing Antony's work;
the recovery of their treasures would reconcile the eastern cities to
Augustus' rule and make him the welcome successor to his
defeated rival. Like Scipio, Augustus could afford the grand
gesture, since the capture of Alexandria provided the Romans
with adequate booty, lawfully Roman from the defeat of her
enemy Cleopatra. She 'had taken practically all the offerings
from even the holiest shrines and so helped the Romans swell
their spoils without letting them incur any defilement'. Augustus
had some interest in persuading people that they had gained by
his victory over Antony, but the memory of Cleopatra mattered
less. As Dio says, 'the Roman empire was enriched and its temples
adorned'. Because Augustus took from Egypt he could afford to
give Ephesus its own; his acquisitions were not impious, since
the guilt was Cleopatra's, and his gifts were the expression of a
true concern for religion.[75] Neither Scipio nor Augustus thought
the Greek cities had a right to recover what they had lost; they
felt the cities were fortunate in having such benefactors, who could
afford to make their name by generosity.

It seems that Greek art was in fact acceptable at Rome if it
came as an offering to a god, an acknowledgment that Rome was
less important than the divine, and the donor of less significance
than the Roman people. The literary tradition, as we saw, was
often hostile to Greek art as such, but the political arguments
about the acquisition of Greek art created another point of view,
which applauded art when on public display at Rome but
denigrated the private ownership of beautiful things. Cicero, in
arguing against the idea that wealth is a true good, maintains
that one does not need money to satisfy a liking for statues and

paintings.[76] There are so many of these at Rome that the poor can get more enjoyment than rich men with private collections. Since these collections are housed on country estates, their wealthy owners see them less often, and, when they do, they feel some remorse as they reflect how they came to own them. It appears that in Cicero's eyes the wealthy art connoisseur is reprehensible because he spends money on himself; his collection is, at best, the triumph of wealth over need, whereas the art dedicated by a general is a sign of open courage shown in war. Similarly the elder Pliny commends a speech made by Agrippa on the theme of making all pictures and statues public property: 'this would have been preferable to forcing them into exile in country-houses'. Josephus approves of Vespasian, who placed some fine works in the temple of Peace, on the grounds that he had collected in one place what men had formerly travelled the whole world to see.[77] It is doubtful whether he would have praised a private collection in these extravagant terms.

But how far did the prejudice against private collections really deter the Romans? In the light of what we have said it is not surprising to find that the younger Pliny says of his Corinthian bronze, 'I did not buy it to keep at home (so far I haven't one at home), but to put it in a much-frequented place in my own country, preferably in the temple of Jupiter. It seems to me to deserve a temple; it is an offering that deserves a god.' We would expect Pliny, who preferred literature, to observe the tradition in favour of public homes for beautiful objects. But many Romans did collect old masterpieces, with the result that the villas of south Italy were provided with more than newly-made mosaics and reproductions. Asinius Pollio was the famous collector of the late republic. Verres,[78] of course, was disreputable, but he survived his forensic defeat by Cicero and lived to see his collection of Corinthian bronzes admired by Antony. Respectable citizens also indulged their taste. Agrippa himself acted against the tenor of his speech on making statues and pictures public property by buying two pictures from Cyzicus (evidently for his own pleasure), though the paintings he put up in his Baths would have been enjoyed by the general public. The Body-Scraper attributed to Lysippus was placed by Agrippa at the entrance to his Baths; but Tiberius conceived such a liking for it that he had it moved to his bedroom and did not restore it until there was a public protest. The emperor was more successful in keeping the picture of a high priest of Cybele, which was also placed in his bedroom. It is fair to add that though we see that Tiberius was very different from

Verres, the elder Pliny is critical of him; he says he was 'ungracious', a comment occasioned by his surprise at having to record that Tiberius did place some pictures in the temple of Augustus.[79]

Some objects were probably regarded as lucky as well as beautiful, which may explain why Nero took with him the famous model of an Amazon whenever he travelled. Perhaps we may surmise too that elegant drinking-cups and table-silver were lent to entertain important men, rather as the Sicilians described by Cicero would pool or borrow to do honour to a Roman official.[80] In this way a private collection might be put, however briefly, to a more social purpose. Yet one has the impression that the would-be true public Roman was conscious of the moralists' disapproval and the tradition that art should be on public display. The great orator Crassus is said to have owned two cups by Mentor, but he was reluctant to use them—from a sense of shame, not because he was afraid of having them broken.[81]

Given the nature of the tradition, it is unusual to find instances of praise for the connoisseur with his private collection. Statius,[82] however, does write enthusiastically about the collector Novius Vindex. Host and guest had not dined lavishly but had enjoyed the pleasures of art instead of the pleasures of the table. They admired a bronze statuette of Hercules supposed to be by Lysippus. According to Statius the statuette had been owned by Alexander the Great, Hannibal and Sulla; Alexander had prayed to it for courage, Hannibal the perfidious Carthaginian had poured libations to it and it had presided over Sulla's banquets. The point of the poem is that the much-travelled bronze has not lost by leaving the company of its illustrious owners. It is appreciated at its artistic worth and will receive due poetic tribute. Yet the Hercules, we should notice, has found a good home in more senses than one. Vindex, the new owner, though he is knowledgeable about art, is also admirable on moral grounds; he has the qualities of 'old-fashioned faith' and loyalty to friends. The Roman morals and integrity of the owner are as important as his aesthetic discrimination. It is noticeable too that private art is not, in this poem, a token of self-indulgent wealth, but represents a true pleasure of the mind in contrast with gluttony.

Both in using the Greek language and in acquiring Greek art the Romans showed that they were receptive to beauty. The sound of Greek was acclaimed and the masterpieces of sculpture, whether genuine or alleged, were welcomed—and not just because they were a good investment. But the Romans did not abase themselves before Greek literature or the visual arts. The foreign language, with its established literature, made them insist on the moral virtues of their own language, and, for a while at least, they tried to exclude Greek from public business. The Roman attitude to the treasures of Greek art shows a different way of admitting the Greek influence. Ideally the sculptures and paintings should be housed in Roman temples where they would be a lasting witness to the success of Roman virtue over the Greeks. The perfect Roman would have confined himself to speaking Greek in private and to admiring Greek art in the temple of Jupiter Capitolinus. In both cases, the Roman was eager to let it be known that the foreign inventions had a limited, though valuable, function in the Roman view of things.

3

GREEK POETRY:
THE INTERPRETATION OF HOMER

A detailed account of the relationship between Roman poets and
their Greek poetic sources is beyond the scope of this book. All I
attempt here is to sketch the different ways in which Romans
might approach the reading of Homer, in order to make the point
that educational requirements imposed a different reading of
Greek poetry from that which would be common today. In Greek
thought the ethical world of Homer had been criticized by some
philosophers and defended by others. Though Romans were
familiar with both views, Homer as a theologian or as the teacher
of all arts and sciences was of little importance. But his reputation
as a great poet fluctuated when the epic form no longer seemed
relevant to contemporary poetic needs.

When the orator Antonius in the *de oratore*[1] speaks about his
leisure reading in Greek, he declares a preference for the orators
and historians, writers who are intelligible to him without too
much effort. Since he reads for pleasure he does not find it easy
to cope with the philosophers, who write on familiar-seeming
topics like justice but make their accounts too crabbed and
precise; as for the poets, he does not even try to handle them. They
seem utterly remote, as though they are using a different idiom,
something quite foreign to the habits of the practising Roman
orator. But if Antonius had been able to look back at Latin from
a vantage-point of about A.D. 200 he would have been surprised
to find that later Roman experience was at variance with his own.
Men who wrote Latin philosophy and poetry were always far
more dependent on Greek originals, whether they translated or
adapted them, than were their fellows who produced histories of
Rome or published speeches; and Greek poets had become en-
trenched in the educational curriculum. I shall examine here
some Roman attitudes to Greek poetry, with particular reference

to Homer, and discuss the theoretical standing of poetry in the Roman educational scheme.

Antonius' attitude to Greek poetry would have been congenial to the elder Cato,[2] who looked back to an earlier Rome when men did not honour poetry at all; but it seems odd when compared with later reactions. Cicero justifies his versions of Greek philosophy and oratory with the remark that he is only setting out to achieve in other fields what has already been accomplished by Ennius and Afranius in their adaptations of Greek poetry. The implied claim—that Latin poets were already the equals of Greeks— seemed strange to the taste of a later age. Horace, for example, did not share Cicero's views about the success of the earlier Latin poets, but he too believed that the study of Greek models was all-important for the would-be Latin poet.[3] In the Augustan age and after, men took pride in the thought that Latin poetry was now the equal of Greek. The comparison was extensive and covered the lighter forms of poetry as well as the serious. In the second century A.D. the teacher of rhetoric, Antonius Julianus, was taunted by some Greeks on the grounds that his Latin exercises were deficient in charm: Latin seemed to have nothing to match the writings of Anacreon. Julianus, of Spanish origin but a true, patriotic Roman, refuted the attack by quoting passages from the light verse of Aedituus, Porcius Licinius and Quintus Catulus.[4] The feeling that Latin poetry had equalled Greek enabled Romans to admire their own earlier poetry without embarrassment.

For many Romans, as for Greeks, the outstanding name was that of Homer, the poet *par excellence*. The prestige of Homer is shown by the fact that the *Aeneid* was praised as a Latin *Iliad* and *Odyssey*, two in one.[5] Those who attempted a Latin epic would hope to hear (even if the compliment was ironical) that they were rivalling Homer; thus the poet Propertius tells the writer of a poem on Thebes that he is in competition with Homer, 'the first and foremost', and prays that fate will be gentle with his work.[6] But admiration of Homer was not confined to Roman poets. Velleius, in his history, digresses briefly to pay his own tribute, and the elder Pliny describes Homer as 'the most valuable work of the human mind', 'the original source of all other talents'.[7] There were, however, one or two voices on the other side. The emperor Caligula toyed with the project of destroying Homer's poetry, though it is not clear that this was more than the passing mood of a megalomaniac absolutist; and Hadrian is said to have preferred Antimachus, the fifth-century poet with a name for obscurity.[8] In general Homer's reputation was secure, though I shall return later to the question whether he remained the poet's poet.

Romans could read Homer in Greek or in Latin translations. Latin poetry began with Livius Andronicus' adaptation of the *Odyssey* into the Saturnian metre, and his work was still used in Horace's time. In the late Republic Cn. Matius translated the *Iliad* into hexameters, and was followed later by Ninius Crassus. The important freedman Polybius, so Seneca says, deserved well of his authors by turning Homer into Latin prose and Virgil into Greek.[9] Later on in the first century A.D. an epitome appeared, the *Latin Iliad*. It is a poem with less than 1100 lines and does no more than scant justice to the original, since some of the Homeric books are treated in a few lines only. But hardly anything is known about the intended readership of these works or, except for the *Latin Iliad*, about their quality. Most upper-class Romans would read the Homeric poems in Greek. Cicero often quotes from the original in his letters to Atticus; when he translates some passages, as in his philosophical works, his aim is to produce a work that is all (or nearly all) Latin. Quintilian requires his pupils to begin Greek at an early age, and says it is established practice to start with Homer and Virgil; though it needs time and maturity to appreciate both, they will be read more than once.[10] It seems justifiable to suppose that he has in mind reading Homer in Greek. Homer was also used as Greek reading at or after meals. The wealthy Calvisius Sabinus, whose memory was so bad that he kept muddling the names of Ulysses, Achilles and Priam, names which 'he knew as well as we know our slave-tutors', had slaves who knew by heart the works of Homer, Hesiod and the lyric poets. Their task was to wait at table and supply him with the lines he wanted.[11] Statius' poem on the dead Glaucias commends him for his recitation of Homer, seemingly in Greek; and according to another poem Statius' father expounded a whole range of Greek poets, including Homer, whom he paraphrased in prose. It would be hard to believe that Statius is here speaking of Greek study done through Latin translations.[12]

Although we know very little about the Latin translations, it should be noticed that theorists and critics did not look kindly on literal translation. As Gellius[13] puts it: 'When striking phrases are to be turned or imitated, we should not strive to turn all the words in the exact way they are put. Many of them lose their grace if they are moved across [into Latin] against their will'. He points out that some of Virgil's successful translations are partial;

Virgil omits parts of the Greek which have charm in the original but would not go well into Latin. Thus literal translation was less highly thought of than imitation, which gives the spirit of the original in idiomatic Latin; and this principle applies in the Roman approach to prose works as well as to poetry. Perhaps then, the Latin translations mentioned above would have seemed inferior to men who believed that Virgil had translated Homer and other Greek poets in the only way that could preserve the sense and do honour to Latin poetry.

For Virgil, as we saw, the *Iliad* and the *Odyssey* were both vital components of his own epic. The *Aeneid* comprises the wanderings of a hero and his battles in Italy; twelve books of Virgil take in the journeys and wars of Homer's forty-eight. In a sense, then, both Homer's epics were equally important to a poet like Virgil; but was it the case that other Romans, many of whom were educated men with less devotion to poetry, were familiar with the *Odyssey* and *Iliad* in the same way? Can we decide which of the Homeric poems was better known or came more readily to mind?

When Horace contrasts his own serious reading of Greek poetry with the declamations of Lollius, he begins with an oblique reference to the 'author of the Trojan War'.[14] He remembers first the Homer of the *Iliad* and alludes to the protracted struggle between Greeks and barbarians, the peace-making activities of Nestor and the royal acts of folly for which the Greeks suffered. But though he mentions the *Iliad* first, he goes on to give the *Odyssey* its due. Ulysses, he says, can provide us with an example of virtue and wisdom, and he is obviously thinking of Ulysses in the *Odyssey*, since he refers to the Sirens and Circe. Other evidence, however, suggests that the *Iliad* was perhaps better known. Quotations from the *Iliad* in Cicero's letters to Atticus outnumber those from the *Odyssey*, and a similar pattern is noticeable in the quotations in Suetonius, Pliny's letters and Aulus Gellius. But it would not be right to put too much weight on mere numerical frequency, especially as there are few such references in two of the authors, Suetonius and Pliny. Quintilian's encomium of Homer may be a more reliable guide, though we should here bear in mind that his test is the rhetorical usefulness of an author. He mentions in order the ninth book of the *Iliad*, with the embassy to Achilles; books one and two, because of the dispute between the kings and the council of war; the introductions to both poems; the death of Patroclus; the battle between the Aetoli and the Curetes; and the moving appeal of Priam to Achilles. To judge by this account the *Iliad* was the more familiar of the two poems to Quintilian. For many Romans, as for Alexander the Great, the *Iliad* was a poem which bestowed lasting fame on the hero Achilles. If serious epic meant a poem about deeds of war, the *Iliad* was the more obvious choice.[15]

In chapter two I discussed briefly why Romans quoted Greek, including passages from Homer. It became clear that this practice had various functions; to make the present seem great and glorious; to render the truth less unpalatable; to make a joke by diverting Homer to a mock-epic usage.[16] It is harder to be sure how well the Romans knew their Homer. Cicero, in his letters to Atticus, quotes lines from more than half the books in the *Iliad*. He often has in mind the content of Homeric verse, as when he quotes the phrase 'I feel shame before the Trojans'[17] while deliberating whether to join the winning Caesarian party in the civil war or to side with the Pompeians. Though his political sympathies are with the latter, he has grave doubts about them and their bellicosity; but since he would feel embarrassed if he deserted the cause, he can express his fear of giving offence by apt quotation from Hector's speech to Andromache. By contrast, the younger Pliny's quotations are fewer and seem to recall the more obvious or memorable passages. He tells how Herennius Senecio, the defence counsel of Licinianus, reported that his client had decided to retire from his case and ask for mercy: 'I have turned from barrister to messenger; Licinianus has withdrawn.' Pliny is reminded of the famous passage in the *Iliad* where Antilochus brings Achilles the terrible news, 'Patroclus lies [dead]'. These are words of unforgettable power, and we can understand that Pliny would remember them without effort; but it is far harder to see the link between quotation and contemporary event. Pliny's point (perhaps it is not quite successful to modern taste) is that Senecio gave his news in a few impressive words. The *Iliad* quotation is here not related through content, but is relevant in a purely formal way since the words of Antilochus were cited by rhetoricians as a proof that brevity can be both timely and effective. It is almost as though Pliny had said, Senecio was as brief as Antilochus.[18] Some of the emperors' quotations, reported by Suetonius, are also from the more memorable passages of Homer; it is not surprising that would-be autocrats like Caligula and Domitian should have quoted phrases such as 'Let there be one ruler, one king', and 'It is not good for there to be many rulers'. But possibly the emperors knew their Homer better than the above would suggest. Tiberius and Claudius were exceptional in that they were closely acquainted with Homer. But Vespasian, who does not seem to have had the same degree of interest in literature, nonetheless made a witty application of the Homeric line, 'Taking great strides, as he brandished his spear that casts a long shadow', to describe a man who was huge and ill-proportioned. This is surely a case of apposite quotation from a passage that would have been much less well-known than the words about Patroclus' death.[19]

Nowadays people read Homer for a variety of reasons. They may set out to enjoy the epics as fine poems, they may be interested in the more technical question of formulaic verse, or they may read with an eye on Homer as a guide to history and the values of Homeric society. The Roman approach to reading Homer was affected by educational and cultural factors that are markedly different from those which obtain today. It will be useful to give a brief account of the diverse motives which influenced Roman interpretations.

We can be helped by Seneca's account of the different ways of reading Cicero's *Republic*. Seneca distinguishes between the story-lover (*philologus*), the grammarian or teacher of literature, and the philosopher, each of whom pays attention to different aspects of the text. The philosopher will marvel that so many arguments can be advanced against the claims of justice. The story-lover, as a sort of elementary historian, will note facts and traditions, for example that Romulus' death coincided with an eclipse of the sun. The grammarian will study changes in verbal forms, different meanings and adaptations made by poets. Seneca, of course, thinks far more highly of a philosophical reading than of the other types;[20] but if we add to his list of readers the orator, we shall have an adequate guide to the principal interests which would govern the Roman reading of Homer.

To some extent the functions of the grammarian included those attributed by Seneca to the story-lover, since the grammarian's task was to introduce Homer as literature and to explain allusions and stories. If we do not take this educational background into account, we shall be surprised that Tiberius could seriously ask his grammarian companions such questions as the following: 'Who was Hecuba's mother? What was Achilles' name among the maidens? What song did the sirens sing?'[21] Aulus Gellius was given a book compiled by an acquaintance who wished to contribute to the making of Gellius' own anthology, the *Attic Nights*. This work was a medley of the most curious information. It gave the names of Ulysses' companions who were snatched and devoured by Scylla, and discussed Greek theories about the route taken by Ulysses in his travels; it explained why Telemachus roused his friend not with his hand but with a touch of the foot, and described the kind of bolt used to fasten the door of Telemachus' bedroom. Gellius was astonished, but not impressed, by this esoteric lore; to him it was a mere exhibition of polymathy, a kind of learning for learning's sake. When he returned the book, he explained that his own interests in literature and learning were ethical. He, like Socrates, was concerned only with questions of good and evil. But though Gellius dismisses the treatise as irrelevant to his concerns, he does not find the questions it posed and answered completely absurd.[22] We may suppose that such 'Homeric questions', like those raised by Tiberius, were a variation or extension of the accounts offered by story-lovers as they expounded Homer. Grown men amused and instructed themselves with stories resembling those which they had learned as children.

The grammarian also explained particular words and forms to the young student of Homer, and discussed the usage of other poets. Comparisons between poets were popular and sometimes focussed on similar passages, either in Latin or in Greek. Just as men of the late republic compared Ennius and Homer, so too the critics of the empire set passages from Virgil side by side with their source in Homer; the exercise was a tribute to Latin epic, showing that it must be taken seriously even if the Latin author came off worse. Valerius Probus made a detailed study of Homer's picture of Nausicaa in the *Odyssey* and Virgil's imitation in the *Aeneid*. According to Probus, Homer compared Nausicaa with the goddess Diana in a way that is poetically appropriate; it was natural to make an analogy between the princess, playing with her friends near the sea, and the goddess, also in the open air. But Virgil's imitation compared the goddess of the chase with Dido, a queen building a city, and to Probus this was a piece of sophisticated incongruity. Also, Homer speaks openly and frankly of Diana's enthusiasm for the chase, whereas all Virgil does is mention her quiver, as though it were a heavy burden for the goddess to shoulder. It seems that this particular passage was thought to be one of Virgil's worst failures. Gellius himself, in writing about another Virgilian imitation, draws a contrast between the directness of Homer and the sophisticated 'neoteric' treatment that he discovers in Virgil.[23] One cannot dispute that an obvious contrast can be made between Homeric directness and Virgilian mannerism, but the form of Probus' criticism will seem captious or pedantic to modern taste. Comparisons of this type originated in the exposition of Homer as practised by grammarians.

Rhetoricians and orators devised yet another use for the Homeric poems. There was no obstacle to reading a poet as a guide to oratorical perfection, since poetry and oratory were viewed as closely related species of the one true eloquence; and, as Quintilian puts it, Homer was outstanding not only in poetic but also in rhetorical excellence.[24] Romans followed Greeks in citing the great Homeric heroes as examples of the three styles in oratory; Ulysses, Nestor and Menelaus were representatives of the grand, the middle and the plain in oratorical discourse.[25] Homer himself was a model of both grandeur and decorum; he could teach one how to match style to the occasion. Different parts and episodes of the poems were valued for their lessons in oratory. The prefaces to the *Iliad* and the *Odyssey* could teach one how to introduce a subject by giving the reader the necessary information and putting him in a receptive frame of mind. The end of the *Iliad*, with Priam's moving prayer to Achilles to return the body of Hector, showed the would-be orator how to treat the emotions in a peroration. Homer's pictorial vividness was much admired; the blind poet had been able to describe places so that the reader would feel he had them before his eyes, and his battle-scenes involved the audience in the action.[26] Vividness of this type was as essential to the orator as to the poet. Particular lines or words were treasured as examples of rhetorical figures. When Ulysses tells Achilles in the underworld how the Greeks 'went down' into the Trojan horse to hide, the rhetorician saw in his words a version of the figure called emphasis: the poet had suggested or implied the huge size of the Trojan horse by indirect means, through signifying more than he actually said. Homer magnifies the beauty of Helen when he says how the Trojans felt it was worthwhile to go on fighting for her sake: this was regarded as a form of amplification.[27] Homer's rhetorical authority was sometimes invoked in the most unexpected ways. The younger Pliny refers to him as a precedent for describing events out of order (*hysteron proteron*). And Nestor's battle-order—he placed the stronger warriors on the outside and the weaker ones in the middle—was taken as a model for the orator's order of proofs; his best proofs should come first and last, enclosing and hence protecting their feebler brethren in the middle of the speech.[28]

A philosopher's interpretation of Homer was obliged to take into account two distinct Greek traditions. In the first place the philosophical attack on Homer had criticized the poet for making gods misbehave in a way that would disgrace human beings, and for portraying humans as the dupes of their own worst feelings. Homer's tales were fictions that were twice guilty: they were unreal compared with fact, and untrue compared with theory. Plato's rejection of Homer as an educational text was no isolated event in the Greek criticism of Homer. On the other hand, what some philosophers had rejected was still popular with ordinary readers and in schools, so it is not surprising that other philosophers tried to save Homer from the attacks of their predecessors. The Stoics,[29] in particular, were ready to explain and defend Homer by means of elaborate allegories. The Homeric poems could therefore be condemned as inferior to philosophy or expounded as the secret doctrine of an author who was conversant with one of the most up-to-date of Greek philosophical systems.

Roman thinkers, or translators of philosophy, do little more than echo the views of Greek supporters or opponents of Homer. Cicero writes in the spirit of Plato when he complains that the rape of Ganymede is pure invention; he suggests that Homer was transferring human actions to the gods. On the other hand both Cicero himself, the critic of Stoicism, and the commonsense Stoic, Seneca, exploited the sect's idealization of Ulysses. Ulysses was famed as the 'sage orator'; the speech-maker of the *Iliad* was combined with the traveller, whose journeys were supposed to reflect his appetite for knowledge. To Cicero the episode of the Sirens is a fiction, but fictions will be accepted only if they resemble the truth; he thinks that the Sirens' song in Homer promises not just pleasure, but knowledge, and would therefore appeal to a man like Ulysses who wanted to gain wisdom even more than he wished to return to his homeland.[30] The Stoic version of Ulysses was alluded to by Cicero and Seneca;[31] hence the portrait of Ulysses the wise, the product of a philosophical reading of Homer, was familiar to Romans, though it was probably less acceptable than Virgil's sketch of Ulysses the foe of Troy, whose wiles and cruelty were depicted in the *Aeneid*.[32]

Romans, however, did not care to adopt the thoroughgoing Stoic allegorization of Homer. Velleius the Epicurean, understandably, rejects the interpretations of Chrysippus, on the grounds that the Greek Stoic was attempting to make the early poets into Stoics, and to foist on to them ideas which they had never imagined. For Horace the *Iliad* is indeed a source of moral doctrine; one can learn from it 'what is fine, what is base', and so the poem instructs as well as entertains—but, he adds, we can learn moral lessons more clearly from the *Iliad* than from the

works of Chrysippus and his fellow-philosophers. Seneca has no
time for the idea that Homer was 'really' a philosopher; that he
cannot be, since all the schools have claimed him for their own,
and they disagree among themselves about the meaning of the
good. Besides (he continues) even if Homer had been wise, it
would not matter to us; it would still be our duty to learn what
made him wise, which can be done without reference to the
Homeric poems.[33]

Many Greeks had believed that Homer was a master of all arts
and sciences. The rhapsode Ion, as portrayed by Plato, holds this
view in a naive form—boys and men can learn morals and military
tactics from a study of Homer. The critique of philosophers made
it difficult for educated men to maintain that Homer was morally
useful, especially if they believed that he told lies about the gods.
But Ion's naive confidence persisted in the guise of sober learning;
men thought that Homer knew subjects like geography and that
he was an authority on natural science. There are signs of this
idea in Pliny's *Natural History*, where Homer is quoted for
information on birds, grasses and air-currents.[34]

These are the more important ideas which influenced the
Roman reading of Homer. Though I have treated them as
distinct approaches for the sake of clarity, it should not be thought
that there was no overlap. The man who expounded Homer as a
model for oratory could hardly dispense with the labours of the
grammarian. But the philosophical allegorist would not have
had much common ground with the student of Homeric oratory.

So far we have not taken into account the theoretical status of
poetry at Rome. We have not considered how it was justified or
compared with other literary activities. Poets themselves were
concerned to maintain that their work was morally valuable as
well as entertaining. Lucretius explains that his poetry is intended
to give pleasure as a way of making moral and scientific truth
more palatable. Horace too commends the poet who can mix
the pleasant with the useful.[35] Both poets in their different ways
defend and justify the poet as a moral educator. Even such poets
as Martial[36] introduce the idea of morality in a curious negative
way; the poet can entertain by writing poems with obscene
expressions, but his life must be proper even if his page is not.
The serious poet, we may say, sets out to improve the public by
his works, and the writer of lighter verse promises his readers
that they will not be corrupted since he is himself, in spite of his
writing, an upright citizen.

Philosophers and rhetorical theorists were less generous to the claims of poetry. For philosophers some words and lines of poetry were serviceable, since they could be lifted from their context and used to illustrate a particular moral truth. But on the whole poems were regarded as 'myths'[37] (*fabulae*), deliberately untrue versions of that reality which philosophers tried to explain by more accurate and becoming procedures. Rhetorical theory allowed that poetry was of some value to the would-be or practising orator. Poets, so Quintilian says, can teach us such things as grandeur of diction and the appropriate treatment of character; poetry can be a welcome respite for the wearied orator who wishes to relax after the hectic bustle of the courts. But poetry cannot be a complete guide for the orator. Its diction and use of figures are too free; the rules of metre compel the poet to take refuge in metaphor, and to depart from ordinary, correct usage; the poet's aim is to do nothing but please, and his productions therefore resemble those of epideictic oratory, the show-speeches which merely entertain and are less important than forensic or deliberative orations. Orators on the other hand are like armed men fighting a real battle; their purpose is to win a victory, not just to entertain. Real events are determined by what they say.[38]

Poets therefore were lesser beings in the eyes of philosophers and orators. The search for truth and victory were aims of more importance than the poet's pleasure. Even the defence of poetry in Tacitus' *Dialogus*[39] is conducted in these same terms. Maternus argues that the poet's pleasure is less harmful than the orator's victory, because the orator makes his way in the world by defending criminals or spreading misery among the convicted; but he does not deny that entertainment and victory are still the respective goals of poets and orators.

If educated opinion was so contemptuous of poetry, we may well ask why poets flourished at Rome, especially in the Augustan age. The reason is that social and political motives were of far more consequence than the critical contempt of rhetorical theorists and philosophers. For a successful aristocrat, the poet was yet another means by which he could establish and broadcast his fame. Thus Cicero applauded the poet Archias for writing about the glorious exploits of Marius and Catulus. Augustus and Maecenas were subtle patrons who had a like interest in the *Aeneid* and Horace's *Odes*. The patron's desire for a glorious reputation spurred on the poet, who had a similar appetite for fame and recognition. Both together were more than a match for the critical judgments which were hostile to poetry as a serious activity.

We would expect to find that Homer's epics enjoyed more prestige among Roman aristocrats and poets than among educators, who gave poetry the honour of starting the curriculum but made it subordinate to oratory or even philosophy, which were the more fitting activities of grown men. The *Aeneid* was acclaimed as Homer made Latin. But Virgil's success as an epic poet had an adverse effect on Homer's standing at Rome. Other poets did not wish to write epic, or felt that the Greek epic had now been so well done into Latin that they looked for other subjects. The epic model was of no use to poets whose theme was their own personality and career or who wrote lighter poetry on the contemporary world. For Propertius, writing love-elegy, the whole of Homer is less important than one line of the poet Mimnermus. The term *Iliads* is transferred to describe the prolonged amorous battles between Propertius and Cynthia. Ovid draws a contrast between Ulysses' hardships and his own—the former are an invention whereas the latter have really happened.[40] For these poets, in their poems about themselves, Homer has become a name for what is archaic or obsolete. They have taken the theorists' idea that poetry is 'myth' (*fabula*) and used it to their own advantage, to claim that their works are about vital, contemporary themes. Their poetry in this sense is a piece of fact not fiction.

There is a similar rejection of epic in Martial's epigrams.[41] The traditional name for lighter verse of this type was 'playthings' (*lusus*). But Martial says it is not fair to call his epigrams by this title; the name should really be given to mythological subjects, for in Martial's own verse there is no bombast or tragic frenzy. People may praise the epic, he adds, but they prefer reading epigrams. When his Muse asks him what he will do if he abandons his trifles (*nugae*), he turns down the possibility of tragedy and epic since the only purpose of such works is to supply material for school-masters. It is noticeable that the epigrammatist's rejection of epic and his cult of light verse would find support in two quarters: the theorists' criticism of 'myth' as falsehood, and the orator's belief that light poetry was a proper relaxation from the courts. The younger Pliny was delighted with Martial's poem about himself and was flattered that his own fame had been treated by the poet. But he was himself a writer of light verse and justified the practice by citing many famous Romans who had relaxed in the same way. The public man might well have preferred commemoration through imitation-epic, but he saw nothing odd about accepting tributes of light verse from good contemporary poets, since this was a diversion he would indulge in himself.[42]

My purpose in touching on these facts is not to argue that Homer's reputation suddenly declined from the heights after or because of the *Aeneid*. Homer remained a classic because he was read in schools, even if he were subordinate to the needs and ideas of rhetoricians and philosophers. But he seemed more remote to those poets who looked for their subject in their own lives or in contemporary Rome. The point is that Homer, ever since the time of Livius Andronicus, had been a stimulus to Latin epic, but could not be of use to personal poets. The epic poet was bound to equal or surpass Homer whereas the elegiac poet felt obliged to deny him. In Rome, then, the significant ups and downs in Homer's fortunes expressed a change in poetic fashion; the epic could not make a satisfying poetry of everyday life. But though Romans relived the Hellenistic experience with regard to Homer the poet, Roman thought was not deeply affected by the need to reflect on Homer as theologian or moralist. The criticism of Homeric content—his gods perhaps, even more than his human characters—had marked an important phase in the development of Greek thought about man's place in the moral universe. The Stoic attempt to save Homer from his critics, to preserve him as a Stoic *avant la lettre,* is further proof that the interpretation of Homer was central to Greek thought. In the Augustan age Strabo[43] began his book with an elaborate defence of Homer as the original geographer—a specific variation of Ion's idea that Homer is the master of all sciences and arts. The Romans did not meditate on Greek epic in this way, though Virgil made a profound change in the character of the epic hero through poetry. Much later, in the age of Macrobius, men felt a need to expound their own great Latin epic as a pure source of religious knowledge; but this belated conservationism was made in response to attacks from outside by Christians, it was not an answer to earlier criticisms made by pagan Romans.

4

GREEK HISTORY AND HISTORIANS

In trying to estimate how much the Romans knew about Greek history, we must always bear in mind that their interpretation of the facts was coloured by their high regard for style. The great achievements of Greece, such as the defeat of Xerxes, were familiar, thanks to the writings of Greek historians and orators. But Romans felt that Greek literary talents had been used to shine too bright a light on the events of Greek history. Roman history, they believed, was really far more serious and important, but looked dimmer than it deserved because Roman historians had not yet done justice to the material. In section one I discuss the idea that Greek history had been made to seem more significant than it really was, and indicate the main sources of information which were available to Romans.

Sections two and three explain Roman opinions about Athens, Sparta and Macedonia. Athens and Sparta were looked on as political and moral opposites; democratic Athens seemed an anarchic state by comparison with Sparta, which was thought to have some of the virtues of earlier Rome. Romans had most respect for Macedonia, both as an empire—however short-lived—under Alexander the Great, and as a power which was still great in the second century B.C. Comparisons with Rome are seldom absent from Roman views on Greek and Macedonian history.

Section four deals with the reputation or later fortune of the major Greek historians at Rome. Romans came to believe that their own historians had equalled the achievement of the Greek historians. But the parallels between Herodotus and Livy, and Thucydides and Sallust, were mostly based on criteria of style; Romans did not see that Herodotus and Thucydides were great historians because they tried to understand the causes that lay behind events.

THE VALUE OF GREEK HISTORY

History was not an autonomous subject either in the Greek states or at Rome. Young men did not study history with a teacher in the sense in which they learned rhetorical theory or the tenets of a philosophical school; these subjects could claim, whatever critics might say about their actual practice, that they offered a body of formal knowledge and devised exercises which would help the pupil to become an orator or a philosopher. Since the would-be historian could not be apprenticed to his craft (the theorists claimed that personal experience in politics was the best teacher) his knowledge of the past was acquired casually, as the by-product of other interests; because history was not a discipline, with a developed theory about how it should be practised, the decisive criteria were imposed by rhetoric. Romans were ready to say that the historian should tell the truth and be impartial; but they did not admit that these are complex and difficult tasks.

When Romans (in the late third and second centuries B.C.) attempted to make a historical literature about their own past, they did so primarily because the story seemed worth telling. They believed, understandably, that the wars between Rome and Carthage were more important than other wars in their own or the Greek past. But the literary record of Greek history made Marathon seem more impressive than Cannae. The Romans felt some resentment about the Greek past, and believed that the skill of Greek writers had made their history seem grander than it was or deserved to be, by comparison with Rome.

One of the first of these complaints about Greece is found in the *Origines* of the elder Cato.[1] He describes the heroic behaviour of an ordinary Roman tribune, who volunteered to lead a small detachment so that the Carthaginian forces would be distracted and the main Roman army could escape from a difficult position. His action succeeded and he even survived to fight for Rome again. Cato observes that when it comes to brave actions, much depends on one's viewpoint. Though Leonidas of Sparta did no more than the Roman tribune, his valour at Thermopylae is famous simply because the whole of Greece has shown its gratitude by erecting statues and writing panegyrics and histories. The tribune, on the other hand, has not received his due share of glory. And this is the more unjust as he succeeded whereas the Spartan was a heroic failure. Cato's remarks are meant to set the tribune in the hall of fame; and his feelings are echoed later by Gellius, who refers to the incident as one which is fully worthy of

'Greek eloquence'. Gellius is like Cato in praising the same Roman deeds, but he differs in his regard for Greek literary excellence, probably because his pride in the achievements of Latin literature enabled him to acknowledge that 'Greek' was a term of praise.

There are other points of interest here, apart from the central idea that Roman heroes have not received their deserts. Cato believed that the particular facts of the tribune's action were as he describes them, but it is significant that it is the story of a tribune, one officer among many such in Rome's armies. Implicit in the story is the idea that Roman excellence is repeatable and does not have to rely on the accident of a great man appearing at the right time. In Cicero[2] this is developed into the theory that the greatness of Rome has come about gradually, through the contributions of numerous Roman statesmen, unlike the single acts of legislation which were believed to have created Solonian Athens or Lycurgan Sparta. When Livy contrasts the greatness of Macedonia with that of Rome, it is a contrast between the one Alexander and the many Roman generals who could have opposed him had he turned to the west. It is the kind of idea that might have impressed Romans as they reflected on the second Punic War and drew a contrast between the great Hannibal and the many Roman generals who fought against him.

In the second place, Cato's manner of comparing Greek and Roman history was unfortunate. It was natural that he should want to do justice to his tribune, but disastrous for the understanding of things Greek that he isolated one particular episode. The relative success or failure of particular actions cannot be grasped in isolation; we can only appreciate the exploits of Leonidas if we view them in the framework of Greek strategy directed against Persia. But Cato was probably not interested in the truth about the Greek past, as long as he made his competitive point that the average Roman was as good as the Spartan king.

Cato does not actually say that deeds are only as mighty as the words which commemorate them, but he comes near it. Sallust[3] uses this idea as a way of denigrating Athenian history and explaining why Roman history has not been praised as it should. Athenian history, he feels, has been exaggerated by talented Greek historians. Early Rome, on the other hand, was a different society, in which action was more highly valued than speaking or writing; men chose to perform actions which would earn them praise rather than to devote themselves to singing the praises of other men. In Sallust's view the greater fame of Athens is an example of fortune's power; fortune likes to bestow fame or obscurity not as events deserve but as it suits her whim. He makes use both of the standing prejudice against Athens as a city of words and of the prejudice in favour of Rome as a city of action; like Cato, he disparages Greek history because he feels that the greatness of the historian has made the events seem more majestic than they are. But perhaps we would be more impressed if he had said which historians or which events, if any, he had in mind.

Pride in Roman history did not make it easy for a Roman to respect or understand Greek history. Praise of Athens or Greece seemed to be taking away from Rome's just due. This sentiment is one of the noticeable features in Valerius Maximus' collection of examples. Valerius claims he is a practical Roman, who is only concerned to supply the reader with historical precedents; it is for others to debate theoretical issues, such as the nature of glory, and to commend their views in fine writing. Though he disclaims skill as a writer, his own flourishes of rhetoric suggest that he had literary ambitions. But he is faithful to his avowed principles (protesting against the unfairness of well-written history) when he mentions a soldier called Acilius who fought for Caesar's side in the naval battle at Massilia in the civil war. 'His heroism is not widely known and fame does not answer to the deed.' Valerius has in mind that an Athenian called Cynaegirus, recorded by Herodotus, acted no more bravely than Acilius . . . 'but Greece, who always sings her own praises, has impressed his name on everlasting memory by the trumpet-voice of literature'.[4]

Valerius' collection of examples is mostly Roman, but he adds instances from the history of other peoples, as an act of fairness and toleration on the part of Rome, though some of these are to be taken less seriously than the episodes from Roman history. Moral and political edification can be well enough served by considering the great history of Rome. He disputes the credibility of Greek history as well as the credibility of Greek historians. He suggests that these historians have not only lied by embroidering the truth, but have also told lies of invention; thus he refuses to accept the classic story that Theseus entered the underworld because of his love for Peirithous—'only an idler would tell the story, only a fool would believe it'. He prefers the true tale of Volumnius, who showed his loyalty to a friend in the civil war between Antony and the liberators.[5] He is accusing the Greeks not merely of literary exaggeration but of falsehood; it is the charge that Greeks are mendacious and will venture any fiction in the field of history.

These complaints against Greece are also found in Tacitus, who feels that the German Arminius has not been properly rewarded by fame because 'the Greeks only admire what is theirs' (but he adds that Romans were also to blame, because of their obsession with Rome's past).[6] The comment does not seem fair; both Dionysius of Halicarnassus and Polybius had admired Rome and had set out to expound her virtues to Greek readers; and one Polybius, at any rate, would have been worth more than any number of Greeks reworking the familiar themes of Greek history. It is probable that Tacitus makes the gibe because it was now a standard practice of the Roman historian; men were not likely to question the idea that Greeks were blind to anything but their own past.

Throughout the great period of Latin, Romans complained about the exaggeration and the mendacity of Greek historians. In the passages I have discussed here, national pride in Rome is shown at its worst; it is constantly making comparisons between Greece and Rome and then belittling the Greek side. There is little doubt that parallels[7] with Greece affected the Romans' interpretation of their own history in many ways, but the Romans either denied their indebtedness or simply did not know that it existed. They were suspicious of Greek historians because of their literary reputation, and they felt in their bones that Roman history was more important than Greek. For both reasons they would be reluctant to think that Greek history was worth knowing. Though envy of Greece helped to give birth to Roman historiography, it was still only one of the factors which affected Roman interest in writing the history of their own city. Roman pride was itself a sufficient cause and was at times independent of animosity towards Greece. Varro's *Antiquities*[8] was intended to acquaint the Romans with their own institutions and make them less like strangers in their own city. In Livy's great work the story of early Rome is worth telling for its own sake; and the contrast to its moral heroism is provided not by Greece but by later Rome, since Livy feels that Rome has declined from her illustrious past.

It seems remarkable, in the light of these ideas, that any Roman should even consider writing about Greek history in Latin. Why, then, did Nepos write short biographies of Greeks and others? His preface[9] suggests that he is attacking the Roman provincialism of those 'who are ignorant of Greek and who will judge what is right by their own [Roman] moral standards'. Nepos' point here is that one must, as he puts it, follow the customs of Greeks in writing an account of their virtues. Greece and Rome have had different standards of approved or acceptable conduct. Thus it

was no disgrace for Cimon at Athens to marry his sister; young
men in Crete were praised for having numbers of male lovers; no
Spartan widow was too grand to accept an invitation to a meal
in return for money; a victor in the Olympic games was sure of
glory throughout Greece. Romans, however, either did not attach
the same value to these pursuits or thought them actually shameful
or unbecoming. Nepos uses this moral relativism to explain why
the biographer of Greeks should mention, for example, the fact
that Epameinondas[10] learned music and could dance well;
otherwise Roman standards would be surprised that such trivial
matters should be thought important in assessing a public figure.
But it is clear that Nepos' talk of relativism is not at all intended
to make Romans question their own code of behaviour or
standards of judgment; it is merely a way of asking the reader to
be patient while the foreign tale is unfolded. The ultimate purpose
is to compare Greek generals with Roman so that we can decide
which are preferable; and it is likely that Nepos decided in favour
of Rome. His apparent tolerance of Greek ways is little more than
a device for making a better informed comparison with Greece to
the advantage of Rome. One passage of his work is of particular
interest as it suggests how ignorance of Greek might limit a
Roman's knowledge of Greek history. Pelopidas,[11] so Nepos says,
'is better known to historians than to the world at large'; it is
difficult to write about him (for an audience which does not
know Greek literature) without seeming to write history or
without failing to make his greatness clear if the treatment is too
summary. Romans, it seems, would probably know the outline of
Epameinondas' life, but would be less well informed about his
friend and compatriot. Perhaps we may conclude that Romans
were more interested in a few famous Greeks than in wider
subjects such as Athenian or Theban history.

   Other Romans who wrote on Greek history were the Augustan
Trogus Pompeius and Curtius Rufus, probably in the first
century A.D. It is difficult to be sure about the motives of Trogus as
his work survives only in the later epitome made by Justin. He is
praised for having assembled in Latin the separate works of Greek
writers and for concluding his work, as a grateful citizen should,
with a brief account of the beginnings of Rome. Thus the Latin
author is commended for giving a synoptic view and the whole of
world-history is subordinated to the importance of Rome. Curtius'
choice of Alexander the Great as his subject is more readily understandable, since (as we shall see) the figure of the world-conqueror
always invited a comparison with the world-empire of Rome.

On the whole, then, Romans were much less interested in Greek history than in rhetoric or philosophy; in these subjects they could not deny their need of Greek theories, whereas in historical matters their own events would supply a more deserving subject for commemoration in Latin. Furthermore, much of Greek history would seem remote from a Roman's consciousness of his own history. The Greek history of the fifth century was a confusing struggle between different city states. The empire of Alexander was soon dissolved into the successor-kingdoms, while by contrast Rome stood for a slow growth towards a unity which seemed enduring. The Greek historians, in their turn, were respected as models for Latin rather than as sources for the study of events in Greece. Cicero,[12] for example, appeals to Greek precedents when he asks Lucceius to devote a separate work to his own consulship; they are called in as authorities who will justify a particular approach to a more important subject than theirs, a subject from recent Roman history.

It may seem mysterious that Romans should have bothered with Greek history at all. We have already seen how they became wearily familiar with Greek arguments from history in the late republic and early empire. But this diplomatic use of Greek history was not a Greek monopoly; Romans had exploited it as political propaganda in earlier times, when, for instance, they promised King Seleucus an alliance if he would allow the people of Ilium freedom from taxation because they were kinsmen of Rome.[13] The Trojan war was a common background for Greeks and Romans alike; neither Greek nor Roman distinguished, except imperfectly, between the legend of Troy and the more credible facts of what we would call historical times. Their Trojan origin certainly made the Romans feel indignant as well as proud; they came to feel, particularly after Virgil's treatment, that the Greek capture of Troy had been achieved by foul means, the calculating treachery of Sinon. In one sense therefore Roman history was a long act of justified revenge against Greek deception. But, on the other hand, the same story said that many of the victorious Greeks had been dispersed from Troy and had settled in Italy. The Greek Evander, in the *Aeneid*, had befriended Aeneas as the founder of Rome. For the Romans, then, the Greeks of the past were friends as well as enemies, since it was believed that Italy was packed with Greek settlements. Their common, Trojan past was a bond of sentiment between Greeks and Romans as well as a source of discord.

We can see that Romans were disposed to think less well of Greek history precisely because they thought highly of the masterpieces of Greek historical writing. But it is difficult to give an account of how they came to be informed about Greek history, broadly understood. Romans, as I suggested earlier, did not take courses in the history of fifth-century Athens or the Hellenistic age; they took in the facts, such as they were (they were often facts associated with great men who could be compared with the heroes of Rome), from their reading of Greek historians, from their studies in rhetoric and philosophy, and from travel or residence in the Greek world.

There is little doubt that Thucydides and Herodotus were respected as the great names among historians, but their high position was decided by criteria of rhetoric, not of historical understanding. Both Cicero and Quintilian value these historians for the contribution they can make to the development of an orator; as we shall see later they make explicit comments on their style but hardly any on their subject-matter. But in the educational scheme outlined by Quintilian, reading in Greek has an important place, and probably included some of the Greek historians. It was the task of the 'grammaticus' to explain the poets and other writers who made up the propaedeutic introduction to the more arduous study of the orators. The 'stories' in the poets, for example, provided a sort of information about the distant Greek past and had been discussed at length by Greek commentators. Quintilian, however, leaves us in no doubt about his opinion on this subject. He thinks that too much detail is arid and useless, and he warns his teacher against this seductive exercise. But though he is talking mainly of the 'stories' in poets, what he says does not suggest that he would have had much idea of historical criticism; 'it is sufficient to give an account of the received version or those which are told by famous authors'.[14] It is hard to believe that this would be a suitable preparation for choosing between or discussing rival versions of the causes of the Peloponnesian War.

At a later stage in the curriculum, rhetorical literature and exercises provided the opportunity to become familiar with subjects from history which might have been exaggerated but were less 'mythical'. The orator learned how to praise or blame since he would encounter panegyric and invective in all three branches of rhetoric. The fullest praise was lavished on the exploits of those heroes who displayed courage and persistence in the face of adversity. 'For this reason', says Cicero,[15] 'teachers of rhetoric have a pageant which embraces Marathon, Salamis, Plataea, Thermopylae and Leuctra . . .' The great battles of Greek history

therefore gave scope for praising men like Leonidas and Epameinondas (though Cicero goes on to remind his reader that there are
innumerable examples to be found in Roman history). Some of
the rhetorical exercises required an outline knowledge of Greek
subjects, such as Alexander the Great, and others were based on
Greek law rather than Roman.[16] The information, of course, was
of minor importance compared with the rhetorical treatment.
Similarly, Demosthenes' speech *On the Crown* was widely read by
Romans; but though this speech is informative about fourth-
century politics, matters of fact were incidental to a study of the
orator's technique. Yet even so his rhetorical training in both
languages gave the Roman some familiarity with examples from
Greek history. To judge by Cicero's speeches, however, Greek
examples were not often quoted by Roman orators; they preferred
their own. When they do appear they tend to form part of an
argument that a course of action is yet more incumbent upon
Rome if it can be said that even Greeks pursued it. Thus Cicero
quotes Themistocles as one who was not deterred by the fate of
Miltiades or the exile of Aristeides from protecting his country
against the rashness of the people; if a Greek could do the right
thing, still more should a Roman.[17]

Philosophy was perhaps the most fruitful source of information.
It had long been the custom for Greek philosophers to use
historical persons and incidents as proofs of their doctrines. Thus
Cicero[18] says, in discussing the right attitude to death, 'It is usual
in the schools to bring forward the verdict of the gods about
death, not by inventing stories but relying on Herodotus and
others'. He goes on to tell the famous Herodotean story of Cleobis
and Biton who died after escorting their mother to a religious
ceremony in a temple. The story was quoted to show that death
could be a grace or reward, not just a punishment, a philosophical
use which is not so far removed from its function in Herodotus.
Cicero[19] also says that the names of great Greeks were 'on the
lips of all the philosophers'; he means that the conduct of men
like Leonidas and Epameinondas was used to show that virtue,
not pleasure, was good for man, except, of course, among the
Epicureans, who could not illustrate their doctrine with such
examples. Historical events were mentioned because they threw
light on principles or famous philosophers. Gellius, for instance,
remembers the great plague of the Peloponnesian War in connection with Socrates, whose temperance was confirmed by the
fact that he did not catch the disease. He mentions the Megarian
decree (excluding Megarians from Attica) not because of its

relevance to history but because Euclid the Megarian used to break the law in order to hear Socrates doing philosophy.[20] This is not to say that these historical facts were known only through the medium of philosophy, but to suggest that philosophical debates about events and persons were more frequent than historical explanation. The Greek instances challenged Cicero to show that Roman examples could be as valuable; it is rare for him to admit that Greek practice, as shown by history, is superior to Roman.

Foreign travel[21] and what can broadly be called the tourist-trade also made the Romans better acquainted with stories about the Greek past. A Roman might go to Athens to study philosophy or rhetoric, but he also visited the monuments and heard the guides. A Greek city's account of the important things in history differed from the Roman; thus Cassius,[22] on his educational visit to Rhodes, was instructed in the Rhodian version of earlier times. He would not have prepared himself beforehand by studying Rhodian history at Rome. On the whole, travel and the guides did not have a beneficial effect on the Romans' understanding of Greek history or add to their respect for Greeks. Many places showed dubious relics of the great past or made claims that were in conflict with others; Homer, for instance, apparently had more than one birthplace.[23] Tacitus is sardonic when he writes about Titus' visit to the temple of Paphian Venus and indicates that there were two different accounts of how it came to be founded. Titus, he adds, departed after listening to all that the Greeks add by way of invention, 'the Greeks, who revel in their past'. Similarly, he reports different stories about the worship of Serapis,[24] perhaps because this gave him the chance for an excursus on a novel subject. The guides influenced Roman opinion in two ways: they helped to whet the appetite of the gullible for Greek marvels and they reinforced the prejudice of the critics that distant Greek history was unreliable and uncertain. They made some Greek history entertaining but incredible in the eyes of competent judges.

It seems that the Romans had a low view of Greek history for several reasons. The very fact that they acknowledged the fine style of some Greek historians led them to believe that the story must have gained in the telling. The various sources of their knowledge, which I have outlined above, gave them information which was often isolated from the context of events or called to higher service in oratory or philosophy. It is hardly surprising that they chose to think of Greece as telling lies about history (whether we mean the plain falsehood or the lie varnished by rhetoric), because the Romans were proud of their own history and had an interest in cutting down the Greek past to fit the size of the Greek present.

But it is important to remember that Greek history was difficult for Romans; it is easy to be misled by such Ciceronian expressions as 'in the whole history of Greece' and 'the annals of the Greeks'[25] into thinking that they knew the subject whole rather than piecemeal. They sometimes referred to events in their own history in such a way as to bring out a relationship between past and present. Thus Tacitus, at the beginning of the *Annals*, gives a brief survey of Roman history by periods. His purpose is to suggest that although absolute and autocratic power had previously existed at Rome, it did not become a permanent feature until the régime of Augustus. Earlier events are here attached to a polemical interpretation of the early empire. We may contrast Sallust's vague reference to a time when 'the Spartans and Athenians began to conquer cities and peoples'. He uses that fact to illustrate his argument that the lust for conquest came to be an important cause of war. But he does not relate Spartan and Athenian aggression to other events in Greek history; the expansion of Sparta and Athens, we might say, is of moral interest to Sallust, but has no historical moorings either in later Greek history or in the Roman present. Cicero's reflections on unjust rule are of interest here; when he gives examples of Greek tyranny and injustice he mentions these in a disconnected way, adding that in this kind of subject he prefers to remember foreign instances rather than Roman. But when he turns to consider the Roman case he makes a distinction between an earlier period, when Rome behaved well, and a later, post-Sullan time when Roman rule became harsh.[26] Whatever one thinks of the distinction, it shows a way of analyzing the Roman past as a whole which is not apparent in his treatment of the Greek examples.

Lastly, it was immensely difficult to be sure of dates. There was some interest in commenting on great men who were contemporaries of each other, such as Themistocles and Coriolanus; the debate over Numa and Pythagoras was similar.[27] But it was unusual to give precise dates; the rule of the Thirty at Athens is more dateable than many events in fifth-century Greek history, but Cicero refers to it vaguely, as occurring 'at a certain time'. But he, we should remember, found it difficult to be sure about the dates of eminent Romans from the second century B.C., when he wanted examples for his work on consolation. The dating of

Greek history would have been more difficult still; and we can imagine that Romans, who were used to dating by consular years or by the number of years since the foundation of Rome, would not at first find much help in a chronology based on Olympiads. There is probably an important clue to the way Romans compared the Greek and Roman past in another passage of Cicero. He writes of Romulus founding Rome 'at a time when Greece was already ageing'. Even though the metaphor of human age was later applied by Florus to Roman history, the Romans in general thought of themselves as the newer people; they did not think that Greek history deserved more respect just because Greece had started earlier than Rome.[28]

ATHENS AND SPARTA

Much Greek history seemed obscure or remote to the Romans. When officials from the Greek cities spoke of events that went back to Homeric times, their Roman audience was inclined to see their remarks more as propaganda than as truth. Later periods of Greek history were confusing for other reasons. Greek power, as Appian[29] observed, was not long-lived; he meant that the effective period of independence had lasted from the early fifth century B.C. to the expansion of Macedonia under Philip II; even then the characteristic of events was rivalry between the various states, without the grand imperial design that seemed so evident in Roman history. Nevertheless we can hope to give some account of Roman opinion about fifth- and fourth-century Greece, with particular reference to Athens and Sparta; and it will be instructive to see what was thought about the part played by Athens throughout the period of Rome's wars with Macedonia in the second century B.C. Our information is sketchy, since many of the remarks about Greek history are incidental or are subordinated to ideas of greater importance to Rome.

There are some Latin panegyrics of Athens which repeat the proud claims that are so pronounced a feature in fifth-century Athenian literature. Lucretius, for example, describes Athens 'with its glorious name' as the city which discovered crops for the benefit of mankind and originated the civilizing influence of a legal code. But he is not just writing a purple patch in Latin on a favourite Athenian theme. His argument rises from the subjects of food and law to assert that Athens' greatest gift to man was the birth and life of Epicurus; in the remote past, Athens had enabled man to sustain an existence, but now, with Epicurus, she was responsible for giving him the means to live the good life. In this way Lucretius adapts the Athenians' boast about their past contribution in order to do honour to his own teacher; it is a neat variation on a well-worn Athenian subject. Cicero, in his speech for Flaccus, touches on other topics which were included in the conventional Athenian portrait of the past. He refers to the story that even the gods (Poseidon and Athena) disputed the possession of the city because it was so beautiful, and mentions its antiquity as evidence for the belief that the citizens of Attica were not immigrants but indigenous. There is no reason to suppose that Cicero himself believed or accepted these Athenian versions of their earlier history; in this speech he is able to incorporate such conventional items because he wants to glorify Athens (which supports his client) as opposed to the Greek cities of Asia (many of which were on the side of the prosecution). Both Lucretius and Cicero, therefore, have their own reasons for acknowledging these Athenian claims. But Velleius, in his epitome, includes a more generous appraisal of Athens that is apparently disinterested, and applauds her as the home of learning and eloquence. Perhaps it is a fair guess that many Romans were willing to admire the Athens of the past for her philosophers and orators; it is less likely that they attended patiently to the Athenian boast that her citizens originated in Attica. When Florus gives Athens her epithet as 'mother of crops', he is merely using verbal rhetoric to emphasize that the city which discovered grain was reduced to famine during Sulla's siege.[30]

These passages show that Athens' place in the Roman history of culture was ostensibly high. However, Athenian myths were less important than other matters; a Roman speaker, by way of illustrating that each city or place is famous for one particular thing, observed that Athens was renowned for her orators.[31] Even so, the cultural prestige of Athenian orators was usually considered in isolation from their political or historical role. Athens the state did not inspire the Romans to admire the Athenians of the past for their political achievement.

Florus expresses his animosity towards the idea of Athens' glorious past as follows: 'Athens should not be self-satisfied. We [Romans] have defeated a Xerxes in Antiochus . . . and we have balanced the battle of Salamis with our victory at Ephesus.'[32] The denigration of Athens went side by side with advantageous reflections on Rome. One verdict on Athens condemned the 'glory of Greece' as a city which had suffered the ill-effects of too much liberty; it was felt that the extreme democracy of fifth-century Athens had been undisciplined and anarchic, and that this form of government was not unconnected with Athens' loss of power at the end of the Peloponnesian War. A speaker in Tacitus links the large number of Athenian orators (often valued as an index to Athens' supremacy in oratory) with the idea that in Athens the people were all-powerful, and though he admits that the same phenomenon has occurred in Roman history, he implies that Rome has now recovered from the excesses of the late republic.[33] Conditions then were politically undesirable, even though they were conducive to great oratory. Athenian freedom was criticized not only as offensive to Roman ideas of a well-ordered society but also as incompatible with philosophy. Thus Seneca[34] condemns Athens for putting Socrates to death. 'Athens the free could not endure the freedom of Socrates.' The paradox is the more extreme as it follows a passage in which Seneca extols Socrates for his opposition to the rule of the Thirty tyrants. His main point is that the true philosopher has scope to show his virtues in times of political deterioration, as under the rule of the Thirty, but he is also saying that more normal political conditions, such as the restored democracy, are full of vices and therefore hostile to the philosopher. Athens, when freed from tyrants, was guilty of destroying a man who had spoken out against unjust rule. It is true that the trial and death of Socrates are no credit to the restored democracy, but it must be said that any judgment on Athens must thank her political freedom for allowing the conditions in which philosophical debate could flourish.

Athenian freedom, it seems, was too high a price to pay for great oratory, and Athens had not been able to accept the orderly criticism made by its leading philosopher-citizen. Roman reservations about the Athenian democracy are expressed somewhat differently by Valerius Maximus, who develops the theme that Athens was ungrateful to her finest sons. He gives a catalogue of eminent Athenians who were exiled in spite of their services to Athens. The list begins with Theseus, to whom Athens owed her existence, includes Solon, Miltiades, Aristeides, and Themistocles, and ends with the stalwart Phocion who was denied burial in Attica. Valerius says it is public madness to punish great virtues as though they were criminal actions; the Athenians had fair laws but an unfair character and chose to be guided by the latter in their treatment of their great men. Although the dead cannot themselves complain, the voice of criticism must not be silent on their behalf. The ingratitude of Athens was the more astounding as the city was said to provide legal redress for an owner who was not treated with proper respect by a liberated slave: a law that was in direct contrast to Athens' own behaviour. Of course Athens is not the only example of ingratitude mentioned by Valerius; he begins his account of this subject with some deplorable instances taken from Roman history. But he introduces his foreign examples with the comment that other cities should not sneer at Romans when they admit their faults, and there can be little doubt that he finds Athens far more culpable than Rome. Athenian ingratitude[35] is no more than a particular case of Valerius' general assumption that foreign history will provide fewer instances of virtue and more examples of misconduct.

In these cases Athens was disparaged as a society marked by the symptoms of excessive freedom. There is a more balanced picture of Athens in Cicero's *Republic* and *Laws*, the only sustained works, fragmentary though they are, of Latin political theory from this period. Cicero, like Valerius after him, makes the charge of Athenian ingratitude, though his main argument is that public ingratitude, whether in Athens or Rome, should not deter one from a political career, the highest good for man. In a later passage from the *Republic*, Athens is compared unfavourably with Rome, on the grounds that Rome's polity has evolved gradually over a long time, whereas Athens was made and remade by a few legislators, such as Solon, Cleisthenes and Demetrius of Phalerum. Several Greek states offered versions of their distant past which gave all or most of the credit to a single law-giver, and Cicero here is showing his antipathy to the 'myth' of the single legislator who imposes his will; he prefers the collective and gradual wisdom of Rome. In the *Laws* there is a more gracious attitude to Athens; the mysteries are praised for having made life more civilized, though Cicero is anxious that there should be no nocturnal religious acts which might encourage immoral behaviour; and Athens is quoted as a state which was advised by the oracle to preserve ancestral customs in its rites, an objective which Cicero also requires for his state. Overall there is no doubt that Cicero has less regard for Athens' contribution to political sagacity than for Rome's; but he does indicate that Athens had admirable and useful features.[36]

So far we have been discussing Roman views of Athens in her prime, and we have noticed that the modern admiration for Athenian democracy was not shared by the Romans. Cicero, for instance, thinks that Athens failed to preserve the degrees of aristocratic distinction after the Areopagus[37] was deprived of its powers, and he does not see this change as a necessary or desirable stage in the evolution of democracy. Yet Romans were interested in other periods too, especially the second century B.C., when Athens was of some importance in Rome's wars against Macedonia. The second of these wars (200–196 B.C.) enables us to judge whether the Romans believed that Athens should be taken seriously as a military or political force. When the consul was persuading the Roman assembly to vote for war against Macedonia, he drew a parallel between the case of Saguntum in the Hannibalic War and that of Athens now. By not helping Saguntum in time, the Romans had allowed its capture and were then invaded by Hannibal's army. Similarly, he argues, if Athens were now taken by Philip V, a Macedonian invasion of Italy would follow. From the Roman point of view, therefore, Athens was now no more than the equivalent of an obscure town in Spain. Although the Athenians would not have been pleased by the comparison, for Rome the main enemy was Macedonia and the importance of Athens was merely incidental. Livy observes that the Athenians had gone to war with Philip V 'for no good reason, as all they had left from their former power was inordinate pride'. Athens had put to death two young Acarnanians who had mistakenly attended a ceremony in the temple of Demeter without having been initiated; the Acarnanians were offended and asked Philip for Macedonian troops in order to invade and pillage Attica. Athens, in Livy's view, was prickly and irritable, but lacked the battalions with which to defend herself. Philip burned temples in Attica but Athens could not retaliate. Quite early in the war Athens expressed her hatred of Philip in the most extreme form, as she hoped for immediate help from other powers. Livy comments that 'in Athens there are always voices which are ready to incite the masses; this class of politician feeds on popular support, especially at Athens, where oratory is all-powerful'. He then describes the measures which were passed to dishonour Philip: his statues were overturned; places which honoured his name were put under a curse; and the death-penalty was pronounced for any Athenian who should speak or act on Philip's behalf. Finally Athens reiterated against Philip all the decrees which had been passed long ago against the Peisistratid tyrants. But the army of the present was not able to make good the proud claims of history. Livy's conclusion is that the Athenians were making war on Philip by means of letters and words, 'the only things in which they excel'.[38]

Second-century Athens, then, was both feeble and pretentious in Roman eyes; she could not compare with Carthage or with Macedonia. The weakness of Athens seemed utterly at variance with her period of strength in the fifth century B.C. But we should not be too ready to draw the simple conclusion that Rome merely contrasted Athens' greatness in the past with her inadequacy in the present. It was not that a city of action had declined into a city of words. In the Roman view the taste for oratory was already noticeable in the fifth century and had helped to cause her decline. The great Athenian orators were of course admired in Roman works on rhetoric, but they were also seen as an expression of demagogic politics which could be detected as a subversive influence on the whole of Athenian history.

Most Roman authors distrusted the political actions of orators who enjoyed popular support. It is, then, not surprising that they preferred Sparta, partly because Sparta had not produced any leaders who were famous for their oratorical skill.[39] Pericles had drawn a sharp contrast between Athens, the home of freedom and opportunity, and Sparta, the closed state with a narrow interest in military excellence. Romans liked to play with the idea of Sparta and Athens as opposites, but they tended to value Sparta more highly as nearer to their own idea of Rome or, at least, nearer to their version of Rome's grandeur in her republican past.

Rome accepted the usual Greek view that Sparta as a state had been created by Lycurgus, and was impressed by the thought that the 'Lycurgan rule' had lasted seven hundred years. Some of Sparta's political institutions seemed comparable with or only a little inferior to those of Rome. Cicero asserts that Rome followed Spartan precedent (whatever that may mean) by instituting a council of sage old men to advise the king. Senate therefore corresponds to *gerousia*, and both terms enshrine the valued principle that old men preserve whereas young men destroy. It was suggested that Rome had improved on the arrangement by increasing the number of elders, which was allegedly too small at Sparta. The ephorate at Sparta was compared with the tribunate at Rome; ephors and tribunes alike were seen as the necessary checks on the assertive power of kings and consuls, Rome's republican substitute for royal power. Cicero thinks that the Romans had certainly improved Lycurgus' schemes in one respect. Lycurgus had designed a form of kingship which was hereditary, and it was therefore believed that the Spartans were obliged to accept whatever king was provided by the accident of birth. But the new people on the Tiber did not make the same mistake; Romulus saw that what mattered in a ruler was virtue and wisdom, and kings with these qualities could be more readily obtained through an elective system.[40]

This political resemblance between Rome and Sparta was completed by a moral likeness. Valerius Maximus, for example, describes how a venerable Athenian citizen could not find a seat in the theatre until he was respectfully welcomed by some Spartan envoys who were also present. Athens, it seemed, knew in theory how to behave, but in practice Spartans conducted themselves more properly. Gellius says that Rome had borrowed from Sparta the custom whereby young men showed respect for age by escorting their elders home. Sparta, so Valerius says, 'was very close to the seriousness (*gravitas*) of our own ancestors'; for a long time she was able to keep her citizens from being contaminated by the luxury of Asia.[41] The moralist's fear that Romans could be corrupted by the Greek east had therefore been anticipated by Sparta. The historical basis for this is that in earlier Greece Spartans were notorious for being led astray by bribes; however, the moralist in Valerius does not take this failing as a proof that the Spartan system was at fault. If King Pausanias went to the bad by adopting effeminate and tyrannical habits, this shows that Sparta was right to keep her citizens away from the taint, not that she was wrong to rear them in isolation from the wicked ways of the world.

Romans idealized earlier Sparta although they knew that recent and contemporary Sparta was governed differently from the Sparta of the past. The tyranny of Nabis in the second century B.C. was probably more objectionable to Greeks than to Romans; but it is true that the power exercised by C. Julius Eurycles and his family was an inconvenience to the imperial government at Rome.[42] These changes were overlooked or forgotten. On the other hand, there was apparent proof of continuity, since Romans could see for themselves the curious rite in which Spartan boys were flogged;[43] this was interpreted as a surviving ritual, and seemed to be present evidence that the Lycurgan discipline still tried to teach manly endurance. But contemporary Athens was known to have changed; the popular citizen-assembly did not meet or had no power, and local government was managed by the wealthier classes. Dislike of the extreme democracy of earlier Athens was confirmed by the feeling that contemporary Athens was directed in the right and proper way.

The preference for Sparta was reinforced by the distinction between Sparta as the city of warlike virtue and Athens as the city of peace, since Romans believed that their own superiority was founded on valour shown in war. And in Sparta a Roman could admire proud independence, the refusal to submit, whereas the characteristic of Athens was an inability to keep quiet.[44] Her reputation for oratory was thereby turned into part of the charges against Athens.

Such were the generalized pictures of Athens and Sparta. They can be supplemented by a study of the famous Athenians and Spartans who are occasionally referred to by Latin writers. This is a difficult subject, since the importance of great individuals in their historical context often mattered less than their usefulness as examples in the works of rhetorical theorists and philosophers. It is not easy to see why, for example, Cicero describes Epameinondas[45] as perhaps the greatest man of all Greece. Perhaps his philosophical training, his self-sacrificing valour (in this he was compared with Leonidas) and his generalship all helped towards this favourable verdict; but it is also possible that he was most renowned as the man who made Thebes great, if only for a while, and seemed to prove that an individual hero can outshine a whole state.

The philosophical and rhetorical bias is clearly shown in the passages where Cicero and Quintilian refer to Pericles. They are mostly interested in his reputation as an orator, though they disagree about whether any speeches are extant. The famous story about Pericles and the eclipse is also mentioned; Pericles, who knew the theory of eclipses from Anaxagoras, was able to use his knowledge to restore morale in his troubled army. The incident had been used by philosophers to show that knowledge of astronomy is relevant to political life.[46] But Pericles the politician is mostly out of sight; we have instead the mere outline of the leader who had been canonized already by Greek theorists.

Perhaps Themistocles was the most discussed of all the Athenian and Spartan politicians. Valerius describes him as the most famous of the Greeks. Romans praised him for leading Greece to victory over Persia and felt that he was unjustly treated by Athens, which sent him into exile. The Greek contrast between Themistocles the astute and Aristeides the just reappears, though in a softened form. His rivalry with Miltiades is held up as an example of laudable ambition. The Roman Themistocles is nearly as many-sided as the original; among other things he illustrates the power of memory (a popular theme with rhetorical theorists), as he is alleged to have learned Persian within a year. Roman interest in Themistocles was increased by the fact that he was roughly contemporary with Coriolanus, who also went into exile. It is worth noticing too that he is among the historical precedents quoted by Cicero when he is discussing whether it would be right for Pompey to employ foreign troops against his own country in the civil war; Themistocles, he says, rightly preferred to die rather than act on behalf of the Persians against the country which had not rewarded him fairly. Cicero, at least, did not feel embarrassed at arguing from the conduct of a Greek long dead, though he did admittedly choose a reputable hero.[47]

On the whole, such details about individuals do not suggest that Romans had much understanding of their historical importance. We have seen that in general the Romans drew an adverse picture of Athens and that they painted Sparta as more like Rome, but still inferior. Any discontent with present conditions in Rome tended to make people look nostalgically back towards the Roman past; men did not feel that they had managed these things better in Greece. The position of Rome, some way inland, seemed preferable to the site of many Greek cities, which were either on the sea or too close to it. Rome was thus more secure from attack by foreign navies and did not encourage the growth of a restless maritime democracy.[48] Greek athleticism was held responsible for making men too proud of their Olympic victories, without promoting that courage in war which was required of the true Roman.

In some ways, the Roman approach to music is most instructive. The traditions made it clear that music had enjoyed a greater esteem in Greece; the criticism of Themistocles, who could not play the lyre, and the praise of Epameinondas, who combined music with politics, were the obvious proofs that in Greece a politician did not have to be ashamed of musical talent. Both Cicero and Nepos urge upon their readers the view that Epameinondas should not be less highly regarded because of his un-Roman accomplishment. But when it comes to theory the Romans do no more than give a limited place to music. Although Cicero agrees in part with Plato's view that a change in music heralds a change in the moral well-being of the state, he thinks that the condition of the aristocracy is a more important guide. Quintilian allows that music can contribute something to the education of his orator; he quotes Greek precedents and believes that music and literature were once parts of one subject. But complimentary though he is, he makes it clear that music is no more than an instructive interlude in his educational scheme.[49]

It seems on the whole that Romans' historical judgment on the great Greek past was based on a few stereotypes of Athens, Sparta and other cities, rather than on detailed knowledge of events, dates and individuals. Their imagination was attracted by the vision of a lasting empire, whereas the hegemonies of the Greek states seemed shifting and transitory. Only Sparta was admirable as it was believed to have retained the Lycurgan system for hundreds of years, and its moral qualities seemed like those of earlier Rome.

MACEDONIA

The history of the Greek city-states seemed insignificant in two respects at least: Rome felt that she had superior institutions and was aware that no Greek empire or hegemony had equalled her own achievement. But it was less easy to make light of Macedonia. Rome's victories over Macedonia in the second century B.C. (notably at Cynoscephalae, 197 B.C., and at Pydna, 168 B.C.) were less hardly won than her defeat of Carthage, but the Macedonians could still muster a formidable army. The fighting qualities of the Macedonian soldiers were respected, whereas in general the armies of the Greek states were by now inconsiderable. Even so, some Romans felt that they had defeated a country which was in decline from a more glorious past. Their imagination was fired far more by the idea of an earlier Macedonia, when Philip II had made it a great power and Alexander had conquered the east. As Pliny[50] observes, Macedonia was famous for its two great kings and its former world-empire. Curtius' full-length history of Alexander is a sufficient indication of Roman interest. Here I shall show how Romans measured themselves by comparison with Alexander and then I shall discuss briefly Livy's account of second-century Macedonia. Speculation about Alexander and the more sober history of later Macedonia are both characterized by the belief that Macedonian history deserved more attention than Greek.

   It is not difficult to say why Romans were interested in Alexander. In the first place, some believed that Rome had in fact had historical links with the great Macedonian. There was a tradition that Rome had sent an embassy to him, and it was alleged that Alexander, after his return from India, planned to lead an army on a war of conquest against the western Mediterranean.[51] Both stories are unreliable, but they probably helped to maintain Roman curiosity about Alexander.

Parts of Alexander's career seemed strikingly topical at Rome. Cicero made a jocular comparison between his own military successes as a Roman governor and the victories of Alexander. He was more serious when he was engaged in writing an advisory tract to Julius Caesar in 45 B.C.; he consulted works addressed by Aristotle and Theophrastus to Alexander but felt that his Greek models had been better placed to persuade an absolute ruler. They could urge a course of action which was honourable for themselves and which would find favour with Alexander. Alexander, moreover, is described as a young man who wanted true glory and sought genuine advice, though even he declined morally after he was called king. But how (Cicero asks) could one expect the autocratic Caesar to be pleased with Cicero's arguments for moderation?[52] In Curtius' history, which was probably written in the first century A.D., no one can read the account of Alexander's attempt to introduce *proskynesis* without thinking of the deification of Roman emperors. In another passage Curtius draws an explicit contrast between the break-up of the Macedonian empire after Alexander's death and the better fortune of Rome, which is said to owe its preservation to the forethought of one particular ruler.[53] It is clear that some of Alexander's doings could be made to look contemporary and relevant.

The principal surviving accounts of Alexander all come from this period. Diodorus' treatment in his universal history, Plutarch's *Life* and Arrian's history all drew on earlier versions; Trogus Pompeius and Curtius made some of them available in Latin. Though all of these are post-Ciceronian, a Roman of Cicero's time still had plenty to read about Alexander; the great Macedonian had been described by many Greeks, though none of them seems to have been a Homer among historians. Probably one of the authors most read was Cleitarchus,[54] who wrote a full history of Alexander in the early third century B.C. Cicero makes it clear that he was an unreliable author, given to exaggerating and sensationalizing the exploits of his hero. But his work seems to have been popular, and the fact that it was easy to read and not intellectually demanding helped to make the subject even more attractive to Romans.

Romans, like Greeks, were captivated by stories about Alexander that, whether true or false, showed him as an extraordinary figure in the thick of remarkable events. Historical analysis did not hold the imagination as much as did the anecdotes and the legend of the marvellous man exploring remote lands.

The elder Pliny and Gellius both enjoyed the story of Alexander and his famous horse Bucephalas.[55] Pliny also tells how Alexander was presented with a dog which would only hunt large animals like elephants. India, so Pliny says, was a land of marvels, and Alexander had opened them up to human curiosity.[56] Alexander's birth had been turned into something of a mystery, since his mother was an adept of snake-worship and a snake was alleged to have visited her bed before his conception. This prompted a Roman comparison with Scipio Africanus, as a similar snake-story was told about his mother.[57]

All these factors, many of which were in poor historical taste, ensured Alexander's lasting appeal. Most important of all, perhaps, were the imitations and flattery of eminent Roman politicians. Pompey, for instance, held his head in such a way as to make people think of the famous pose in Alexander's statues, and his title Magnus was the subject of uncomplimentary comparisons with Alexander's name. Julius Caesar expressed his discontent with his own achievements on seeing a statue of Alexander.[58] The emperors, in different ways, continued this Alexander-comparison. Augustus, for a while, used an image of Alexander as his seal; one of Nero's legions was called Alexander's phalanx;[59] and it was no more than apposite flattery to see a resemblance between Trajan, victorious in his eastern wars, and Alexander. Augustus' attitude to Alexander's sarcophagus is evidence of Roman respect; he honoured it by offering a golden crown and showed his scorn for the Ptolemies by saying, 'I wanted to see a [true] king, not a corpse'.[60]

We might expect to find, in view of all these instances, that Roman writers would show some sympathy and understanding for Alexander, as the ruler of an extensive empire comparable with their own. But the judgments of Livy, Curtius and Tacitus are surprisingly adverse. They did not have the critical ability, or, more likely, were not sufficiently interested, to see that many details of the traditional literary portrait of Alexander were coloured by Greek hostility[61] to the Macedonian. Stoics and Peripatetics, for example, had portrayed Alexander as an unsatisfactory king who misused his power and was not in control of his own violent temper. Yet although Roman accounts of Alexander reiterated the criticisms made by earlier Greeks, they were not inspired by sympathy for Greece as the victim of Macedonia. By Livy's time there were Greeks who had changed their tune and had begun to argue that Alexander was a greater ruler than Rome. Thus it is understandable that some Romans exhibit bias against Greeks as well as a patriotic pro-Roman sentiment directed at Alexander.

In a lengthy digression, Livy[62] gives his opinion on what might have been had Rome been involved in war with Alexander's Macedonia. He says he was impelled to write it for two reasons: he had often reflected on the possibility and he was anxious to refute 'some lightweight Greeks' who felt that Parthia was more than a match for Rome and alleged that Rome would have been defeated by Alexander. Some Greeks, we see, had apparently put aside their enmity and adopted Alexander as a means with which to denigrate Rome. Livy cannot believe that the Roman people would have been unable to withstand the majesty of Alexander's name. Even in Athens, when it was defeated by Macedonia and daunted by the recent sack of Thebes, men ventured to speak freely against the victorious enemy; it is hard to believe, he continues, that the Roman nobles would have failed to speak freely against Alexander. Thus one of Livy's aims is to criticize Greeks who carped at Rome and to suggest that aristocratic Romans were more free and independent than the Athenian politicians who were anti-Macedonian.

Livy's assertion of Rome's superiority turns on two ideas. He contrasts the one Alexander with a multiplicity of Roman generals who could have led Rome's armies against him. Roman prowess, he means, had been incarnate in many individuals, and he is therefore deploying a variant of that 'repeated excellence' which lies behind Cato's vindication of his tribune and Cicero's praise of Rome's collective political wisdom. Secondly, he claims that Roman military discipline and organization, an art developed over the many years since Romulus, were better than the Macedonian.

Though he acknowledges the fine generalship of Alexander, Livy also portrays him as a man who succumbed to the temptations of power and success. After defeating Darius he came to resemble him; the victor's adoption of Persian clothes and his attempt to introduce *proskynesis* as a mode of greeting are not seen as political measures but as the expression of a growing personal arrogance. The theme is that Alexander's success was too much for his moral character and he is therefore exposed not as a man of virtue but as one of fortune's creations with imitation virtues. Thus, if Alexander had attacked Rome he would have come as a half-hero in decline, leading an army that had likewise been made soft by the ways of Asia. Romans often liked to commend their own generals as men who had both virtue and good luck, since it was felt that merit and divine favour were essential elements in winning victories. It is in these terms that Cicero commends Pompey or even quite minor figures like Fonteius, when he is defending him against a charge of extortion.[63] Hence Roman readers of Livy would be prone to think that his Alexander, with his mere good fortune, would have compared badly with the great Roman generals of the past.

Less extensive character-comparisons occur in Tacitus and Gellius. Tacitus[64] reports that when Germanicus' funeral was held (A.D. 19) some compared him with Alexander because the two men were about the same age when they died; both died far from home among foreign peoples, and were thought by some to have been poisoned. From these unpromising or remote circumstances the comparison advances in favour of Germanicus: he was gentle to his friends, sparing in his pleasures, married once only and was as fine a soldier, though without the Macedonian's rashness. Here Alexander's faults are described allusively, an indication that they might be easily identified by Tacitus' readers. The historical basis for this belittling of Alexander is as follows. He had some of his disaffected generals put to death and killed Cleitus in a fit of temper; he was alleged to have been a pederast; he married twice; and in battle he led his troops at great personal risk which could look impulsive. It is a fanciful comparison, if only because no one could seriously compare the two men as generals; Germanicus was no Alexander. It shows that Romans liked to dwell on the supposed weaknesses of Alexander as a way of emphasizing the contrasting strength of the Roman character. A similar point is made, though more good-humouredly, in Gellius'[65] remarks on Alexander and Scipio Africanus; it would be entertaining, he says, to ask which of the two was more chaste—Alexander, who would not even set eyes upon Darius' wife, or Scipio, who admired a beautiful female prisoner but nevertheless sent her back untouched to her father. Gellius sees the subject as providing no more than a civilized, rhetorical diversion, but the comparison made as an innocent pastime is very close to those more earnest, more Roman comparisons in Livy and Tacitus.

The fullest study of Alexander is in Curtius' history. It is true that his Alexander does not have to be disinterred from comparisons with Rome; but though he gives his hero some qualities he also attributes to him many of the conventional defects— deterioration after victory, drunkenness, anger and so on. Some of these defects had been exaggerated, or even entirely fabricated, by earlier Greeks who were hostile to Alexander. But Curtius, even though he repeats and transmits Greek prejudice, does not take sides with Greeks against Alexander. He complains of their 'time-serving character'; he describes a Sicilian Greek as one who 'like all his people was a flatterer'—though by contrast he admires Callisthenes for his speech against introducing *proskynesis*—and he disparages the Greek love of lies when he refers to the story that Dionysus was hidden in Zeus' thigh. He is not a persuasive moralist, since, after criticizing the Greeks for their addiction to falsehood, he goes on to tell a sensational story himself. There is something of a clash between his Roman severity towards Greeks and the fact that he saw Alexander through traditions which had been established by Greeks and which he could not evaluate properly.[66]

It is obvious that there was some ambiguity in Roman attitudes to Alexander. In one sense they could only gain by acknowledging his prestige as a general since this would add to the stature of Romans who might be compared with him. But stories about his moral weaknesses were not altogether unwelcome because they could be used to argue that any comparison should ultimately find in favour of Rome. Many of the hostile elements in the tradition were derived from Greek fear or hatred of Macedonia, but the Romans were probably less aware of this distortion (and the historical reasons for it) than of the usual Greek faults as they conceived them—argumentativeness, as in Livy's view, adulation and mendacity.

Roman philosophical writing is more one-sided in its approach to Alexander's character; the great conquests are not viewed as the work of a character which was partly admirable but still plagued by weaknesses and failings. Seneca, for instance, takes Alexander's continuing progress to the east as evidence of an insatiable appetite for glory; true philosophy would aim at self-mastery, control of one's own emotions—a difficult task admittedly, but one which can be attempted without moving far from home. Alexander's eagerness to master more and more territory is therefore an act of ignorance, proving that he did not know the right objectives of philosophy. To seek for more worlds to conquer is to claim more for man than satisfies nature herself, for she accepts the limits imposed on the earth. This is to condemn Alexander by the rigorous criteria of Stoicism; the more common-sense approach of historians found much to admire as well as blame. Seneca[67] uses Alexander as an example of what to avoid in conduct because this was a familiar theme in Greek philosophy, both Stoic and Peripatetic; he was not taking sides with Rome out of hurt patriotism but judging Alexander as his view of the truth required.

Alexander's fame is also an important theme in Livy's account of Rome's wars against Macedonia, especially the wars against Philip V (200–196 B.C.) and the war which ended with the defeat of his successor Perseus in 168 B.C. For Livy these wars are in a sense no more than episodes in his chronicle of Roman expansion; he is hardly interested in the history of Macedonia for its own sake. He prefaces his account of the war against Philip by saying that it was not as difficult as the recent war with Carthage; neither the general's 'virtue' nor his army was comparable. But he finds glory in the fact that Rome triumphed over a people who had once had great kings and ruled a large empire. The greatness of Alexander is evoked as a glorious compensation for the in-adequacies of Macedonia's leaders against Rome. An Aetolian spokesman contrasts Philip V with Alexander, alleging that the kings of old fought open battles and spared the Greek cities. Perseus' army, in the later war, is said to have been larger than any Macedonian force since Alexander, but Livy accuses Perseus of incompetence as a general and of parsimony towards his allies.[68]

The character defects of these kings are the main cause of their defeat. Philip was too witty for a king, in Livy's view, and prone to insult where he might have been diplomatic; for instance, he was unnecessarily cruel to Greek communities.[69] Perseus' lack of sense and his vanity (in the Roman view) were apparent in the way he addressed his Roman victor; he still called himself king at a time when omitting this title would have been more realistic.[70] But though they were unworthy successors of Alexander they were not contemptible adversaries. Livy finds a compliment for Philip's courage and royal attitude. The importance of Philip's army is emphasized by Hannibal in a speech of advice to Antio-chus (191 B.C.). Hannibal[71] points out that Antiochus should seek an alliance with Philip, not waste his time in Euboea, Boeotia and Thessaly; these are places which have no independent strength of their own but merely flatter the power on the spot. Thus, even in decline, Macedonia was still a force to be reckoned with, unlike the Greeks, who had no battalions to back up their words.

Livy ends his account of these wars with a brief sketch of Macedonian history. It was, he says, an obscure country until Philip II; even then it was confined to Europe and did not expand into Asia till Alexander created his huge, but transitory empire. Then it was destroyed and divided by men who sought to satisfy their own greed and ambition.[72]

Romans did not do justice to Macedonian history, it is true, but clearly they had more respect for it than for Greek; they felt that here was an imperial power with some resemblance to their own. They were impressed most by Alexander's fame as a general and conqueror, and they wished to assert that individual Romans were equal or even superior to him. They believed that the reason for their superiority to Macedonia was in principle the same as their superiority to the Greek states—the one or two great kings, like the single legislators of Greece mentioned by Cicero, were no match for the many-headed genius of Rome. They felt too that their own empire was more important because it was enduring as a coherent whole whereas Macedonia had rapidly become fragmented into smaller kingdoms.

GREEK HISTORIANS

Roman judgments on the Greek historians are seldom concerned with the quality of their insight into events. Their comments and discussions are guided by other interests, even though they agree with modern opinion in acclaiming Herodotus and Thucydides and in criticizing Cleitarchus. The important questions from their point of view were (1) Does the historian tell lies or improbable stories (*fabulae*)? and (2) Does he make useful reading for the orator-in-training? They were suspicious of anything that seemed outlandish or remote and their respect for the leading historians was governed by stylistic values. Here I shall illustrate Roman contempt for Greek lies and consider the bias towards a rhetorical evaluation, and then discuss some Roman opinions on the three principal Greek historians, Herodotus, Thucydides and Polybius.

We have already seen how Romans were offended by encomia on Greeks such as Leonidas. They did not doubt that he had fought the Persians but they thought that his exploits had been exaggerated. Stories about the size of Xerxes' army also seemed incredible, as Juvenal[73] shows when he jokes about the rivers that were drunk dry by the invaders. Romans were more sceptical still about those Greek stories which concerned people or events from early times or purveyed information about marvels in remote lands. Disbelief of this kind was not the preserve of Romans alone, since criticism of tall stories was as much a Greek tradition as was the story-telling itself. But Romans liked to give

the credit to their own commonsense rather than to the spirit
of Greek criticism.

This attitude is clearly shown in the elder Pliny's encyclopaedic
work, even though he makes the general point that 'we should
not turn up our noses at following Greek authors—they have
been more diligent and their enquiries started earlier than ours'.
He writes scornfully of a plane-tree at Gortyn in Crete, which was
said to have given shelter to Jupiter's amour with Europa; the
story was evidently associated with the alleged fact that the tree
always kept its leaves. This was perhaps a guide's or traveller's
tale, but Pliny sees it as an instance of the Greek taste for historical
fictions. Mythological creatures were as suspect as the deeds of
gods; thus Pliny says that we should not believe in sirens, even
though Deinon, the father of Cleitarchus, asserts that they are
found in India. Euanthes, 'a respected Greek author', wrote
about werewolves which returned to human shape after nine
years and even recovered the clothes they had been wearing: 'it
is astonishing how far Greek gullibility will go, there is no lie so
brazen that it cannot find a witness'. Such adverse criticisms occur
only occasionally in Pliny,[74] but the fervour with which they are
expressed shows a deep distrust of the Greek addiction to stories.

These were stories in the works of minor Greek historians, it is
true, but if we add to them the apparent fictions of those who
were better known, historians such as Herodotus and Cleitarchus,
we shall begin to understand the Roman feeling that there was
much to beware of in the Greek historians. How, then, did they
account for this taste for falsehood among the Greeks? Pliny,
clearly, believes that it was a bad national habit. A more charitable
explanation can be discerned in a passage of Cicero.[75] In a
jocular exchange with Atticus he gives a version of Coriolanus'
death which is different from that advanced by Atticus. 'Do as
you like' replies Atticus, 'orators are allowed to tell lies in history
so that they can write more eloquently.' He then goes on to cite
the dramatic versions of Themistocles' death as told by Cleitarchus
and Stratocles. Cicero, with a certain amount of humour at his
own expense, is admitting that some Greek fictions can be
explained as rhetorical licence. Neither explanation reflects much
credit on the Greeks, but Cicero's idea of rhetorical licence is
kinder and also does more justice to the literary facts. The
influence of rhetoric on Greek historical writing was such that
writers were often more interested in a tale that could be presented
with style than in the truth about dull facts. Rhetorical licence
seems apt as an explanation of the exaggerations in Cleitarchus,

but we cannot be sure that Cicero would have invoked this idea to account for the 'stories' in Herodotus.

The Greeks had no monopoly of tall stories. To judge by Pliny, the Flavian politician Mucianus included much incredible information in his work on marvels. But Romans were inclined to treat some of their own tales by different standards. Thus Pliny records a story about a dolphin which took a boy to school; he says that he would not have believed it were it not guaranteed by dignified Romans like Maecenas and others.[76] Livy comments that one does not have to put complete trust in mythical tales about the origins of Rome; but, he adds, if any city is entitled to believe that it has a divine origin, that city is surely Rome. The authority of great Romans and the prestige of Rome itself made some Roman stories seem less implausible than Greek ones.

Though Greek historians were blamed for their lies, they were praised and valued for writing well. The subject of the style of the Greek historians enters into the debate between Antonius and Catulus in Cicero's dialogue, the *de oratore*. When Antonius observes that oratorical skill is a pre-requisite for writing history, Catulus is not wholly convinced; he agrees if the historical work is to be judged on the Greek standard, but finds himself disagreeing when he looks at Roman historical works. If these latter are our guides, then the bare facts without rhetoric are all that is required. Antonius then argues that plain historical narrative preceded more stylish writing both in Greek and Latin. He says that rhetorical perfection in history was attained only slowly in Greece, and he draws a parallel with Roman historical writing to date, which started with a plain story and has only now begun to rise to greater heights of style. Subsequently he makes the point that Roman orators have not yet excelled at history because their talents are taken up with practical oratory in the courts and senate. On the other hand, he continues, the eloquent historians of Greece did not plead in the courts; he seems to think of them as orators manqués. Even Thucydides, who was a public man at Athens, was excluded from oratory when he was sent into exile.[77]

It is difficult to know whether Cicero means us to take seriously this alleged parallel between the beginnings of Greek and Roman historiography. If so, he does not give a satisfactory account of Greek historical writing in relation to the development of rhetoric, and he conveniently overlooks the fact that some early Roman historians wrote in Greek. It may be that the parallel is no more than a character-item in the polemical argument of Antonius, who is the staunch exponent of native Roman wit against Greek

doctrine and surprises his hearers by saying that Latin history
will be as good as Greek when our orators have more time to
spare. His most serious point is that great history needs to be
presented with eloquence or rhetoric; and he praises the Greek
historians for their success in achieving various oratorical effects
in their work.

Antonius is portrayed as a man who reads Greek historians
when he has the time. But even though he is reading for pleasure,
not for any practical end—it is noticeable that he says nothing
about historical content—he feels that their language and style
are affecting his own. The merit of the Greek historians for him is
that they write well and are commonly intelligible, unlike the
philosophers and poets, who have a special language. If oratory
is the one true end of reading and study, then historians, whether
Greek or Latin, will be valued for their stylistic qualities. The
younger Pliny[78] makes a like point about the subordinate use of
history. He tells a correspondent to relax from his serious work of
oratory by doing various exercises which will eventually help him
to wage war with words in the courts: letter-writing, light poetry
and writing on a historical topic are all useful. Pliny here probably
means exercises to be done in Latin. But if historical exercises in
Latin are useful merely as a support for the tired orator, the works
of Greek historians are likely to be read and cherished for their
qualities of style, not their content.

Does he tell something credible? How well does he write?
As we have seen, these two questions would often decide a
Roman's assessment of a Greek historian. It is fair to add that
neither criterion would give much insight into the works of Greek
historians. Style was too much regarded, to the exclusion of
subject-matter, and credibility was often measured by whether a
story happened to seem likely to the reader, solely in the light of
his own experience or ideas. Furthermore there was some inconsistency between blaming the Greeks for writing lies and
praising them for their fine style; rhetoric was held responsible
for the best literary effects, but it was this same rhetoric which
had led men to alter the facts so that they could write a fine
page.

Some Roman historical writing was little more than the
continuation in literature of the political struggle to assert one's
own status (*dignitas*) or the status of others. Cicero[79] wanted
Lucceius to write a study which would make as much as possible
of his own consulship and his defeat of Catiline. Caesar and
Augustus, more effectively, were both concerned to justify their

actions. Under the empire, self-justification and the criticism of others could be more embarrassing; men who had been important under an earlier emperor were made uncomfortable when contemporary historians criticized their actions. Flexibility was required in order to survive in politics, but it would not look like a great moral quality on the historian's page.[80] These pre-occupations with personal status did not make it easy for Romans to see the wider issues involved in a reading of Herodotus and Thucydides, to see the latter's work, for example, as the history of a paradox, the democratic empire of Athens, not merely as the sum of so many famous individuals—Pericles, Nicias, Alcibiades and so on.

These general points should be kept in mind as we consider Roman opinions on particular Greek historians.

Though Cicero[81] gives Herodotus his title as the father of history, he also says that Herodotus' work contains numerous 'stories'. He is here drawing a distinction between history, which aims at truth, and poetry, in which the standard is set by pleasure; untrue stories, he means, would be acceptable in poetry but seem out of place in history, even though they are found in Herodotus and Theopompus. Herodotus is criticized for failing in the historian's duty to the truth. Among the Greek critics he had a reputation for lying which was taken over by the Romans. In a polemical attack on divination Cicero mentions the oracle given to Croesus—'if Croesus crosses the Halys he will destroy a great empire'. He asks why he should think this oracle was ever delivered to Croesus. 'Why should I think Herodotus more truthful than Ennius?' Normally, of course, a historian was by definition bound to be more truthful than a poet, but in this case, it seems, Herodotus' reputation is so bad that one can reasonably question whether he is more reliable than the poet Ennius. And since Ennius' story about the oracle given to Pyrrhus is known to be a fiction, doubt is cast on the story of Croesus' oracle by implication.

Most of the stories for which Herodotus was attacked come from those parts of his work in which the traveller is more prominent than the historian of the Persian Wars. Aulus Gellius repeats the accusations and shows that Herodotus' name was still suspect in the second century A.D. He calls him a man 'who tells stories' (*fabulator*); Gellius is here discussing the number seven, and follows an authority which gives seven feet as the maximum height of a human being—a truer idea, he thinks, than Herodotus' story that Orestes' corpse was seven cubits in length. In another passage Herodotus is mentioned as 'the famous historian', but the compliment is swiftly followed by the remark that he was wrong to say that the pine is the only tree which can never grow again from the same roots. Again, Herodotus was in a minority of one in saying that the Cimmerian and Scythian seas are subject to freezing. Perhaps the best-liked of Herodotean 'stories' was the tale of Arion, saved from drowning by musical dolphins; though Gellius takes pleasure in re-telling it, he evidently thinks of it as a fiction.[82]

Many of these tales aroused interest because they touched on natural science, broadly understood, and folk-lore. Thus the elder Pliny[83] discusses and rejects the story (given by Herodotus, though Pliny does not name him) that the lioness can bear only one cub, since the offspring tears the womb with its claws. There are signs that Gellius'[84] acquaintance with Herodotus was incidental to other interests. He looked up 'old books' and found Herodotus' story about the *Psylli* with their power over snakes because he was interested in a similar tradition about an Italian people, the Marsi. It seems that he heard about Herodotus' views on the freezing of the Cimmerian sea from the philosopher Taurus, who raised the question why rivers freeze and seas do not. It is perhaps doubtful whether Gellius knew the text well enough to be able to recall it himself or find a passage he wanted. And many stories about Herodotean characters such as Croesus, Cyrus and Themistocles were familiar because they were used as examples by philosophers and teachers of rhetoric.

These Roman criticisms merely repeat the Greek attacks on Herodotus as a liar and marvel-monger. No one seems to have excused Herodotus in the light of his own avowed principle, that he is bound to give an account though he does not always commit himself to believing it.[85] But Romans seem to have ignored or overlooked one feature of Greek criticism. It is clear from Plutarch's work *On the Malignity of Herodotus* that some Greeks objected to Herodotus' account of the Persian Wars on the grounds that he was unfair to particular Greek states and had shown them up as traitors. They felt that Herodotus lied about matters of fact as well as about the marvels of nature; he was too fond of foreigners and not patriotic enough. The Romans, however, were probably not interested in this argument, which—assuming they knew about it—would have seemed provincial and irrelevant.

Comments on Herodotus' style are best taken in conjunction with those on Thucydides, for the two are seen as complementary; the general standpoint of the criticism is rhetorical. Cicero praises both historians for having steered clear of the more extreme sound-effects which are noticeable in Gorgias and others; they avoided this form of Greek folly. Herodotus is compared to a gentle, flowing river whereas Thucydides is more vehement and sounds an urgent, warlike note. Great but imperfect, that is Cicero's view of the two Greeks. He argues that they were outstanding in their time, but he also thinks that they were in a sense primitives, writing when Greek rhetoric had not yet reached maturity. They are said to be deficient in rhythm, a key element in Cicero's analysis of oratorical appeal. Thus, though some of their work is rhythmical, they achieve this effect not by their awareness of rhythm as such but by felicitously juxtaposing the right words. Quintilian agrees with part of this. He sees Thucydides as a master of brevity and compactness, whereas Herodotus is charming, clear and relaxed; there is a contrast between the power of Thucydides and the attractiveness of the other. So far the critics are alike, but Quintilian tersely differs from Cicero's view that these historians neglected rhythm. It would seem that he read them more carefully or else that Cicero was simply carried away by his picture of them as writing early in relation to the development of Greek rhetoric.[86]

Thucydides was a difficult author, for both Greeks and Romans. The Roman comments perhaps show a narrower form of the rhetorical approach than is found in Dionysius of Halicarnassus, who is mainly concerned with style and expression, it is true, but does criticize Thucydides for an unfortunate choice of subject—civil wars among the Greek states. The Romans would not have been perturbed by this alleged failure in patriotism. Cicero[87] quotes Thucydides twice in his letters, the longer quotation having to do with Themistocles, who was a familiar figure from the treatment of rhetoricians and philosophers. The younger Pliny[88] also quotes Thucydides. In one passage he refers to the famous Thucydidean distinction between two types of history, the serious, which he calls a 'true possession', and the mythical or pleasing, which is called 'a competitive performance'; but Pliny applies the distinction to the difference between history and oratory. In another passage he quotes Pericles' maxim on the Spartans—'ignorance gives them confidence but thinking about things makes them timorous'—but does not mention the context. This is not to say that he did not understand the contexts; the point is that he was clearly more interested in adapting well-known phrases.

Even so, Thucydides was paid the greatest compliment that Rome could bestow: he was described as weighty and serious, having the virtue of *gravitas,* which was so important in the Roman's ideal self-portrait. His brevity of style and his trenchant maxims (*sententiae*) were much admired, especially by self-styled Latin Atticists both in Cicero's time and in Quintilian's. They affected a kind of pithy abruptness which they called Thucydidean. Neither Cicero nor Quintilian was sympathetic to this form of plain speaking. They point out that Thucydides is not likely to be a good model for the orator, as his speeches, fine though they are, do not resemble the oratory of real life; the orator cannot afford to be obscure, and brevity, though a virtue, is only one among many.[89]

By Quintilian's time there was enough Roman historical writing to justify a comparison with Greek. Quintilian[90] sees Livy as the Roman Herodotus, though he adds that Livy's speeches are better, and he matches Sallust with Thucydides. This last comparison had been made earlier, as Sallustian brevity and conciseness seemed to be a patent Latin imitation of the Greek. It is difficult to say whether Sallust himself was deliberately putting into Latin dress some or all of the Thucydidean phrases which some modern scholars maintain are parallels. Whether such parallels[91] are convincing will depend on the standard of proof. It is certain, however, that Roman standards of proof were lower than ours. Thus Gellius[92] says that Sallust's description of Sertorius was modelled on a Demosthenic passage on Philip II, but this view does not seem compelling now. Perhaps we may assume that Romans were prone to think of Sallust as a purposive imitator because he and Thucydides were both distinguished for brevity. It should also be said that if Sallust did set out to imitate Thucydides he did not pay much attention to Thucydides' care about chronology, and he analyzed political morals far more partially than did his model.

Herodotus and Thucydides, then, had qualities of style which seemed relevant to rhetorical education in Cicero's time and later. Polybius' style did not earn his work the same degree of attention; it is too ordinary and prolix, and he wrote much later than the great period of Attic prose in which Romans looked for models to surpass. But he was respected as a man and as an author; Cicero praises him as the friend of the great Scipio Aemilianus and speaks of him as a reliable authority.[93] Most important of all, Polybius was essential as a source for Livy, particularly in the books of the third and fourth decade.

Livy's high regard for Polybius is clearly shown by the fact that they give like accounts in many places. It is true that Livy makes some mistakes[94] about items of Polybius' Greek and he tends at times to put a gentler construction on Roman policy. But these are understandable errors or points of difference. Livy's attitude to Polybius is made explicit in a discussion of the number of Macedonian casualties in the battle of Cynoscephalae; Valerius Antias ('who exaggerates the number beyond measure') gave a figure of 40,000, Claudius Quadrigarius 32,000, whereas Livy contents himself with a mere 8,000. 'I do so not because it is the smallest number, but because Polybius is here my chosen authority —he is reliable on all matters to do with Roman history, especially events in Greece.'[95]

This is sensible praise and gives a true Greek no more than his due. But Livy does not seem to have derived much benefit from reading and using Polybius other than to turn him into Latin. He went to Polybius for facts and details, he does not seem to have made contact with his mind. Had he done so he might have sought for experience as an administrator, since Polybius believes that political experience is a pre-requisite for a historian. Livy might also have done more travelling to see the places which are mentioned in his history, since Polybius thinks that practical geographical knowledge of this sort is very necessary. But Livy did not enter public life nor did he move far from Rome. It is something of a curiosity that the Roman who used Polybius so extensively did little or nothing to put some of his excellent precepts into practice. In some ways he resembles the literary gentleman historian Timaeus, who is attacked by Polybius for writing about events without sufficient experience of public affairs or foreign parts.

Yet this may be too harsh a verdict on Livy. Why should one expect him to have taken in Polybius when there is no sign that other Romans had any real understanding of Herodotus and Thucydides? On the other hand we might reasonably expect that a professional historian such as Livy should have responded to the ideas of his source as well as accepting his facts. But he was not a historian of the contemporary and near-contemporary world as Polybius was. And because of his rhetorical background he naturally sought to describe the character of Rome's greatness in ways that were less analytical but could make Romans proud of their past. It is important to remember that if the ideas and discoveries of these Greek historians had no message for Rome, the Roman historians did succeed in adapting to their needs a rhetorical form of history which was itself a Greek invention from the Hellenistic age. Though rhetorical licence encouraged men to make the facts more interesting than they deserved to be, there was a better side to rhetoric which aimed at the artistic discovery of truth. The use of speeches in a dramatic setting and the colouring of episodes to make them seem vivid or present to the reader are two of these rhetorical fictions which did some service to the cause of historical truth and were skilfully used by Roman writers.

5

RHETORIC

Greek rhetoric, like philosophy, was a formal subject, taught by men who could document their theories by referring to the acknowledged classics of oratory.

The history of Greek oratory for its own sake was of little interest to Romans. But it did provide a familiar and convincing demonstration of the idea that oratory was an art which had developed gradually to reach its perfection in the time of Demosthenes. From this history the Romans took two key terms, Asianism and Atticism, which they used to discuss the best kind of oratorical style. Of all the Greek orators Demosthenes was the best known and most admired, though Lysias also had his Roman adherents.

Rhetorical theory was known from the technical manuals on the subject and from the arguments of philosophers directed against the claims that rhetoric was an art. Cicero and Quintilian believed that the orator had more to learn from philosophy than from the text-books written by professional rhetoricians. They had two main objectives: to assert that Plato and other philosophers were not ill-disposed to true oratory, and to make the manuals more interesting by introducing general ideas which could loosely be called philosophical. The manuals were obviously thought to be useful since they were translated into Latin.

THE GREEK ORATORS

Romans were more at home with Greek orators than with Greek historians. It is true that in neither case were they interested in the substantive issues which had been important to Greeks; they did not prize Thucydides for his discussion of the causes of the Peloponnesian War, and, similarly, they did not value Demosthenes as the spokesman for Greek freedom against Macedonia. But they learned more about style from the Greek orators, especially the kind of style which would be useful in law courts and political debates. Though teachers of rhetoric used the academic skills of their subject to analyze the merits of literature other than oratory, this sort of exposition made speeches more accessible and enjoyable than narrative; and the speeches in the Greek historians, important though they are as a key to the writer's mind, are still less than half the whole.

Education and training made the Greek orators of the past seem relevant and familiar. Cicero and the younger Pliny both practised translation, and Pliny describes how he would read a Greek or Latin speech to help his digestion, as well as to practise his voice.[1] Though Greek orators of the present did not have scope for great political oratory, they were often heard as diplomats, entertainers and teachers. The elder Seneca quotes the maxims and epigrams of declaimers in both languages, so that his readers can see how easy it is to turn Greek eloquence into Latin, always allowing for the greater freedom of the Greek language. In the early empire the famous declaimer Latro was an exception to the general rule in despising Greek declaimers and their works. Later still, in the second century A.D., the Greeks of the second sophistic made an even more brilliant impression than Seneca's Greeks.[2] Contemporary Greek oratory was thus more important than other forms of contemporary Greek literature in educating the Roman mind.

Romans, however, continued to pay most attention to the oratorical classics of an earlier age. They drew on the history of Greek oratory as evidence, to show that oratory was important and difficult, and as a source of critical terminology in arguments on style. In both kinds of discussion, the Greek orator with the highest standing was Demosthenes, and we shall see why the Romans admired him as a model, an instance of near-perfection in oratory.

Cicero's main concern in the *de oratore* (55 B.C.) was to argue that in Greek culture rhetoric had become divorced from philosophy and that the two should be reunited. But even in that work he alluded in passing to the history of Greek oratory, and returned to the subject at greater length in the *Brutus* (46 B.C.). His sketch in the *Brutus*[3] acclaims Athens as the homeland of oratory and discounts Greek orators from other places as hardly worth mentioning. He deliberately puts on one side the claim made in Greek text-books, that the antiquity and importance of oratory are attested by the speeches in Homer, and says that Homer's Menelaus is no proof that Sparta had great orators; Menelaus had only one of the oratorical virtues, brevity. Cicero's account of Athenian oratory begins with Pericles and culminates in a salute to the several orators of the late fourth century, Demosthenes, Deinarchus, Lycurgus, Aeschines and Demades. Though most of the great Greek names are present, there are some curious assertions, judgments and mistakes. Cicero thought that some of Pericles' oratory was still extant and that the judgment of the comic poets on Pericles could be confirmed by these remains; but Quintilian later is doubtful whether these are genuine. The oratory of speakers in Thucydides is used as evidence for the rhetorical taste and style of his contemporaries like Alcibiades— a curious view, since Thucydidean oratory would obviously have been too difficult and pithy for delivery before a real-life audience. Cicero says of Isocrates that he gave up his practice of writing speeches for others because he was tried for breaking the law, and that he subsequently took to writing manuals, or arts, of rhetoric. The alleged trial and charge seem to be an invention, and the important fact about Isocrates is that he taught a broad general culture of ideas, which he called 'philosophy', not the orthodox pedantries of the manuals on rhetoric.

But these mistakes are not the most instructive feature of Cicero's version. It is more important to understand why he includes this history of Athenian oratory in the *Brutus*, which is after all a survey of Roman orators. His case is that oratory is one of the most difficult attainments in the world. He wishes to show that even at Athens, with all its enthusiasm for speakers, oratory developed late, after the other arts, though he does not specify what these arts are. Thus the late acme of the activity, in the age of Demosthenes, adds prestige to the subject. Secondly, his comments on oratory before Demosthenes are designed to bring out the principle of gradual development towards perfection. He allows that particular orators achieved mastery in certain areas; Isocrates, for example, excelled at rhythmical prose and Lysias was a master of the plain style. But no one orator before Demosthenes was able to range successfully over the whole field of oratory. This idea of a slow evolution towards the perfect specimen is then applied in Cicero's account of Roman orators from the elder Cato onwards; particular successes of earlier oratory are part of a groping after perfection that is attained (or nearly so) in the Ciceronian age.

The history of classic, Athenian oratory does not interest Cicero for its own sake; it is of service as a precursor that illuminates Roman oratory. Cicero ends his sketch with the remark, 'But that is enough about the Greeks; indeed what I have said may well be superfluous'. Though Brutus demurs politely, they at once turn to the main subject, Roman orators of the past. We may compare this sort of interest in Greek oratory with the excursus in the earlier *de oratore*,[4] on the role of imitation in creating the style and taste peculiar to a given age. The idea is illustrated by referring to the Greek or Athenian experience, because Roman orators (it is said) have not left as many written speeches as have Greeks on which to form a judgment. This is to introduce the case of Athenian oratory without having to show too much deference. Though Roman oratory is still developing, it will eventually have enough written speeches to prove again what can at present be demonstrated more clearly by an examination of Greek speeches. ·

In these ways Greek oratory was of use to Romans because it demonstrated certain truths which apply to the oratory of all countries. Greece was not so much a model to follow and emulate as a source of general rules and principles; it was Rome written more clearly because the development was complete. Yet Romans also believed that the perfection of the Demosthenic age did not last. If Athenians were the best orators of Greece, they were followed by other Greeks with inferior standards and tastes. The history of Greek oratory *as a whole* suggested to Romans a story of gradual perfection followed by decay. The Greek experience in this case supplied Romans with the key critical terms in which oratorical style was discussed in Cicero's time and later on. When critics of Cicero spoke of his being florid, they charged him with Asianism; they advocated instead the idea of Atticism in style, though both they and Cicero disagreed on the definition of Atticism.

A short account of the Greek decline will explain how these terms came to be adopted at Rome. There was, allegedly, only one Greek orator of repute at Athens after the age of Demosthenes: Demetrius of Phalerum. His style was not corrupt, but he was more placid than his immediate predecessors in Athens and could not sway the emotions as they had done.[5] He too, so Cicero says, must be regarded as Attic. The more significant change came when, as Cicero puts it, 'eloquence left the Peiraeus ... and travelled all over Asia, so that it became smeared with foreign ways and lost its healthy Attic style; it almost unlearned the gift of speaking'. Quintilian gives a similar version, attributing this view to the grammarian Santra.[6] The Greek orator Hegesias was sometimes said to be responsible for the later vices of Asianism, especially the fault known as turgidity. Both Cicero and Quintilian suggest that the different quality of Asianic oratory is to be explained by the different quality of the audience; the discourse of Asianic orators reflects the more vulgar and theatrical tastes of their hearers. The exception is the island of Rhodes, which was thought to have been improved by the teaching of the exiled Aeschines. Rhodian[7] oratory was said to be closer to the refined Attic taste, and thus occupied a middle position.

Asianism and Atticism were terms borrowed from the history of Greek rhetoric and then used as 'polemical slogans' in Roman discussions of oratory at the end of Cicero's life. It is relatively easy to understand the different Roman interpretations of Atticism; it is far more difficult to define the content of Asianism. It would seem, from the historical sketch above, that it should always stand for a less pure or even corrupt oratory; perhaps there was a tendency to put down as Asianism all the qualities which were opposed to one's particular version of Atticism. In the *de oratore*[8] Cicero does not touch on the subject, except to compare the sound of Attic and Asianic Greek; even the uneducated Athenian voice is said to be more pleasing than the sound of Asianic Greek. In the *Brutus*[9] he speaks at greater length about Asianism but does not pronounce the death-sentence. He there distinguishes between two types of Asianism in oratory: the speech packed with maxims and epigrams, which are not stern and serious but intended to charm and please, and the discourse in which maxims occur more rarely and the characteristic is rapid flow. He illustrates both types by referring to contemporary Greeks whom he has heard, and says that the Greek representatives Hierocles and Menecles were as orators 'praiseworthy given that their style was Asianist'. He explains that Asianism as a style is best suited to young men and considers that Hortensius the orator was a master of both types when he started his career. But he failed to change as he grew older and he did not practise. The Asianism of his youth was less becoming to the older man, with his consular dignity, and his failure to keep in training meant that he could no longer give his maxims the proper dress or ornament of language. Cicero had considerable respect for Hortensius the orator and would not have described him as an Asianist if the term were wholly damning. Perhaps Cicero has two purposes in view in the *Brutus*: first, he might wish to point out to the narrow Atticists who condemned him that Asianism had achieved great results in the Roman courts, as no one could deny Hortensius his success; secondly, since Asianism as such is not wrong, the mistake being not to grow out of it, he can be proud that he is himself no longer an Asianist—in later life he has modified the rhetorical exuberance which was noticeable in his first speeches. His self-defence, then, is partly a denial—he is no longer an Asianist—and partly an assertion that Asianism has a legitimate place in a good orator's development.

Asianism was perhaps more significant in Greek thinking about oratory. Dionysius of Halicarnassus[10] believed that Greek literature in all forms was about to return to the classic purity of Atticism, and thought that the credit should be given to the sensible government and good standards of Romans. If this is anything more than an enthusiastic (but not necessarily in-sincere) compliment, we might perhaps infer that Roman taste has here led to a change in Greek. There is still a difference; for Dionysius had in mind a revival of Attic Greek, whereas the Roman Atticists, of whatever kind, were intent on creating a new Latin unlike the past.

The more significant dispute at Rome turned on the content of Atticism. We may usefully distinguish between the specialized or narrow Atticists, such as Calvus and Brutus, and those with a broader conception, like Cicero. Some critics of Cicero thought that even his mature work was long-winded and exuberant, and advocated the plain terse style of Lysias as a model for Roman orators. Political conditions during the régime of Julius Caesar may have affected the issue; it is possible that the critics of Cicero thought that there was no longer a place for the grand style of deliberative oratory and that one should therefore strive after the terse forensic competence of the Greek logographer. The narrow Atticists added Thucydides as another model of Atticism.[11]

Cicero agrees with his opponents that Atticism must be a term of high praise; his disagreement is over which Greek writers should be admitted as Attic. He disposes of the imitators of Thucydides with the remark that Thucydides did not write speeches for the courts, and so his trenchancy cannot be a model for practical orators. He has two principal arguments against the restrictive cult of Lysias. If men take pleasure in this Greek, who is an example of early and unemphatic oratory, why do they not also recognize the virtues of the elder Cato as worth studying? Atticus wonders whether Cicero can be wholly serious in suggesting that Cato, at the start of Latin oratory, is really a Latin equivalent to Lysias, who is 'more successful in every point that can be praised'. Cicero introduced Cato for two reasons. He wanted to point out that earlier Latin oratory had many virtues: it would be an injustice to the principle of gradual development to omit Cato, whose speeches were good but lacking in rhythm and verbal arrangement, qualities which were then unimaginable and had only been discovered since. And also, if the narrow Atticists accepted this equation of Lysias and Cato, they would be obliged to admit that they were admiring an orator who stood in the same relation to Greek oratory as Cato to Roman—an early orator, admirable, but still imperfect.[12]

The other argument against the Atticism of Calvus is probably more important. It cannot be right to say that you wish to model yourself on the Attic orators and then confine yourself to one or two orators among all those who are entitled to be called Attic. If Atticism is an excellence, which Cicero admits, it must be compounded of the different perfections found in all the various Attic writers; Demosthenes, Hypereides and Aeschines cannot be omitted. Cicero makes his view clear in a letter to Atticus about a speech by Brutus. It is a good speech which could not be improved in respect of neatness. But, he says to Atticus, if you remember the thunderbolts of Demosthenes you will realize that oratory can be both Attic and powerful. Cicero's search for grandeur in oratory compelled him to bring in Demosthenes as a counterweight to Lysias; if moving the emotions is the true test of an orator, then Demosthenes must be the model. If Cicero had had to speak on Brutus' theme he could not have done it more neatly, but there would have been more passion and fire; Brutus and Lysias are in too low a key.[13]

The argument over Atticism was no more than a passing affair. The taste and style of later orators were influenced not so much by Greek models from the past as by educational exercises (like declamation), restrictions on barristers' time, the presence in court of emperors or their advisers. Interest in Atticism survived · because the subject was attached to Cicero's reputation. Quintilian,[14] for example, says that Cicero's worst (posthumous) enemies were those who wanted to appear as 'followers of the Atticists', the admirers of Lysias. He repeats both forms of Ciceronian argument. If Lysias, why not Andocides? In other words there are other, earlier Greeks, if we must have an ancient as our model. In the second place the category must include other Athenians, like Isocrates and Demosthenes; if not we shall end by calling the inspired Plato an Asianist. Quintilian believed that Cicero had won the argument but he alluded to it in order to defend his esteemed Latin classic. The younger Pliny[15] seems to have preferred broad Atticism, as would befit a follower of Cicero; he says of one of his speeches that he tried to imitate

Demosthenes and Calvus, evidently a hint that he had both Atticisms in mind.

It will be clear that the Roman critics who have prevailed, Cicero and Quintilian, had most admiration for Demosthenes, though they did not exclude Lysias and others. For Cicero he was the perfection of Greek oratory; indeed, to a large extent his Roman reputation was the work of Cicero himself and those later 'friends' of Cicero who compared the two orators.

Demosthenes' prestige is attested by warm words of praise from many writers. Brutus, apparently, read all Demosthenes with a Greek enthusiast at Athens, and continued to read him, even though he was himself a narrow Atticist and was the only person known to Quintilian to criticize the word-order in a passage in the *Philippics*. Brutus also acquired a bronze bust of the orator. And for Quintilian, Demosthenes is 'to be read before all others, or, better, to be learned by heart'. The quality for which he was most admired was his force or power. Roman critics felt that he had been able to give fitting expression to his powerful feelings—the orator, so theory held, must himself feel the emotion which he wished to inspire in his audience—and to move his hearers so that they would vote as he required. Cicero's admiration is clearly expressed in the remark that Demosthenes achieves what others (Romans, in this case) merely attempt.[16]

Brutus and Cicero were probably acquainted with the whole range of Demosthenes' speeches. So too was the younger Pliny,[17] who refers to passages from several speeches in order to illustrate the thesis that orators should be bold and attempt high flights of language; he would hardly have looked them up for the first time, though he may have verified them from note-books. But one speech was far more important than the rest, the *de corona*, the speech on behalf of Ctesiphon. The speech on the *Crown* has often seemed the obvious choice as Demosthenes' masterpiece. Other considerations apart, Romans were especially drawn to it because Aeschines' counter-speech had also survived and could be compared.[18] Educational theory greatly valued those speeches from the past which enabled the reader to see how the pros and cons of a particular case had been treated by great orators. Cicero wrote an introduction to a Latin translation of the two speeches, though it is not certain whether the project was finished. His preface, the *de optimo genere oratorum*, explains that true Atticism can only be understood if we read Demosthenes, for he can stoop to be ordinary whereas Lysias could not rise to the heights. It was to be a free, not a literal, rendering, done by an orator, not a mere translator. Cicero explains the circumstances of the case and admits that it is foreign to Roman custom, but he argues that it is valuable because it concerns interpretation of the laws on both sides of the question and involves a comparison of the two speakers' services to the state.

Quintilian's high praise of Demosthenes is confirmed by his references to the *Crown*. The speech will show the budding orator how to begin with propei modesty, and is also commended for its narrative; rhetoric teachers evidently used it to show how the main parts of a speech, as they conceived them, should be handled. The *Crown* will teach counsel how to base a successful defence on different principles from those already used by the prosecution. The circumstances of the speech obliged Demosthenes to speak at length about his own career; to Quintilian and others this illustrates the rhetorical principle that self-praise is occasionally admissible, when it does not appear as boasting but is a necessary part of self-defence.[19]

Romans put some of the stories about Demosthenes to didactic use. According to Greek tradition Demosthenes had been a pupil of Plato,[20] a story repeated by Cicero, Quintilian and Tacitus. To these Romans the anecdote was a proof (if proof were needed) that the orator has far more to learn from philosophy than from text-books on rhetoric. To Quintilian, for example, the famous oath in the *Crown*, by the men who died at Marathon and Salamis, was sure evidence that Demosthenes had been taught by Plato. Another story about the two Athenians was less popular; it tells how Demosthenes, then a student with Plato, went to hear the orator Callistratus defend himself in court. He was so impressed that he left Plato for politics and oratory.[21]

Another group of stories concerns the role of delivery in persuading an audience; voice-control and stance were both important. Demosthenes' remark that delivery is not only the first thing to aim at, but also the second and third, was often quoted. Lucius Cicero is said to have visited the beach at Phalerum where Demosthenes practised speaking against the waves. Romans liked the story of Aeschines who was said to have confirmed his rival's views on delivery. When in exile at Rhodes he gave his own speech against Demosthenes and followed with Demosthenes' speech in defence; his audience marvelled, but was told that it was even more wonderful to have heard the orator in person.[22]

Demosthenes, then, was read and admired, and some details of his life were used to teach object-lessons in rhetorical principles. His reputation at Rome was secure, and it was only natural for

Romans to make comparisons between him and Cicero. The habit of comparison begins with Cicero himself; he contrasts the Greek's achievement with his own endeavour, and when he wants an example to show that orators must feel the emotion they wish to rouse, he goes, not reluctantly, to the *Crown*.[23] Cicero disparaged himself by comparison with Demosthenes, but many later Romans felt that the two were equals, that Cicero was the Roman Demosthenes. Livy made the brief but pointed remark that one should read Cicero and Demosthenes, and those who are most like them. Quintilian makes it clear that both orators are the high points of rhetorical development; before them there was a less sophisticated style of oratory.[24] Quintilian's main comparison of the two says that they resemble each other in all those oratorical virtues which are concerned with discovery (*inventio*). In style there are many differences, though each is excellent in his own way. When it comes to wit and pathos, Quintilian gives the prize to Cicero, though he was aware that Cicero had been criticized for his misplaced or excessive wit. Perhaps most Romans were content to put both orators on the same high plane, but it is noticeable that Quintilian is inclined to give Cicero the preference, since he is judging him as a writer and takes into account his letters and dialogues. Cicero, according to him, was three Greeks in one, as he gives to us 'the power of Demosthenes, the fluency of Plato and the charm of Isocrates'.[25]

Most of the stories about Demosthenes illustrate his effectiveness as a speaker and stylist; Romans were in general less interested in those tales which condemn his avarice and cowardice, though these too were known.[26] He was valued as a model which would set the Roman tongue standards of excellence; the Roman character was more self-confident and did not require lessons from other peoples. It is probable that enthusiasm for the greatest Greek orator did not induce Romans to read extensively in other Greek orators. If Demosthenes was the best, there was no need to waste time on lesser Greeks who had not achieved his kind of perfection. The Romans would naturally think it good enough to measure themselves by the best Greek orator.

RHETORIC AS AN ART

The speeches of the Greek orators were fine specimens of what could be achieved by political rhetoric in a civilized society. They set standards which the Romans wished to emulate or surpass, and they also provided evidence which could be used in critical discussions of oratorical style. But the extant speeches were only part of the Greek rhetorical tradition. The Romans learned much from Greek discussions on the theory of rhetoric in the text-books produced by professional teachers and from the arguments by philosophers refuting the claim that rhetoric was a true art. The manuals, the so-called *artes*, offered an analysis of the skills which would teach men how to become good orators. But though their title seemed to prejudge the question of the status of rhetoric, the claim was continually challenged by philosophers, who were doubtful whether rhetoric really was an art with its own subject-matter, like medicine or geometry. In short, Romans inherited from Greeks a long-standing debate about the value of rhetoric, whether we mean by this the actual oratory of public life or the theory as prescribed in text-books. Here I shall discuss, first, what the Romans thought about the anti-rhetorical arguments of the Greek philosophers, and, secondly, their criticisms of the ordinary rhetorical text-books.

As Crassus observes in the *de oratore*, the ultimate source of the philosophical attack on rhetoric is Plato's *Gorgias*.[27] In this dialogue Socrates argues against those who claim that rhetoric is the most important art available to man. Gorgias' follower Polus, for example, rates rhetoric highly because he thinks that it will enable the politician to do what he likes and to get his own way; the successful orator-politician can persuade his citizens to pass the measures he wants, will be able to defend himself in law-suits, and have his opponents convicted. Polus does not actually say that the politician will apply this art to political objectives which he knows to be merely selfish, concerned with his own power rather than with the welfare of the community, but he is only a step away· from this view. Socrates, in reply, denies that rhetoric is an art in the sense in which medicine is an art. The doctor knows what he is doing and can give reasons for it; his methods are not merely based on the hope that a particular treatment will cure a disease because he happens to have tried it before, successfully but without understanding why. Also the doctor will try. certain remedies which may be distasteful to his patient in the short run, but which have the long-term aim of restoring the sufferer to good health. How, then, does the orator-politician differ? He happens to be acquainted with the opinions of his electorate, but this is, unlike the doctor's skill, not based on principles. Also he aims to please his audience, not to prescribe what is best for them. The consequence is that rhetoric is dismissed by Socrates as no longer an art, but a sub-species of flattery, a flattery of the soul like the bastard arts, confectionery and cosmetics, which set out to pamper the body instead of training it in the right way.[28]

This is no more than a small part of Socrates' complex case against Polus and rhetoric. But it is enough to make clear that, if his views are accepted, rhetoric has been degraded. The advocates of oratory, who claim that it is important, will see their creature shorn of its prestige, since it has lost its title among people who are used to speaking of most activities as arts. It is at best a knack, won through experience, of finding the right answer. Socrates is not impressed by Polus' claim that orator-politicians have power to do what they will. He will only respect oratory if it is used for good ends. This is why he asks Gorgias at an earlier stage of the dialogue if he will teach his students justice, in order to make sure that they will not misuse their skill when they address political meetings.

Towards the end of the dialogue Polus is replaced by Callicles, who does not have the regard for conventional morality which causes the downfall of Gorgias and Polus. He draws an antithesis between nature and law; it is the nature of things that the strong should rule over the weak, but the weak make use of law and convention in order to defend themselves against the strong. If human beings were true to nature—if they obeyed the law of nature, the only law that matters—they would seek their own advantage and pleasure at the expense of others. The argument here shifts away from the enquiry into the essence of rhetoric. The dispute now, so Socrates says, is about the most important subject of all, how should a man live? Should one, like Socrates, pursue truth and philosophy, devoting oneself to educative argument? Or should one, like Callicles, aim at mastery and power over society, using oratory as a means to that end and thinking only of the advantage to oneself? Callicles is a particular case of the orator-politician who does not scruple to make what Socrates would call an unjust use of his rhetorical talents.[29]

In the *Phaedrus*[30] Plato returns to the subject. It seems at one point that Socrates now admits that rhetoric can be an art. The true orator, he says, needs to have a thorough knowledge of the soul, so that he can see which arguments or speeches will have the desired effect on a given group of people. But I am inclined to think that the concession is playful rather than serious; it is obvious from Phaedrus' answers to Socrates that this new rhetoric is going to be immensely difficult, if not impossible. It would certainly mean that existing orators would have to be re-trained in parts (at least) of philosophy. If the new, true rhetoric is somewhat futuristic, Socrates is in earnest when he turns to criticize the existing writers of manuals for suggesting that orators should use 'probable' arguments for unjust purposes. The standard example was as follows: a physical weakling who is courageous beats up a man who looks powerful but is a coward. When the case is heard, neither should tell the truth but both should employ the probable; the weakling, for example, should ask the jury whether it is *likely* that he would take on a giant, let alone maul him. As before, Socrates is critical of rhetoric for providing arguments that can be used against the truth and justice; he advises the manual-writers that 'probable' or 'likely' should mean 'resembling the truth', and he adds that they will only be able to say what is probable in this sense when they have learnt the truth by means of the more difficult art outlined above.

The *Gorgias* and the *Phaedrus* provided later philosophers with a fund of arguments to use against the pretensions of rhetoric. Romans met these arguments live when they conversed with Greek philosophers, and some read the Platonic dialogues where they originated. Crassus says that he read the *Gorgias* with the philosopher Charmadas at Athens, and Quintilian speaks somewhat severely of those who have a wrong idea about Plato because they have not read this dialogue as a whole but only in selections.

Both Crassus and Antony, in the *de oratore*, give accounts of their reactions to philosophical debates at Athens. We cannot say that the views expressed were actually held by these men—their language is, of course, Ciceronian, and the dialogue was written more than thirty years after the conversation took place—but even so they are not wholly in the realm of fiction.[31] It is worth noticing that these men did not feel that the philosophical attack on rhetoric was hostile to them. Their oratorical fame had preceded them and the Greek critics of rhetoric were complimentary about their achievements.[32] They were therefore listening to an academic discussion about the value of an activity which they knew to be indispensable in Roman public life.

Crassus says that the philosophers he heard all rejected the idea that part of the orator's function is political leadership. They would restrict the orator to forensic activity and a minor deliberative role. Crassus, however, did not agree, nor did he agree with Plato in the *Gorgias*. His only comment on this work is to say how he marvelled at Plato for his great rhetorical skill in making fun of orators and rhetoricians. Crassus seems to have been most impressed by the style and literary qualities of the *Gorgias*; he has

turned Plato the philosopher into Plato the orator.[33] His remark
suggests a trivial reading of the *Gorgias*, but Crassus, as he makes
plain, has no real interest in the question whether rhetoric is an
art. In his eyes this is a mere semantic quibble, typical of Greeks,
who have always had more enthusiasm for disputation than for
truth. Crassus believes that the orator has to have many subjects
at his finger-tips, even if his role is confined to law-courts and
does not embrace politics; he has to know about law, customs,
history and so on. The orator's business is therefore complex, and
the argument about art is just hair-splitting. Also (he goes on) if
by oratory we mean no more than good style, it is still true that
style is a distinct attribute, separate from other arts. Some philosophers, for instance Plato, write well; others, such as Chrysippus,
do not. Presumably, if oratory were not something real and
tangible, there would not be this difference between men who
know the same subject equally well.[34]

Crassus' objection to Greek quibbling suits his case. He makes
great claims for the orator and does not want to be tied down to
the close analysis of words; the term 'art' hardly appears in his
account, with the result that the reader who does not know the
Gorgias will find it hard to realize what the Greek question is. In
this he is speaking in accord with rhetorical precept, which advised
pleaders to avoid close definitions that might be used against
them. He adopts what might well be called the Roman motto,
'study things not words', as if it were possible to study this sort of
subject without reference to verbal niceties.[35]

Antonius is less coy in speaking of art and artifice when he
reports *his* conversation at Athens, but this is not surprising, as in
the *de oratore* he at first takes the opposite view to Crassus and
diminishes the scope of the orator. He enjoys repeating some of the
criticisms which had often been levelled at rhetoric, such as the
view that oratory cannot be an art since the orator deals in
opinions whereas art (or science) is about certainties. Antonius
does criticize one of the philosophers, the Stoic Mnesarchus, but
his reason is that Stoic definition claims more for the philosopher
than a Roman would allow; he is here thinking of the Stoic
maxim that only the sage is a true orator. The other philosophers,
especially the Academic Charmadas, were more attractive to
Antonius, who approved of the attack on the teachers of rhetoric.
Charmadas argued that it was pointless to use Demosthenes as an
example of the view that the orator's function extends to political
leadership; no one, he says, denies that Demosthenes did have
prudence in political matters; but if arts of rhetoric are going to

make men orator-politicians, why are these books stuffed with 'prefaces and perorations and suchlike rubbish'?

Clearly, the war between philosophy and rhetoric was still alive, in Greece at any rate. The dispute, as far as can be seen from the comments of these two Romans, was between rival groups of intellectuals, all of them professional teachers. Antonius and Crassus happen to have called in for a while, are interested enough to eavesdrop, but are not intimately concerned with the validity of the argument or its consequences for them. They are glad to see the manuals abused (after all, their own rhetorical success was won through experience), but their own way of life will not be affected. Both Romans are far closer to each other than the philosopher is to the teacher of rhetoric. There is no conflict between them like the opposition between Socrates and his interlocutors in the *Gorgias*, for in that work the issues discussed symbolize contrasting political objectives. Roman orators, one feels, will continue as before to make speeches as and when they want. In short, the debate between rhetoric and philosophy has left the market-place to become a set piece of the schools. In the world of Socrates as described by Plato there was a real contest between the philosopher and the would-be or existing politicians (Polus and Callicles), men with influence and power. But in these conversations from Cicero the intellectuals set about one another while the Roman men of the world are mere onlookers, sometimes rather contemptuous of the spectacle.

Both Antonius and Crassus here express opinions which they may have held and which are in part those of Cicero himself.[36] He believes, with Crassus, that the philosophers' attack on rhetoric is unjustified, since in his view the good orator is more than a forensic labourer; the orator is rather a culture-hero who persuades men to accept the rule of law and thus maintains civilization against anarchy. But he is also at one with Antony and criticizes the text-books for being trivial and irrelevant. Cicero, like Quintilian after him, goes further than both his Roman models in his eagerness to save the orator, since he wishes to bring about a reconciliation between philosophy and rhetoric.[37] Both writers believe that philosophy has taken away from rhetoric the study of ethics; it is therefore time to give rhetoric her due, since the orator must be concerned with questions of what is just, good, and so on, and should recover his stolen property from the philosophers. Some of the developments in later Greek philosophy after Plato encouraged the Roman theorists to think that not all philosophers were as hostile to rhetoric as was Socrates. Aristotle's

Rhetoric, even if it was known from the tradition rather than at first-hand, was proof that an eminent philosopher had thought rhetoric a subject worth analyzing. The practice of the later Academy, whereby one argued on both sides of a case, became a useful exercise for barristers-in-training, who would learn how to anticipate the arguments of the other side. Though Epicureans despised rhetoric, Epicurus was in turn despised by Cicero and Quintilian. On the other hand, Stoic theory offered rhetoric more scope; Zeno's image compared rhetoric to the open hand and dialectic to the closed fist, and Chrysippus' definition of rhetoric as 'the knowledge of speaking well' was accepted by Quintilian. This definition was useful to the advocates of rhetoric for two reasons; it implied that rhetoric was not just opinion, and it seemed to Quintilian to ensure that the orator would not misuse his art, since 'no one but a man of good character will speak well'.[38]

In the light of these remarks we may now examine Quintilian's comments on the Socratic criticisms.[39] He objects to the view that Plato is a foe of rhetoric and thinks that the error comes about from reading selections from the *Gorgias,* rather than the whole work. He says that although there are criticisms of rhetoric in the *Gorgias,* there is a distinction to be made between those Platonic dialogues which are concerned with refutation and others which are 'dogmatic'. The *Gorgias* is a work of refutation; the views of Gorgias, Polus and Callicles stand for a disreputable, contemporary rhetoric which Plato and Socrates reject; but Quintilian thinks that Socrates the critic also has in mind 'the true and noble rhetoric', rhetoric as she really is. This analysis is supposed to show that in Plato's view rhetoric is not really an evil, that the true rhetoric cannot be practised by any but the just, good man. Quintilian completes his explanation by referring to the *Phaedrus,* which he evidently takes to be a 'dogmatic' work; he has in mind Socrates' sketch of the comprehensive rhetoric based not on the lore of the manuals but on knowledge of souls, though he gives no hint of Socrates' admission that this is a difficult or unattainable science.

This interpretation is partly supported by some curious historical arguments. Quintilian thinks that Plato's approval of rhetoric is shown by the fact that he also wrote the *Apology* and the *Menexenus*; but (in answer to this) the rhetorical form of the *Apology* was imposed by the occasion, and the *Menexenus* is probably best read as an ironical exercise that makes fun of professional encomiasts of Athens. In both cases a rhetorical form is parodied, but there is no reason to believe that this shows respect for rhetoric. Again, Quintilian cites 'evidence' to support his view that Plato's target was corrupt contemporary rhetoric. He repeats the often-told story that Socrates refused to make use of a speech which was composed for him by Lysias,[40] on the grounds that it was unworthy of him; and he adds that Greek logographers, by writing speeches for other men, were in effect practising deception[41] on the law, which did not allow one man to conduct the legal case of another. It is indeed true that Athenian law in theory disallowed this practice, but the fact that it was breached is not a proof that contemporary rhetoric was wicked in the sense in which Socrates thinks Callicles is wicked.

Even though we may smile at this corroborative evidence, Quintilian's view of the *Gorgias* could still be right; the interpretation might hold in spite of the fact that it is supported by specious and irrelevant bits of history. But this reading of the *Gorgias* seems untenable. If Socrates in that work does have a true rhetoric in mind, its only purpose is to help unjust men to secure their own conviction, so that punishment can then remedy their character; and this is not the kind of oratory for which there would be much room according to normal Roman values. Quintilian[42] wants his orator to defend others, not to convict himself.

The Romans did not rise to the serious questions which are posed in the *Gorgias*. Crassus pooh-poohs the argument as a mere quarrel about words, and Quintilian, in effect, believes that Plato is not really an enemy of rhetoric proper. The *Gorgias*, though still read by Romans, has disappeared as an argument because of their unshakeable certainty about the valuable role of orators in real life. Quintilian, especially, interprets the *Gorgias* as he does because of his conviction that philosophy and rhetoric had once been bed-fellows and should be restored to their state of compatibility; hence it helps his cause to say that the enmity ascribed to Plato was based on a misreading. There is, however, one respect in which Quintilian[43] differs from Crassus; he sees that there are difficulties ahead if one denies that rhetoric is an art. Can we go on speaking of humbler activities like weaving and pottery as arts if we say that rhetoric has accomplished its marvellous works without having the status of an art? Oratory is prestigious in the eyes of Cicero and Quintilian, because they think that the peculiar distinction of man is speech: the more we perfect our discourse, the higher we rise towards the gods, and it seems likely that this ascent cannot be made without the help of art. Quintilian does not *argue* his view that rhetoric is an art—he settles the matter by 'proofs', such as the titles of manuals and the fact that many philosophers speak of the art of rhetoric—but he rightly sees that if oratory is thought to be important, one cannot just recklessly dismiss its claim to be an art. He would be shocked if he had to accept that rhetoric is not an art, just as Polus is outraged by Socrates' remark to this effect.

If the Romans did not do justice to the issues raised in the *Gorgias*, they paid the manuals of rhetoric, the *artes*, the compliment of translating and adapting them into Latin. The Latin manuals[44] are represented for us by Cicero's *Rhetorici Libri* and by the so-called *ad Herennium*; the latter is a complete text-book, embracing all the parts of rhetoric from invention to style, whereas Cicero's work deals only with the first part of the subject—hence its usual name, the *de inventione*. Cicero's *de oratore* is too ambitious to be called a text-book in the ordinary sense, because of its literary and philosophical aims, but even so it touches on most of the standard subjects. Quintilian's *Institutio* is in some ways similar; if it does not have the grand pretensions of the *de oratore* it is still not just a text-book though it covers the pedagogic ground more than adequately. Thus, even though much Latin writing on the art has not survived, we can form a clear impression of the Latin writers' approach to turning the *artes* into their own language. We shall examine Roman judgments on the Greek manual-tradition, and then see whether there is a common element in Roman criticisms of the Greek text-books as a whole and the second-century B.C. rhetorician Hermagoras in particular.

These are several Roman versions of the history of Greek rhetorical theory. In the earliest account (the *de inventione*[45]) pride of place goes to Aristotle, who is said to have collected pre-Aristotelian views so efficiently that interested readers consult his book rather than the original sources. Aristotle is here applauded because he wrote tersely, and made agreeable reading. But he is not only significant as the epitomator who saved Romans (and perhaps later Greeks) the trouble of hunting for the views of earlier writers. He is the cardinal representative of philosophical authorities and thinkers who wrote on rhetoric though they devoted most of their interest to philosophical subjects. Aristotle's contemporary Isocrates, together with his pupils, stands for the other type of instructor; Cicero says (although he has not actually come across Isocrates' text-book on rhetoric) that he was concerned with nothing but rhetoric. Later on, Cicero adds, the two families were in a sense brought together; writers of text-books incorporated whatever seemed relevant from both traditions, the

Aristotelian and the purely rhetorical represented by Isocrates.

It is probable that Cicero is here giving a schematic account of what he heard from a teacher or gathered from a brief history of rhetoric.[46] (He does not seem to have a first-hand acquaintance with Isocrates, or he might have commented on Isocrates' claim that he too taught 'philosophy', the practical sort.) Perhaps there are two features in this sketch which should be emphasized. One is the prestige of Aristotle; the other is the assertion that later manual-writers combined the broadly philosophical and the narrower rhetorical traditions. This is a bold generalization for which no evidence is given; Cicero may have thought that Hermagoras' text-book, with, for instance, its distinction between general issues and particular questions, was proof of a sort that later rhetoricians did not confine themselves to technical matters.

Other accounts of the history of Greek rhetorical theory are slightly different. In the *de oratore* (55 B.C.) Cicero was deliberately attempting a work on the grand scale, something far more substantial than the text-book of his first youth. He gives his general view in a letter:[47] 'These books steer clear of the commonplace precepts and embrace the whole of Aristotelian and Isocratic theory.' It does not seem that we can say how Cicero discriminated what is Aristotelian from Isocratic theory, but it is certain that he is contrasting the trite formulae of the text-book with a more intellectual approach to rhetoric ascribed to the fourth-century thinkers. Indeed, Catulus[48] tells Antonius that his ideas on the sources of argument resemble those of Aristotle, whether he is following the steps of the master because his own nature is like that 'divine genius' or because he has actually read the Greek. (Antonius is portrayed as one who knows far more about the Greeks than he thinks it prudent to admit.) In reply Antonius says he has read Aristotle's account of pre-Aristotelian theories and the books 'in which he gave some views of his own about the art' (evidently an allusion to the *Rhetoric*); the difference between Aristotle and the professional teachers of rhetoric is that he applied his general philosophical insight to a subject which he despised, whereas the professionals, who dealt with nothing but rhetoric, had less insight and wisdom but more experience. Now it is doubtful whether Antonius could have read the *Rhetoric*,[49] but the important point is that he is made to acclaim Aristotle for providing the would-be orator with more serviceable principles than can be found in the technical manuals.

Quintilian's brief history of the subject is different yet again; for one thing it is better documented with the names of manual-

writers both Latin and Greek, and naturally includes a reference
to the opposing rhetorical schools of the early empire, the followers
of Apollodorus and Theodorus respectively. He speaks of the
'different routes' taken by rhetorical theory in the fourth century;
he seems to mean the philosophical approach, in which his first
name is Aristotle, and the Isocratic, though he does not make it
clear whether this is the forefather of the technical manuals.[50]

It is not necessary to speculate on the reasons why these
accounts vary. Pehaps the important point is that in the Roman
view (in Cicero's case certainly) Aristotle was the king-theorist,
though it is far from clear whether the *Rhetoric* was actually read.
Cicero's spokesmen in the *de oratore*, Cicero himself and Quintilian
all admire Aristotle for having taken a wider view of rhetorical
argument than could be found in the manuals. They made very
little use of Aristotle's treatment of the enthymeme and his
discussion of ethos and pathos, but they respected his place in the
history of rhetorical theory as one who had made rhetoric intellectually acceptable and interesting. Perhaps we can explain
Cicero's regard for 'Isocratic theory' in his letter on the *de
oratore* in a similar way; 'Isocratic theory' is valued here because it
represents the claim that the orator must be a master of many
subjects, not just the crabbed distinctions of the manuals.

To some extent Roman criticism of the manuals expresses a
like dissatisfaction. The voice of complaint is heard from the
early first century B.C., right through to Quintilian. The author
of the *ad Herennium* says that he would prefer to devote his leisure
to philosophy; however, a manual can be useful if one leaves out
all the material that Greek writers have introduced 'because of
their empty arrogance'. He means that Greeks have tried to
make the subject more complicated than it really is. Antonius
makes several criticisms in the *de oratore*; his main point is that
the manuals are deficient in intellectual acumen and offer pre-
scriptions and recipes that no practising orator needs to learn. As
Quintilian observes, the manual-writers showed a perverse zest
in avoiding the terms used by their predecessors and introducing
their own. These works developed a huge and varied technical
vocabulary but were lacking in genuine intellectual discoveries.[51]

It is instructive to look more closely at some Roman observations
on the second-century rhetorician Hermagoras. According to
Cicero in his 'first rhetoric',[52] he divided the orator's subject-
matter into two, consisting of general issues and particular
questions. As examples of general issues Cicero gives the following:
'Is there any good apart from virtue? Are the senses reliable?

What is the shape of the universe? What is the size of the sun?'
Cicero then complains that these are philosophers' questions and
that Hermagoras is guilty of trespassing. He adds, caustically, in
case anyone supposes that Hermagoras was discussing his own
abilities rather than the scope of the art, that 'one would sooner
deprive him of rhetoric than allow him philosophy'. Evidently
Cicero was not impressed by Hermagoras as a thinker.

Unfortunately, we do not know how Hermagoras meant his
distinction to apply. It is true that the examples of general issues
given by Cicero are philosophical questions, and seem far removed from questions with named persons, such as: Is so-and-so
guilty of murder? Quintilian gives what seems a more plausible
illustration: as a general issue one may discuss whether man
should marry, and as a particular question, whether Cato should
marry Marcia. Obviously both such questions could be regarded
as falling within the orator's scope.

Clearly, the young Cicero found fault with Hermagoras for
intruding into philosophy without having any ability for the
subject. But in the *de oratore*[53] he understands the distinction in
the manner given just above, and now finds fault with the
manual-writers (Hermagoras perhaps) for suggesting that one
can handle particular questions without also taking into account
general issues. It is far from clear that the text-books *said* this; but
Cicero takes advantage of the possibility that they did to make a
contrast between the practical Roman orator, who knows from
experience that one cannot discuss the particular without involving
the general, and the rhetoric-teacher with his artificial distinctions.

Quintilian,[54] who was convinced that general issues, as he
defined them, come within the orator's art, was baffled by the
whole business. He says there were books attributed to Hermagoras
which maintained the opposite. But perhaps the title was forged
or possibly it was some other Hermagoras. How could it be the
same Hermagoras who wrote so well on the art of rhetoric? It
will be noticed that Quintilian is a kinder critic than Cicero; he
admits that Hermagoras was too pedantic, but says that otherwise he was subtle, a man to marvel at.

The case of Hermagoras is instructive for two reasons. It shows
how difficult it was, even for Quintilian, to be sure what an
important and influential Greek had written, even when (perhaps
we should say especially when) he had been discussed by Cicero.
Secondly we can notice that the young Cicero is not unlike the
author of the *ad Herennium*; both have a certain intellectual

contempt for the manual-writers whose works they adapted into Latin. It is easy to understand that Romans found these text-books academic and pretentious; they were narrow and fussy compared with the broader views ascribed to Aristotle and, some-times, to Isocrates. But we should remember that the prejudice against them is most noticeable in Cicero, who gave the credit for his own oratory to philosophy, in the form of the Academy, and who believed that his oratorical heroes, Antonius and Crassus, were both men with a greater vision of oratory than could have come from a manual.

But this is not wholly a case of Roman ingratitude to leisured Greeks. Cicero himself says there was a time (after the Roman empire was established) when Romans were eager to excel as speakers but did not believe that practice had any effect, or that there were such things as 'precepts derived from art'. Then they heard Greek orators and were introduced to Greek teachers, so that the age of rhetorical innocence came to an end. He is admitting that the manuals and rhetoric-teachers did make a difference. A speaker in Tacitus' *Dialogus* draws attention to the unsophisticated taste of the earlier Romans in the Ciceronian age compared with the imperial present (about A.D. 75). At that time, he says, any and every precept that can be found in the dry-as-dust books of Hermagoras was held in great honour, and an orator who included a passage from philosophy in his speech was praised to high heaven. All these things were novel at the time, and very few of the practising orators were then familiar with rhetorical precepts or philosophical opinions. Thus the manuals had more effect on Roman education and taste than one might gather from the criticisms in the *ad Herennium* and Cicero's rhetorical works. [55]

The Romans, in general, chose what might be called a middle way when they sought to assimilate the Greek rhetorical tradition. They distrusted or explained away the philosophical intolerance of rhetoric, as shown in the *Gorgias*, and they found that the ordinary text-books or 'arts of rhetoric' lacked intellectual depth. Their preferred authorities were those philosophers who had made rhetoric respectable by expounding it in separate treatises. Both Cicero and Quintilian want to make rhetoric more philosophical but they carefully point out that they do not ask their orator to talk in syllogisms. Eloquence is respectable as the counterpart of logic, but it is logic made expansive. The orator's discourse should therefore be fluent, not closely packed with sequential arguments, which was apparently a fault of contemporary Greeks, about whom Quintilian says, 'this is the only thing they do worse than us'.[56] That was not the Roman way of trying to reach the excellence attained by Demosthenes.

But Roman writers on this subject do not offer a satisfying wealth of argument to refute the *Gorgias* or take the manuals down. In discussing the manuals, for example, the characters in the *de oratore* appeal to Roman experience as a counter to the idea that an 'art of rhetoric' by a professional can teach a man to be a good orator. Greek theory of this sort was felt to be an impertinence to those who were making the speeches that really mattered. Romans liked the story of Phormio, the academic Greek who addressed the experienced Hannibal for several hours on the function of a general. They felt that Hannibal's response was boorish and uncivilized, but they agreed that theorists should not lecture men of experience, whether generals or orators, in this way; hence Antonius begins a speech with heavy humour aimed at the self-advertisement of Greek teachers.[57]

Nature (natural talent), art and experience are given as the three separate factors required to make an orator. One purpose of the *de oratore* is to suggest that practical training—writing out one's speech, making a new version of an earlier orator's speech, translating a Greek speech—is of far more importance than knowing the manuals. Given ability, training and practice will accomplish more than theory. The *de oratore* also tells us about certain qualities, valued by Romans, which cannot be found in manuals or taught by Greek teachers. It is more important to show modesty at the start of a speech than to know all the text-book rules about the exordium. Thus Crassus shows that he is overcome by confusion, so that the others are amazed and impressed, and take the lesson to heart. In turn, Crassus admires the modesty of the younger man Sulpicius.[58] Such decorum is felt to be right and proper, a world apart from the arrogance of Phormio lecturing Hannibal. And Crassus says more about the visible presence of a successful orator than can be learnt from Greek theorists.

The manuals were useful, or they would not have been translated. But the Romans were quick to say that more philosophical content was necessary; even Cicero's account of style in the *Orator*[59] is introduced by a short study of Plato's theory of forms, in order to explain that what he means is ideal or absolute excellence, not the stylistic virtues of actual orators. They believed too that there were qualities demanded of an orator which could not be found in any text-book, but which were visible in the behaviour of respected politicians and orators at Rome. The modesty of Antonius leads him to doubt whether success as an orator, much though he is admired by his companions and by Greek philosophers, deserves to be called an 'art'. He is embarrassed by the pretensions inherent in the name, it is true, but he is also making a grand defence of the practical Roman as against the Greek theorists. This modesty of the successful Roman is itself not without arrogance, an impatience with the tradition. Roman critics therefore agreed with the Socratic attack on the manuals in the *Phaedrus* and tried to raise their standard by a curious mixture of Roman experience and Greek philosophy.

6

PHILOSOPHY

In this chapter I discuss some of the more important questions which were raised when Roman writers tried to present Greek philosophy in Latin. In this subject the Romans were at a greater disadvantage than in oratory or history. Their barristers and men of action could readily be seen as equal or superior to those Greeks whose praises had been so freely sung. But Roman philosophers (in the usual sense of the word) were very few until the Ciceronian age, and even then most were dependent on the learning of Greeks, whether they met them abroad or invited them into residence.

If philosophy was not a native product it was perhaps desirable to justify an activity which might well seem un-Roman; even when the value of the subject was conceded, Cicero felt he still had to contend with the prejudice against studying it in Latin. Could it not be left in Greek? Cicero, Seneca and others then found that they had to choose between translation and creative imitation, which led them to reflect on the suitability of Latin as a medium for philosophy. I shall outline their ideas on these subjects in the first part of this chapter.

Secondly, the history of Greek philosophy did not attract the Romans as an academic subject and they did not conceive of the familiar modern emphases on the pre-Socratics, Plato and Aristotle, and the post-Aristotelian schools. Cicero, for example, dwelt mostly on Pythagoras, Socrates, and the later schools. He looked at the history of Greek thought with an eye on Roman history and tried to show that Rome had produced her sages to equal the thinkers of Greece.

It is clear that Romans were derivative when they discussed Greek philosophic ideas. But though they acknowledged their borrowing they made some attempt to seem original, either by reviving traditional methods of thought or by criticizing some of the Greeks whose works they used. A sketch of these attitudes is given at the end of the chapter.

THE ROMAN APPROACH

Latin philosophical writing is not an extensive literature. Apart from Lucretius' poem, Cicero's dialogues and Seneca's treatises and letters to Lucilius, we have to take into account some poetic discussion of philosophical themes, especially Stoic ones. Yet it is hard to believe that much of value has failed to survive. Quintilian's reading list, composed near the end of the first century, gives pride of place to Cicero and (with reservations) Seneca among Latin philosophical authors, though it is fair to add that his criteria are literary and aesthetic rather than philosophical.[1] Further, it is doubtful whether Cicero and Seneca are now read for the sake of their philosophical ideas; they appeal, rather, to historians of philosophy who are looking for clues to the lost Greek originals. Thus Latin philosophy failed on two counts: it did not originate nor was it cherished with the kind of affection felt by teachers who expounded Virgil or a Ciceronian speech. Rome's relationship to Greek philosophical models was always a dependent one, and even if later Romans did discuss philosophy in both languages, they often wrote in Greek, as we see from Musonius Rufus and the emperor Marcus Aurelius.

A possible reason for the Romans' lack of success in philosophy is that they despised the subject as such, considering it to be an improper pursuit for a Roman worthy. There is some evidence to support this view. Cicero was nicknamed 'Greek' and 'man of the schools',[2] and, in his philosophical works, he several times admits that there may be objections from, among others, those who disapprove of philosophy as such. His own *Hortensius* had been intended to urge the claims of philosophy as a subject. We hear of other objections later on. Seneca says that his father was hostile to his vegetarian habits, not because he was afraid of slanderous charges but 'because he hated philosophy'. He alleges too that his father's 'old-fashioned strictness' did not allow his mother Helvia to have more than a superficial acquaintance with 'all good arts'.[3] The future emperor Nero, perhaps unfortunately, was forbidden by Agrippina to study philosophy, and the future general Agricola showed more interest in the subject than his mother thought proper.[4] However, only Agricola's enthusiasm was curbed; we are told that he did profit by his studies and learned the hardest lesson, moderation. Finally, Fronto, as one might expect from a teacher of rhetoric, does not seem to applaud Marcus' interest in philosophical studies.[5] All in all, it might appear that many Romans, Greek speakers and non-Greek speakers alike, would agree with the sentiment expressed by Neoptolemus in Ennius: 'I must philosophize, but only a little; for on the whole it [philosophy] is displeasing'.[6]

But these instances are perhaps not enough to prove that philosophy as such was generally disliked. On the other side one can point to enthusiasts from the Ciceronian age, most notably Cato and Brutus. Later Romans also were keen students, especially Thrasea Paetus, Helvidius Priscus and their friends. In the second century A.D. Aulus Gellius, though not primarily a philosophy student, nevertheless included many philosophical items in his anthology. Indeed it is instructive to see how Romans used the quotation from Ennius given above. Cicero criticizes the statement on the grounds that it is impossible to do just 'a little philosophy'. He asserts that one cannot know just a little, for in philosophy 'a little' either means selection from wide knowledge or implies an enthusiasm that will carry one on more deeply into the subject. This is of course special pleading, designed to grant philosophy an entry, but Aulus Gellius, who twice refers to the passage, adapts it to show his dislike for certain subjects in philosophy. He first objects to the much-debated question, is the voice incorporeal or not, because it has produced various answers, seems to be insoluble and does not yield any solid lesson for the conduct of life. Similarly, he says, one should not linger over theories of vision; so he quotes the Neoptolemus passage to show that one should merely taste philosophy, not drink deep.[7]

If we are uncertain whether Roman critics outnumbered the advocates, we can be sure that both groups agreed on finding some parts of philosophy more useless or irrelevant than others. Romans were well aware of the threefold Greek division of philosophy into the study of nature, ethics and epistemology and logic. Ethics was usually felt to be in some ways useful since it defined what was good for man, whereas many of the questions discussed by philosophers under the other two headings seemed remote from everyday concerns. Hence the criticisms made by Gellius above; they express the feeling that a little natural science goes a long way. These views are more characteristically Roman than the panegyric on scientific theory that is found at the start of Seneca's *Natural Questions*.[8] Where such theory touched upon theology, it was felt to be respectable and worthwhile, but otherwise it tended to raise questions to which there were no answers or just a bewildering number. Similarly, too, there were objections to the constraints of logic and to refined definition. Quintilian, for example, advises the orator to put his case forward in broad outline and warns him against tying himself to a definition that may give a hold to his adversary—precise definitions, he feels, have their place in philosophical discourse but not in the courts. The same caution is expressed about philosophical disputes taken on their own, not compared with oratory; thus Seneca says that verbal quibbling lost the ancients (Greeks) much time, as do captious arguments that train the intelligence, but to no effective purpose.[9]

The demand for moral relevance led to some neglect of two whole areas of philosophy. A Roman's feelings on the subject were strengthened by his tendency to see his ancestors as men of action, men who had actually achieved what Greek theorists had pre-scribed without doing. Cicero portrays Cato as one who deserved the title wise (*sapiens*) even more than did Socrates, the archetypal wise man among the Greeks, 'for in the one case we praise his actions, in the other his words'.[10] The school of experience is felt to be superior to the school of argument even when the master, Socrates, is acknowledged by the Romans as an exemplar of right living. It is, then, not surprising that the school of experience is felt to have the advantage over the claims of bogus philosophers. Thus Gellius quotes approvingly the view of the poet Afranius that wisdom is the daughter of experience and memory;[11] this is a useful reminder that wisdom (the standard term for the goal pursued by moral philosophy) must be sought from life as well as from books; and he ends by saying that there is nothing more intolerable than indolent people who divert the true character and profit of philosophy to the arts of mere words.

But although real-life Romans were extolled by comparison with inactive Greeks, this does not mean that philosophy, properly pursued, was dismissed as worthless. One might expect to find that Romans would have scorned philosophy as mere words (*verba*), by contrast with real events or hard facts (*res*). Yet Cicero says:[12] 'If the manner of expression makes so much difference in philo-sophy, in which things (*res*) are the object, whereas words are not weighed, what must we think will be the case in law-suits, which are entirely governed by language?' Is it not surprising to find him saying that philosophy has to do with 'things'? His point about oratory is the familiar assertion that the most persuasive speaker is the one who can use all the resources of language to sway the jury as he wishes. But he is not contrasting oratory as a mere art of words with philosophy as the study of real events or facts. Both arts deploy language to win assent, but the orator uses more of the resources. Both the *ad hominem* persuasion of a philosopher and the verdict rendered by juries to the orator are real events (*res*); but even in philosophy the more or less persuasive language can make all the difference.

The reason for emphasizing facts rather than words as the object of the philosopher's quest becomes even more apparent when we consider Greek and Roman attitudes to moral philosophy. It was felt by Greek teachers and their Roman adherents that the philosopher should not merely define the good but also exemplify it in his own life. Disagreements about language should find a solution and have the consequence of making teacher and pupil better men.[13] Philosophers who did not do this were considered shocking. Hence the complaints of Gellius and others about the sham philosophers who grew a beard and wore the *pallium*, but did nothing except lounge about. Philosophers like Epicurus, who defined pleasure as the goal, were suspect because they were expected to act out what they had spoken and, furthermore, enact it along conventional lines of self-indulgence.[14] On the other hand, merely to *say* that virtue was the good was not enough, even though the statement would make an audience favourably disposed. Socrates, as we have seen, was admired because he was a good man, not just because he asked interesting philosophical questions. Thus Seneca says that Plato and others derived more benefit from Socrates' character than from his words, and he advises Lucilius not only to meditate on what he has heard but also to show by results that he has really understood. 'For the most shameful charge that can be laid against us is that we handle the vocabulary of philosophy but not its works.'[15]

There were, then, two reasons why the verbal element in philosophy received less than its due from the Romans.[16] For one thing they tended to value action higher than argument; the Roman examples in the pages of Cicero and Seneca are so many philosophers of real life, men who have exemplified the best without always having learned the theories of a philosopher. In the second place they insisted that the philosopher should not only discuss virtue but himself be virtuous. In this at least they were in agreement with Greek philosophers of the past and present alike. Yet the Roman emphasis, as in Seneca, is often over-critical of the argumentative or defining side of philosophy. The urge for moral improvement sometimes leads to impatience with syllogisms on the grounds that they are less morally effective than an exhortation.

The prejudice against words meant that even the philosophically

minded would give logic less than its due; there were other
Roman values which affected the start of philosophical literature
by Cicero and its continuation by Seneca. In general, Romans
valued fame and glory that came through success in oratory,
office-holding and war; such activities were thought to be the
proper business (*negotium*) of life. On the other hand they looked
down on leisure or inaction (*otium*), since it did not produce the
highest reward, and it was disallowed except as a respite between
labours. It was felt that inaction or retirement should be time
well spent, as in composing a history; it should not be used
for self-indulgence.

It follows that serious discussion or writing about philosophy,
though a commendable use of leisure, was considered second-
best to the life of political action. Cicero's philosophical works
were written quickly during a time when he was excluded from
politics, especially in 45 B.C. and the beginning of 44. He makes
the point that philosophical discussion is a proper activity for
Roman nobles when they are at leisure. But he draws a contrast
between his own leisure—enforced because 'the senate and the
courts were dead'—and the more voluntary leisure of a hero like
the first Scipio Africanus. 'My leisure has come about through
sheer lack of occupation, not from a positive wish to have a
respite from affairs.'[17] If Caesar's government had been different
it is doubtful whether Cicero would have composed his philosophical works at all.

However, though he felt compelled to lead a life of leisure,
Cicero sometimes suggests that this form of inaction can produce
rewards similar to those offered by the life of affairs. He says that
his account of philosophy will serve his country and win fame for
Latin literature; the author's glory, begotten in leisure, is therefore
a substitute for the active triumphs of the general and orator. It
is not surprising that Greeks, who have no public business in the
Roman sense, should be copious authors; but Cicero, in praising
the number and variety of his speeches, says that no orator 'even
in Greek *otium*' has equalled his achievement.[18] Though he
declares that philosophy is important (and there is no reason to
doubt that he means what he says), he is still a politician turned
philosopher who would prefer public life: but while he is at
leisure he attempts to win from retirement a reputation similar to
that acquired by successful orators and statesmen.

The same distinction is employed by Seneca, but he does not
treat *otium* as a kind of second-best substitute for public life; he
reverses the values completely. In his treatise (the *de otio*) he

makes the point that the man of action is concerned only with the affairs of his own state, whereas the man of leisure is conducting the affairs of the universal community to which all mankind belongs. Leisure, therefore, enables one to do a more important service than action, which is restricted to a corner of the world. In the letters to Lucilius he does say that philosophers are grateful to rulers because they provide the opportunities for leisure; but it is clear that leisure or inaction is valued more highly than the pursuit of a career. 'Those who seem to be doing nothing are in fact doing more important things; they are considering the affairs *both* of men and of gods.' It is only through abstention from public life that one has the chance to improve oneself morally (the effective use of philosophy), by avoiding the waste of time and flattery that are attendant upon ambition. At the same time the philosopher's inaction should not be paraded. 'I would not advise you to try to make a name for yourself from your leisure . . . it should be noticeable but not ostentatious.'[19] Just as men work for money and office, so too one must act boldly on behalf of leisure.[20]

Why do both writers, in presenting Greek philosophy in Latin, make such play with this contrast between action and leisure? The reason is largely political. Cicero felt excluded from his usual sphere of action—he returned with enthusiasm to politics after Caesar's murder—and Seneca, certainly when the letters were composed, had retired from politics and felt that Nero's government was not to be approved. But why the difference? Why did Seneca reverse the values and make the life of non-involvement in public affairs supreme? Perhaps the reason is that Cicero had not given up political hope, so that for him it was enough to stress that philosophy was a proper use of leisure. Seneca, on the other hand, does not give the impression of one who will return to office; he is waiting for death and uses his letters to show that the philosopher's business is an extended meditation on dying. And his particular form of Greek philosophy, Stoicism, far more than Cicero's Academic eclecticism, is directed towards self-improvement; it would seem to follow that for such a thinker the life of retirement must have a higher value, since it avoids distraction and drives man to concentrate on his moral state. Also the Stoic can always say that though he does not take part in local politics, however grandiose, he is doing the business of posterity and showing his allegiance to the larger political community, mankind as a whole.

Thus political circumstances affected the thinking of Cicero and

Seneca when they presented philosophy in Latin. They had also
to consider how or whether Greek ideas could be rendered in
Latin and which literary form should be used. There were
questions of language, involving a comparison of Greek and Latin
as media for philosophical thought, and questions of genre. It is
possible to outline different views about the language question[21]
from the Ciceronian age through Seneca to the second century
A.D. when Aulus Gellius provides some evidence.

Lucretius makes two main points in his references[22] to this
topic; he speaks of the poverty of Latin, as compared with Greek,
and says that it is difficult to give a clear account of the 'dark
discoveries of the Greeks' in Latin verse, since he has to use new
words because of the novelty of the subject. If we leave aside the
special problems of the poet, who has to accommodate words to
metre, Lucretius has succinctly defined the problem as the
Romans saw it. The relative poverty or wealth of Latin was an
obvious subject; 'name-finding' seemed important because the
language of Greek philosophy by this time had become rather a
jargon, at any rate remote from ordinary Greek.[23] These matters
were the more significant for Cicero as he felt that philosophy was
the last of the arts to be taken from 'Greece in decline'; Rome
had taken poetry and had also, he says, developed oratory almost
beyond perfection; philosophy was still to be provided for.

There was obviously some resistance to the very idea of turning
Greek philosophy into Latin. If there were Romans who had
'Greek doctrine' surely they would prefer to read Greek, and
those Romans who disliked Greek arts would not care for a Latin
version, because it could only be understood by the help of 'Greek
learning'. That case is attributed to Varro in the *Academica*,[24] and
he goes on to say that he sends his friends who are interested in
philosophy to the Greeks, 'so that they can drink from the
fountain-head'. Varro's own contribution to Latin erudition—he
is made to say—has been in an area which could not be obtained
from the Greeks, studies of early Rome. Cicero replies that Latin
philosophy will be useful to those who cannot read Greek and will
not be scorned by those who can. He cites the example of poetry,
maintaining that just as Latin poets, like Ennius, give pleasure
by their versions of Greek tragedy, so too philosophers will give
pleasure if writers 'imitate' Plato, Aristotle and others. Cicero's
enthusiasm for his cause makes him beg the question whether
philosophy should be compared with poetry, even if one accepts
that the task of poetry is to give pleasure. As he goes on to describe
philosophy as the medicine of the soul, perhaps we should not

make too much of his parallel with poetry, except to say that it expresses his determination that there is a place for Greek philosophy in Latin.

It is worth noticing that Cicero did not on the whole set out to be a translator; to do literal translations, as of the Platonic dialogues, would have been to deserve well of his fellow-citizens, as he says, and he produced a translation of the *Timaeus*. But in general he drew a distinction between translation (*interpretatio*) and imitation, in which the Greek original, one or more, is used more freely by the adapter.[25] The Latin writer can then use his own judgment and arrange the subject as he wishes. And this kind of work, when brilliantly expressed, not just a verbatim translation, would make it difficult for the critics of philosophy in Latin to prefer the Greek. So Cicero's aim is to produce works that have their own Latin aesthetic but are dependent on Greek substance; he appears to imply that because Greek philosophical authors sometimes cover the same ground, there is no need to read them all, and a Latin imitation, being selective, will therefore supply what is necessary. This reveals Cicero's attitude: he tends to think of philosophy as a collection of dogmas rather than a continuing debate, some of which is bound to appear repetitive if only because earlier views can only be refuted through quotation. One should also add that his literary reputation, which Cicero naturally wished to enhance, would be better served by an original-seeming imitation than by a translation, in which the Latin consular would appear in too humble a role.

Cicero would have agreed with Lucretius that the main language problem was to supply new words, though he would not have agreed that Latin was poor or inadequate for the task. He is fond of instances which, according to him, show that Latin has a richer vocabulary than Greek, or that Latin terms are more perspicuous. He says, for instance, that Latin has two words for pain (*labor* and *dolor*) where the Greeks, 'whose language is more copious than ours', have only one.[26] The obvious irony is underlined by his saying 'O Greece, you who at times lack words, which you think you always have in plenty, I tell you that *labor* is different from *dolor*'. The distinction is that between the pain involved in hard work and, say, the pain of a wound; in fact Greek has two words to render the distinction, though it could use one. Here, as in other places, Cicero's enthusiasm leads him to exaggerate the resources of Latin and to belittle Greek. The greater perspicuity of Latin is shown, in Cicero's view, by his comments on madness (*insania*). Because this term denotes *dementia*, which in turn means malfunction of the mind (*mens*), he asserts that in Latin these ideas are better delineated than they are in Greek; for, he continues, 'I cannot easily say from where the Greeks came to speak of *mania*.'[27] Similarly, the Roman term for a common meal (*convivium*) is preferred to the Greek *symposium*;[28] it is a moral preference since the Latin is held to refer to the fellowship of living together whereas the Greek word suggests that the main purpose of the gathering is drink. Thus Latin terms can be credited with greater clarity or a higher moral purpose, by an argument from etymology. Plato in the *Cratylus* makes fun of the attempt to construct philosophies out of etymology, but the device was still popular, as with the Stoics.

Cicero's attitude was probably affected by the rhetorical doctrine that one of the main virtues of language is correct diction. Yet finding the right word is only one of the translator's tasks. Cicero thinks that because some Latin words have the characteristics described above, Latin is as good as or superior to Greek. He neglects the fact that many of the Latin words required— especially the ordinary or 'public' words like *bonum*—had not been analyzed until they were chosen as equivalents to Greek words which had been so debated. He used some Greek words which were accepted into Latin, though without ever being as gracious as Quintilian,[29] who says that one has to use many Greek terms; Cicero coined new terms and adapted existing ones; in the long run he was influential, since some Greek originals were lost or no longer read.

Seneca's attitude to the language question is more difficult to decide. He makes a general distinction between the languages, characterizing Latin as powerful, Greek as having more grace and licence. The compliment to Greek is perhaps disingenuous since Latin is left with a quality which would be convincing in earnest exhortation, a main concern with Seneca. He also refers to Greek as distinguishing between different kinds of anger,[30] which 'with us do not have their own names'; so, he goes on, he will omit the different kinds, but he nonetheless gives a host of Latin adjectives that in effect do stand for differences. This is hardly a serious discussion; the rhetorician's device, praeterition, is used to make the reader forget the feigned modesty of admitting to the weakness of Latin. Rhetorical and aesthetic factors also affect what Seneca has to say about the word *essentia* (essence).[31] He says that in talking about Plato he found that many things needed names but did not have them, while other names had gone out of use because they were distasteful. The word essence seems to be an example; it had been used, he says, by Cicero and Fabianus, both eloquent men, but he is clearly afraid that it needs some apology before Lucilius will accept it. He says too that several Latin names have been used for the word *sophismata* (sophistry) but none is really successful.[32] But he does not use this alleged fact to show the inadequacy of Latin; the failure over a word is for him a symptom of the earlier Romans' resistance to sophistry as such. His theme, then, is the moral superiority of Romans to Greeks, but he also implies that present Romans have declined. Perhaps we can draw two conclusions here: one, that Ciceronian terminology did not always stick, second, that Seneca does not on the whole accept the Ciceronian contention that Latin is richer than Greek in words for things.

Aulus Gellius has many remarks on the two languages; his views are of particular interest because he was both proud of Latin literature and also a devotee of Greek, including philosophical Greek. One might expect him to be an out-and-out advocate of Latin, but this is not so. In one passage he reports a debate between Favorinus the philosopher and Fronto the rhetorician; Favorinus, the Gaul who preferred Greek, says that Latin is poorer in colour-words than Greek. Fronto replies (not impolitely) that Greek is indeed more comprehensive and richer, but Latin is not so poor as the other thinks. After this speech Favorinus says that without Fronto Greek would have won the race, but now the result is in doubt.[33] The conversation is urbane and friendly; there is a sense of competition about the merits of the languages, but neither speaker is as aggressive as Cicero. Perhaps the passage shows that the usual position was to ascribe poverty to Latin, the claims of which had still to be asserted.

Though Gellius praises Latin, he often says that Greek is superior to a translation because it has more charm. Thus he translates some Greek sophistic arguments but observes that in Latin they are 'almost without charm'; his apology seems to be serious. When Taurus teased him about a passage in the *Symposium*, saying that it was rhetorically perfect but still more valuable as a means to Platonic truth, Gellius was tempted to translate it, but he does not set out to rival Plato, only to give the outline of the passage. In one case he describes how he tried to explain to a Latin ignorant of Greek the title of Plutarch's treatise on inquisitiveness; he found that he could not give a single-word rendering and that compound literal translations and paraphrases were also unacceptable. His attempted explanation was a failure since the Latin speaker supposed that Plutarch was commending a virtue; so Gellius finally remarked that the cause of the man's mistake was his own lack of eloquence—he had not been able to say in Latin what in Greek is stated perfectly clearly in a single word.[34]

This evidence suggests that Roman writers tended to concentrate on the problem of finding suitable Latin words to render Greek terms, many of which had never been part of ordinary language but were technical inventions. Cicero's confidence in Latin as a richer medium than Greek was not borne out by history. Seneca, for example, admired the Augustan figure Q. Sextius as one who philosophized in Greek but had a (truly) Roman character.[35] Both Latin and Greek were used in philosophical ·converse by Romans, but one suspects that Greek persisted as the familiar medium for writing. Secondly, all these writers were highly conscious of the aesthetics of the translation problem; Cicero's view that philosophy should please, Seneca's anxiety about the word essence (*essentia*), Gellius' remarks on the charm of Greek, all betray a concern that philosophical Latin should be agreeable to read. No one would wish to argue that philosophers should not write well in this sense. But the Latin writers give this objective too high a place.

Just as aesthetic considerations affected the way Romans translated, so too they determined the choice of form. One reason for disliking Epicurus was his advice to flee every form of culture; a reason for admiring Plato was that he could be regarded as the most eloquent of the philosophers. A work of philosophy in Latin, though ultimately concerned with realities (*res*), attracted Cicero because it gave him scope for his eloquence and 'supply of words'; Seneca for his part tends to look down on concern with style, but his scorn is belied by his studied manner.[36]

The dialogue form chosen by Cicero gave him some difficulties. He praises the Socratic manner of those Platonic dialogues in which the debate proceeds by question and answer, and thinks it a pity that contemporary philosophers lecture while the auditor, having posed a question, says no more. He says in the *de finibus* that he will not hold a school, like a philosopher, but use question and answer; his opponent, however, is soon made to tire of this and expresses a preference for long speeches.[37] Cicero agrees to this, saying that he will use the rhetoric of the philosophers, not of the courts. In general, Ciceronian dialogues take the form of fairly long speeches which are sometimes answered by others. The method, whatever Cicero said, certainly suited the barrister in him. Also, he could rightly claim that some of his works were in the Aristotelian manner, in which longer speeches were used and sometimes the author appeared in person.[38] But Cicero's marvellous Latin does not succeed in making the dialogues seem natural or easy. This is partly because his Roman characters often disclaim any experience of philosophical speaking, which then makes it hard to accept the following copious discourse as in character. It is also true (even allowing for the different method) that Socrates, as man and philosopher, gives to Platonic dialogues a vitality which Cicero's Romans never display. He was a philosopher all day and every day, not a part-time thinker and reader making literature out of an enforced retirement. Cicero had picked out some of the more external problems of the dialogue form, like vouching for the narrator's credibility and omitting the 'he saids',[39] but he did not get near the essentials.

The dialogues of Seneca are not of the Ciceronian type. They can only be called dialogues because the writer at times imagines objections, from the addressee or others, which he proceeds to answer. Much the same technique is at times employed in the letters to Lucilius. The result is an interrupted meditation, which deploys philosophy, poetry and historical examples with a view to directing the reader by means of moral instruction. At times heroic behaviour is illustrated by examples taken from the lower orders of society, as if to rouse the respectable by showing what the ignoble can achieve.[40] The ancestor of the form is probably the diatribe,[41] but in this Roman form the plea for the simple life is relaxed by the amble of Seneca's prose.

Philosophy at this time largely took the form of lectures, comments on texts and (less seriously) dinner-party conversations, for which the authoritative model was Plato's *Symposium*. It would not have been easy to use any of these contemporary forms as the basis for a philosophical work of literary and artistic merit. There are reasons why we might have preferred straight accounts of lectures, but the Romans aimed at a literary annexation of Greek, not just a record. Perhaps Aulus Gellius is a more reliable guide than Cicero or Seneca to the kind of subject which attracted the Romans. We have already noticed his distaste for questions in philosophy that admit of several, uncertain answers; on the other hand he shows a positive liking for the discussion of moral problems which seem to him to be relevant to Roman life. In one passage the philosopher Taurus discusses, in the presence of a Roman official and his father, which of the two should be seated. There might appear to be a conflict between the respect due to a father and the honour which should be paid to the office-holder.

Taurus' view of the matter is presented briefly, and Gellius concludes his account by reporting an incident from Roman history which shows how a Roman father had in fact acknowledged the precedence of his son, a consul, on a public occasion. The philosopher's theory is therefore confirmed by Roman practice. Other topics discussed concern the duty of a judge, the task of a commander when a subordinate acts for the best against orders, the control of anger and the endurance of pain;[42] all these can be treated theoretically, they seem relevant to problems of public or private life and they allow Roman history to be introduced. It is credible that Romans consulted philosophers on such matters, both in Cicero's time and in the second century A.D.

But if it is more difficult to accept Cicero's dialogues as an imaginative account of how Romans philosophized at the time, there are signs that some philosophical questions were both contemporary and potentially subversive.[43] Plutarch refers to a conversation in which Favonius the Stoic and Statyllius the Epicurean gave their opinions on the evils of monarchy and civil war. The topic was introduced by Brutus to see if the philosophers would make reliable conspirators against Caesar, but their answers discouraged him. This was the kind of philosophical debate which governments feared, at any rate at times in the first century A.D.; yet the matters discussed in Gellius suggest that philosophy was often in the position of a servant rather than a revolutionary. It is tempting to suppose that the Roman Stoics who opposed the emperors in the first century A.D. were enacting in politics the convictions of their philosophy, and that later on, when Marcus Aurelius was emperor, *his* Stoicism was expressed in the legislation of his reign.[44] But this sort of direct political connection between philosophy and behaviour is often obscure or debatable. Stoicism was not ideologically committed to the active pursuit of any one form of government but it did offer the individual the means of enduring both good and bad fortune, especially adversity. Perhaps it was typically Roman to use philosophy either for private consolation (as with Cicero's grief for his daughter) or for guidance on restricted problems from the public sphere (as with the above instances from Gellius). The first-century Stoics and Marcus are alike in the sense that they exploited philosophy in order to alleviate the world rather than change it.

THE 'HISTORY' OF GREEK PHILOSOPHY

Although philosophy was important in higher education, there was little by way of disinterested history of the subject. Some Greek doxography attempted to be objective, but an account of the opinions of one's predecessors would often be conducted in the light of one's own presuppositions or theories. Aristotle's version of the pre-Socratics is of this type; he records their views to show that nearly all of them had in fact made use of one or more of the four causes, his own doctrine. When Lucretius criticizes some of the pre-Socratics, his argument is based on assumptions that are only valid for a convinced Epicurean; he does not try to see each thinker in his particular context of thought. Perhaps it is to be expected that practising philosophers should value their predecessors only or mainly for their failure to anticipate or agree with their own views. We might then expect that Romans like Cicero and Seneca, who were not original thinkers, would have been less partial in their reflections on the history of Greek philosophy. But here too we find that Roman accounts of Greek thought are highly selective, designed to meet the needs of Roman observers. In these sketches one or two individuals are named and a few lines of development are indicated.

The main outlines of a history of philosophy are to be found in Cicero, whose range of interest obliged him at least to consider the relationships of the different schools. We may profitably distinguish between two Ciceronian versions of this subject. In one, Cicero discusses the parts played by Pythagoras, Socrates and the later schools, whereas in the other, Socrates is again important, but mainly because of Cicero's special emphasis on his alleged place in the struggle between rhetoric and philosophy. The former shows the Roman emphasis on practical ethics and will enable us to see how the Romans sought to make up for their dearth of thinkers; while in the latter the Roman sense that rhetoric should be restored to her rightful position is not just Ciceronian, but is echoed later by Quintilian. These different views are expounded in the *Tusculan Disputations* and the *de oratore*.

Cicero introduces his discussion of whether virtue alone is sufficient for happiness by an encomium of philosophy, calling it 'the leader of life, seeking after virtue and driving out vices'. It is a general praise associated with his personal feelings of gratitude to philosophy for educating him when young and for providing a refuge in the storms of life. Philosophy, he says, needs this defence because ignorant men do not realize that philosophers were those who discovered the rules of social and political life. The subject is itself of great antiquity though the name is relatively recent. Wisdom (*sapientia*) and related words were the terms first applied to this idea, both by Greeks and Romans—'the famous seven, whom the Greeks called *sophoi*, were by our people believed to be *sapientes* and were given that name'. The term philosopher did not become current until Pythagoras used it to explain what his art was; 'he knew no art but was a philosopher'. As well as inventing the new word, Pythagoras developed the subject, and on visiting Italy improved the political quality of life in Magna Graecia. Somewhat later Socrates deflected the course of philosophy; 'he called it down from the heavens, placed it in cities . . . and compelled it to put questions about how to live, and about good and evil'. Socrates' style of discussion was commemorated by Plato and 'brought about many groups of philosophers all in disagreement with one another'.[45] And Cicero ends by describing himself as making use of the Socratic method (a claim which I discuss later).

Only two names—Pythagoras and Socrates—are important in this historical sketch and only the former is (elsewhere) linked with Roman history. To take Pythagoras first: his describing himself as a philosopher (or lover of wisdom) was, in a Greek version, an admission of human weakness as well as an account of his aims, since 'only god is wise'.[46] Cicero omits this part of the story, possibly because he does not wish to emphasize the point that wisdom is difficult to attain, but does wish to criticize those who might argue that the idea is new because the word philosophy is recent. In asserting that the seven sages, Ulysses and Nestor were all wise men, he is able to make the history of philosophy reach back to earlier times; it becomes almost co-extensive with the history of man because of the evidence offered by the Greek heroes. It is true that no Roman parallels are mentioned, but it is implied that the history of the words is similar in both languages; that is, 'wise' preceded 'wise-loving' in both Latin and Greek.

In another passage Cicero writes at greater length about the alleged influence of Pythagoras on Magna Graecia and thence on Rome. The theme here is the *practical* virtue of the early Romans, clearly shown in their political and religious organization. It is not remarkable that theoretically based learning (*doctrina*) was welcomed and cherished; there was the nearby example of Pythagoras, now described as a man of wisdom, whose influence spread far and wide and would therefore have no difficulty in finding its way from Great Greece to Rome. Cicero's view that

Pythagoras influenced Rome is based both on likelihood and on so-called evidence. In the first place he thinks it improbable that the earlier Romans would have closed their ears to the fame and reputation of Pythagoras and his followers. Secondly he believes there was evidence of similar customs; Pythagoreans used songs in order to convey certain doctrines more secretly and to create a sense of moral tranquillity, and Cato had asserted that it was the custom of the early Romans to celebrate the glories of great men in song.[47] The exact nature of this similarity is not clear, nor is it easy to accept Cicero's claims that 'many of our customs are derived from the Pythagoreans'; this evidence is withheld 'lest it seem that we have learned from others things which we are thought to have discovered ourselves'. Quite suddenly, the assertion of a Roman debt to Pythagoras is seen to be incompatible with claims of Roman originality.

In short 'Pythagoras the philosopher' suggested to Cicero two lines of argument which might make Greek philosophy more familiar or less forbidding to Romans. The verbal argument indicates that wise men (*sapientes*),[48] because they preceded lovers of wisdom, are a surer indication of a society's regard for philosophy than technical teachers of the subject. Romans need not be embarrassed by their lack of philosophers with pupils and schools since they can point to a host of real-life sages, drawn from the pages of Roman history. In the second place, Roman respect for the subject was (we are told) attested at an early date, when Pythagoras visited Magna Graecia.

Although these ideas in effect simplify earlier Greek philosophy so that it can more readily be absorbed by a proud Roman, Cicero's comments on the other great philosopher, Socrates, seem at first to recognize that Greece and Rome are, in philosophy, a world apart. Socrates, we are told, 'called philosophy down from the heavens', and later there arose 'many groups of philosophers in debate with one another'. This is clearly an explicit, though terse, acknowledgment of the post-Aristotelian schools, especially the Academics, Peripatetics, Epicureans and Stoics. The way in which Cicero affiliates them to Socrates makes rough and ready historical sense. Yet he is talking of a Greek tradition with named philosophers (however obscure some are to us), to which there is no Roman equivalent at all. Can we then say that Cicero, in admitting the complexities of later Greek philosophy, is now at last fairer to the claims of truth while at the same time making it more difficult for Romans to feel that they can compete in philosophy with Greeks?

An answer to this will in part depend on what Cicero says elsewhere about the disagreements of the post-Aristotelian schools and their relationship to Socrates. In several places he distinguishes between the different phases of the Academy, and works like the *de finibus* and the *de natura deorum* are carefully arranged to take account of the different opinions of the Stoics and Epicureans. Yet in some ways Cicero does not register the full philosophical importance of the differences between the schools. Aside from his treatment of Epicureanism, the arch-deviant philosophy because it does not acclaim virtue as the goal, he sometimes tends to emphasize points in which the other philosophies agree. Thus, in speaking of his own method of discussing both sides of a question, he calls this 'the custom of the Peripatetics and the Academy'; he writes too in praise of that 'true and elegant philosophy which was derived from Socrates and is still found among the Peripatetics'.[49] So, as far as method is concerned, these two schools are here assimilated; and, rather similarly, there are also passages in which the originality of Stoicism is minimized. There is an instance of this kind when Cicero replies to Cato's defence of Stoic theory. He speaks ironically of Stoicism as a 'revision and a correction of the old philosophy'.[50] He means that Stoics have given different names to concepts they have in common with other people; they have not really changed the face of ethical philosophy by denying the name of good or bad to ideas which would be so called by other philosophers and by commonsense. Where others speak of 'good', Stoics use the term 'preferred', and according to Cicero this is to change the nomenclature without making a change in the idea referred to. As a criticism this is not fair; by denying that there is any good but virtue Stoics had effectively challenged any theory which claims that virtue is good and also admits other, though lesser, goods such as beauty and wealth. Thus Cicero describes Stoicism as a mere verbal revision; it is not an *improvement* at all. He points out that Stoicism is unrealistic; it would be absurd if a politician were to argue like a Stoic and deny that it is evil to be taken prisoner at the very moment when the enemy is about to capture the city.

Thus, although Cicero does rather more justice to post-Socratic philosophy, there are still signs that he obscured the differences between the schools. His version is fairly simple; after Pythagoras it was Socrates who made the great change, confining the main quest of philosophy to ethics, and it was also Socrates to whom the later schools looked back; but even though the whole process was made more comprehensible, it was still the case that Romans could not match Latin philosophers against the Greek. One has to except Cicero's ambition to be the Plato of Latin letters,[51] since we must of course search for pre-Ciceronian figures. Cicero, and others after him, met this difficulty by invoking those whom they could regard as Roman sages (*sapientes*) as well as that undifferentiated group, the ancestors (*maiores*). Since they could not appeal to Roman philosophers, they deployed instead a host of illustrious Romans. These had already been used to defeat the claims of Greeks on the field of history and were now required to show the superiority of Rome in the conduct of real life. Whether the Romans had any thoughts, however vague, of justifying this manoeuvre is a question that can be raised when we have examined some instances.

The superiority of the earlier Romans is acclaimed at the start of the *Tusculans*, where Cicero states that 'our ancestors' devised better laws and customs than did the Greeks. In any accomplishment that depends on 'nature, not literature' the Romans are supreme; indeed Cicero declares that where Romans have been originators they are wiser than the Greeks, and when they borrow they improve what they have taken. This appeal to the ancestors is particularly marked when the subject is religion; thus Cotta introduces his refutation of Balbus' defence of Stoicism by reminding him that he is both 'a Cotta and a pontiff'. His authorities in religion are not Greek philosophers like Zeno, but the great pontiffs of Roman tradition. He will believe these ancestors even without grounds for his belief. Other passages make less extreme claims for a general Roman superiority, but they still proclaim that in religion ancestral authority is comparable with philosophical argument.[52] Balbus is made to say that if we make comparisons between Rome and others, we shall find that except here Rome is either equal or inferior—but this is only a modest way of bringing in the claim that Rome is far and away the best in religion.

It was natural for a Roman, even when writing in Latin, to make use of Greek historical examples which he would find quoted in his Greek philosophical sources. Even so, it is hardly a surprise when Quintus Cicero is made to say: 'But why should I give Greek examples? In a way our own examples give me more pleasure.' But this preference for Roman forebears is not merely aesthetic. To some extent Greek history is felt to be suspect and unreliable compared with the solid proofs offered by Roman history. This doubt becomes even more acute when the shadowy creatures of

Greek myth are discussed. Thus Balbus the Stoic admits that the stories of Mopsus, Teiresias and others may be 'over-free, mythical fictions', but he then claims that 'our own internal history' will prove that there is a divine power. On the other hand, the Epicureans, who could hardly quote the great Greek heroes like Lycurgus as a witness to their ethical theory, would be obliged to omit a still more numerous army of Romans. The Epicurean Torquatus is challenged to say what his great ancestor would have thought of his doctrine that pleasure is the good; would the ancestor have behaved as he did, holding the beliefs of the descendant? There is a slight qualification to this prejudice in favour of Roman examples. When Cicero is discussing unjust rule he first mentions Greek examples, adding the remark: 'in a matter like this I remember foreign incidents rather than our own'. In general he prefers Roman examples because they are native, good and reliable; he can look to foreigners (including Greeks) to supply him with illustrations of wrong conduct.[53]

Seneca too shows his admiration for Roman ancestors. He contrasts the extensive baths of the present with the dark and constricted room used by the great Scipio Africanus. In part therefore he is pitting the Roman past against present decadence; but it is a past which has deteriorated mainly because foreign materials like Alexandrian marble and Thasian stone have been imported to defile the original Roman austerity. When he deplores the fact that cruelty has come to Rome along with other foreign vices, he is in effect idealizing an earlier period, when Roman ancestors behaved impeccably. Yet his list is not entirely confined to the orthodox figures of the early Roman canon; some Greek philosophers, he says to Lucilius, 'are your ancestors, if you show you are good enough for them'; and a Cynic relish for low-life heroism leads him to extol the gladiator who escaped his lot by committing suicide in the lavatory.[54]

In some of Gellius' stories, the object-lessons derived from great Romans of the past are equal or superior to the instruction of Greek philosophy. In discussing punishment Gellius points out that the idea of punishment as exemplary is attested not only in Greek political theory but also among 'our ancients'. The communal association of the Pythagoreans is compared with an old Roman partnership based on not dividing an inheritance. It is the same with speeches as with the actions of great Romans. The antiquarianism which made Gellius admire the elder Cato led him to comment on changes in the meaning of words and to look for permanent moral lessons. Thus he approves of Cato's remark that it is not a vice to *be* without many things, whereas the inability to *do* without is vicious. This 'undiluted realism' on the part of the man from Tusculum does more to encourage abstemiousness than the 'Greek ingenuities of those who say they are philosophers and invent empty verbal games'. One should add the reminder that Gellius' enemy here is not the Greek philosopher as such, but the specious imitation, who wears the right clothes without having the heart of the matter in him.[55]

A curious version of the esteem in which 'ancestors' were held is found in some references to the decemviral laws of 454–451 B.C. Writers of our period often recognized that the *Twelve Tables* were expressed in archaic language and contained provisions that had lapsed or been changed. There was also a tradition which maintained that some Roman officials were sent to Athens to write down the famous laws of Solon and to investigate the laws of other Greek states. But though the *Twelve Tables* were thought to be obsolete or to imply dependence on the Greeks, some Romans felt that they embodied a wisdom that was distinctively Roman. Cicero praises 'our ancestors' because, many years before Socrates, 'from whom all this ethical philosophy is derived', they discovered or maintained that all disturbance of the mind is madness; he draws on the *Twelve Tables* to show that they anticipated the Socratic-Stoic view 'that all who are not wise are mad' and to praise the Latin language for discriminating between degrees of madness. Gellius compares the *Tables* favourably with the harsh and cruel laws of Draco.[56] Speakers both in Cicero and in Gellius express the view that the *Tables* are worth all the books of philosophers or are as valuable as Plato's *Laws*.[57] These early Roman laws were therefore endowed with a philosophic content which could help Romans to feel less inadequate before the mass of Greek political and moral theory.

In this Ciceronian sketch of philosophy the important figures were Pythagoras and Socrates; the former, in his own terms, was a lover of wisdom (*sapientia*) while the latter was declared by Apollo to be the wisest of the Greeks. If the Romans felt that they could match the learning of Greek philosophers by pointing with pride to the collective wisdom of their *maiores*, they would perhaps tilt the balance by claiming that some individual Romans deserved the name wise. In the *de amicitia*,[58] Laelius commends the elder Cato for having this quality, because of the way in which he bore his son's death; and he adds the warning that one should not give a higher place 'even to that man whom Apollo, as you say, adjudged the wisest'. Both men are praiseworthy, Socrates for his words, Cato for his actions—and, clearly, these latter are felt to be the more important. Laelius himself was nicknamed *Sapiens*—it is doubtful whether he acquired the title, as Plutarch alleges, because of his prudence in withdrawing a controversial law—and, appropriately, is made to speak on the subject of Greek and Roman wisdom. He criticizes the Stoic view that only the wise man is good, for this is to speak of a wisdom that no mortal has yet attained. He admits that great Romans like M' Curius, C. Fabricius and Ti. Coruncanius—'whom our ancestors adjudged wise'—were not wise according to the Stoic norm, but this does not mean that the Stoics were right. It is implied that the Roman description of these men is right for the practical purposes of life. There is irony at the expense of the Stoics and satisfaction that Romans have lived rightly whereas Socrates was a teacher, rarely involved in politics.

Yet however much these pre-Ciceronians were declared wise, many of them could only thank nature, not the learning of the Greeks. As Crassus says, the elder Cato, for all his many Roman interests, did not have this 'polished foreign learning from across the seas'.[59] The Romans did not acquire their own Socratic sage[60] until the younger Cato committed suicide at Utica. Here was a Roman who had lived creditably, was known to have studied philosophy and chose to die by his own hand. It might seem that the suicide of Cato is not comparable with the execution of Socrates, but since both rejected courses of action which would have meant life with dishonour, both could be portrayed as men who accepted their fate and did not run away. The argument that we may depart this life when god provides just cause seemed to fit both the Greek and the Roman. Cicero's comparison of the two men was the more plausible because Cato had read Plato's *Phaedo* on the night he committed suicide. Seneca mentions that Cato's death was a stock subject but makes no apology for referring to it and for coupling Cato's sword with the hemlock that 'made Socrates great'.[61] It is of course apparent that even when the Romans had acquired their own philosophical sage, they were in effect comparing the two men for their manner of living, not for their philosophies. In short it was Cato the man who was regarded as a match for Socrates the man, though it is likely that Cato's avowed Stoicism helped to suggest and keep alive the comparison with the good Greek who was also a philosopher.

The Romans, then, created their own national academy of real-life sages. They were needed to make up for the lack of

Roman philosophers; and the absence of a key-date, like the Socratic revolution described by Cicero, does not seem to have mattered, since it was felt that the Roman past was in general a match for Greece. This same Roman past was also extolled as a challenge to the moral feebleness of contemporary Rome; both in Cicero and Seneca the Romans of the past are put forward as the models to which the pygmies of the present should try to conform. But this is merely to describe the purposes for which these Roman sages were enrolled; can we not ask how Cicero and others might have justified what they did? Perhaps they would have said that ethics is not only theory but must be judged by action; the aim of the moral philosopher is not merely to preach the truth, but to be good. Then, if one can point to Romans who are agreed to have been good men, Roman history will provide actual examples of the virtue which the Greeks had taught—with the advantage for Rome that these heroes were virtuous in politics as well as in private life. Secondly, the defenders of Roman virtue might well have said that precepts are inferior to examples, since a familiar name gives substance and colour to a general moral exhortation.[62] Lastly, one finds not merely that the Romans take pride in their history, but that they incline to the view that it is more reliable than Greek history; the alleged mendacity of some Greek historians rubs off on their subjects; thus it becomes possible to introduce Roman examples as a more accurate complement to the examples from Greek history which Romans found quoted in the lectures and works of Greek philosophers, or even to substitute them altogether.

The Romans admired Socrates partly because they recognized his philosophical originality, but perhaps even more because he lived and died creditably. This interest in the man is clearly shown by Seneca, who sometimes gives Socrates as the only Greek example together with three or four Romans, such as Mucius, Regulus, Rutilius and Cato. In his last philosophical works Cicero sometimes discusses the thinker (particularly on questions of method), at other times it is Socrates the man he has in view; but in an earlier work, the *de oratore*,[63] he is almost exclusively concerned with Socratic thought, and creates a different picture of the development of Greek philosophy.

Cicero's spokesman in this book, with its dramatic setting in 91 B.C., is the great Crassus, who theorizes on his experience for the benefit of his aspiring audience. Part of his function is to argue that the ideal orator needs an acquaintance with many arts and to deny that he can be produced by the art of rhetoric narrowly conceived. Though he opposes Roman experience to Greek theory he admits that in this kind of discussion one cannot do without the Greeks; it is therefore not unexpected when he ranges broadly across the history of Greek thought. He recognizes an early stage when 'thought and public speaking' (i.e. philosophy and rhetoric) were united, and this faculty was called wisdom (*sapientia*) by the Greeks of old. He gives Lycurgus and Solon as examples and compares certain earlier Romans 'who were not perhaps as learned but had a similar drive and purpose'. Teachers, like politicians, were then masters of more than one skill; they did not teach successful speaking alone, but also right action. This happy period lasted till the fifth century; even then there were men like Pericles who showed in their own person this twofold wisdom of action and discourse; and there were still men like Gorgias who taught this wisdom, though they themselves abstained from public life. But now there came people who had learning in abundance but rejected public affairs utterly, and these proceeded to abuse and despise oratory. Chief of these was Socrates (he is here praised both for his wisdom and for his eloquence), who separated wisdom from the knowledge of successful speaking and withdrew the common name, philosophy, from the unified art. 'Hence this divorce between tongue and mind . . . with the consequence that we now have different teachers of rhetoric and philosophy.'

In a later passage Crassus returns to the subject, when his theme is that all good arts and virtues are members of one family and should not be treated in isolation. According to this version, the phase of unity lasted till the end of the fourth century; there are various Greek instances which are intended to show that, throughout this period, politicians (who must perforce be good speakers) acquired their learning from philosophers. Public oratory therefore was not yet divorced from the content supplied by philosophers. The final example is Aristotle, who is said to have introduced rhetoric into his courses in order to vie with Isocrates, and was appointed tutor to Alexander to teach him both how to act and how to speak.

The most important feature of Crassus' discourse is his attack on specialization. Cicero wanted his ideal orator to be acquainted with all arts; neither mere experience (however valuable) nor technical rhetoric will suffice. At the same time he knew well that he was living in an age when subjects were in the hands of specialists, who often maligned one another. How tempting, therefore, to create a historical golden age when the great rivals, philosophy and oratory, were not at war! This would suggest that there was a good precedent for his recommendation that the orator needs to study philosophy. As often when the Greeks *are* praised, it is because they exhibit qualities which are also found in Romans; Crassus makes the point that earlier Romans, like Sextus Aelius and Cato, were also men of many parts, not mere specialists. So the desired state of affairs had occurred in the earlier stages of both Greece and Rome.

Though Cicero's motive is understandable, this account of Socrates comes as a surprise.[64] The Greek who elsewhere is praised for his emphasis on ethics is here replaced by one who put asunder subjects which are meant by nature to cohere. It is noticeable too that the sophists are praiseworthy[65] compared with Socrates; Crassus says that they taught practical wisdom, and, later on, Catulus speaks highly of their versatility, where, again, Cicero is making a plea against specialization. It is possible that Cicero cast Socrates in this role because of his attack on rhetoric in the *Gorgias*; he may also have taken a hint from Socrates' life, since he was famous for not taking part in politics (which would necessitate oratory) except when compelled. Yet Cicero is not so much interested in the intellectual villainy of Socrates as in providing reasons (historical of a sort) for thinking that present-day specialization is wrong and that one must return to a unity cherished in the past.

Compared with the sketch of Greek philosophy in the *Tusculans*, the account in *de oratore* is less informative about Roman attitudes. Yet it is instructive for more than one reason. In the first place it was accepted by Quintilian, who, like Cicero, did not wish the orator to be restricted to narrow rhetorical theory. He agrees with Cicero that the orator must now acquire the moral content of his speeches from philosophy, because 'it seems to me that philosophy [more than rhetoric] is now in control of those subjects. That is why Cicero says, in several books and letters, that the faculty of discourse proceeds from the very springs of wisdom, and for that reason there was a time when the same people taught ethics and oratory.'[66] Quintilian has retained the essential idea—that there was a time of unity—though he does not mention Socrates. However, he does not want his ideal orator to be a philosopher, remote from public life, but a Roman sage, a true citizen educated by experience. It is because of the divorce, as Cicero put it, that orators now have to apply to philosophers for subjects that are missing from the curriculum of rhetoricians.

Secondly, the Ciceronian idea that rhetoric and philosophy

rightly belong together affected his manner of writing philosophy.
If the orator gains from the philosopher, when his discourse is on
moral themes, so too the philosopher can be assisted by rhetoric.
There is an interesting example of this at the end of the first
Tusculan,[67] where the topic discussed is that death is not an evil.
After the philosophical proofs Cicero asks the interlocutor: 'Do
we still need a rhetorical epilogue? Can it be that we are now
leaving that art behind us?' 'No' is the reply—'What is that
epilogue you mention? I long to hear it, whatever it is.' Cicero
then gives a number of examples from Greek history which help
to give evidence that the theory is true. And he ends by saying
that the Greeks quote numerous examples of their own, but 'they
do not know our instances, though it would be a lengthy task to
enumerate them; there are so many [Romans] in whose eyes
death with honour was a thing to be desired'. The philosophical
discussion is here completed by a persuasive collection of instances, with the Greeks given in detail and the Romans presented
as the larger, unparticularized mass.

It is true that on some occasions Cicero refers to a different
principle, which should be upheld in philosophical argument,
namely that reason outweighs witnesses.[68] But in this case the
witnesses add authority to the proofs offered by reason; his use of
witnesses at the end of the first *Tusculan* is a good illustration of
the ideas expressed in the *de oratore*, that oratory and philosophy
should not be separated. The philosopher cannot do without
eloquence, the orator uses the moral ideas expressed by the
philosopher. Rhetoric has here taken on the role which in a
Platonic dialogue is often filled by the culminating myth. Thus
oratory, in Cicero's view, would bring philosophy closer to
experience and real life, whereas myth, being for him essentially a
fabrication, would only add to the remoteness of philosophy.

In both these schemes Cicero, however strangely, recognizes
the importance of Socrates and distinguishes the post-Socratic
schools, though he tends at times to merge their differences. But
he often slides the discussion from philosophy as an activity to
that wisdom (*sapientia*) which is the goal of ethical philosophers.
Thereby he was able to produce a number of Roman sages who
had been virtuous and wise in real life even when they had not
had the benefit of formal instruction. This form of reference to
the Romans of the past is also apparent in Seneca and Aulus
Gellius, though the actual content of Roman wisdom varies. Thus
Cicero tends to have in mind the qualities of the public man who
can take a creative part in politics, whereas the Senecan sage is

more often a political victim who can for that very reason exhibit moral grandeur in adversity.

ROMAN METHODS AND THE CRITICISM OF GREEK PHILOSOPHERS

I have suggested above that some Romans, when philosophizing in Latin, looked for a counterpoise to the many famous names of Greek philosophy, distributed among the several schools. They discovered grounds for believing that their past was not wholly unphilosophical—perhaps one should say not without benefit of wisdom—when they remembered the virtues of their ancestors and the prudence of individuals like Laelius. The examples provided a sense of equivalence or even superiority to Greeks, and helped to make this difficult subject seem less remote. Yet even though the Romans were proud of their own sages, they relied on Greek writers and teachers for most of their content and method. And in order to sustain the idea that he had some independence as a philosopher, it was natural for a Roman to criticize the Greeks, even when he was making use of their works. He would then appear to be striking out on his own and escaping, however briefly, from too close a reliance on his authorities. If he were well-disposed towards his source, he could express his gratitude but still attempt some improvements; if the Greek original was from an alien school, his criticism would be more severe. In general the Epicureans were treated most harshly, but the Stoics did not escape modifying censure, even from their fellow-Stoic Seneca. Disagreement with the spirit or the letter of a text is an obvious way of asserting one's own claims as a thinker. But the belief or pretence of originality can also be pursued by proclaiming that one is faithful to an old tradition which has come to be neglected. Cicero's avowed following of Socratic method is an instance of this fidelity to the past, which is in part used by the writer as a form of self-assertion. Before considering the Roman criticisms of Epicurus and the Stoics I shall examine Cicero's Socraticism to see how far it conforms to the practice of the master.

The *de natura deorum*[69] opens with a short explanation of Cicero's position as an Academic, a summary of his longer treatment in the *Academica*. 'I am not acting as the defender of something which others have forsaken. It is not the case that ideas die with their authors, but they do perhaps need a sponsor to illuminate them.

This is true of that philosophical method which began with Socrates, was restored by Arcesilaus and, when reaffirmed by Carneades, has flourished up to our own time. I know that nowadays it is almost without an heir in Greece itself. And I think this has happened not through any fault on the part of the Academy but because of human dullness. If it is difficult to know *one* subject, it is much harder to be acquainted with all; which is essential for those whose aim is—for the sake of discovering the truth—to speak against all philosophers and also in defence of all.' He goes on to say that this form of two-sided scepticism does not mean that there are no rules to guide one's actions. It is not the case that there are no truths, but that all truth has an admixture of falsehood and uncertainty. The basis for human action is therefore not truth or certainty but what is probable, which can be sufficient to guide the life of the wise man.

It is instructive to see how the method is actually applied in this dialogue. The *de natura* is a discussion between an Epicurean (Velleius), a Stoic (Balbus), and the Academic Cotta. Cicero himself is present as a listener, while Cotta's function is to deny, first, the positive views of Velleius and, later, the Stoic certainties about the gods. He makes the point that he could not offer views of his own but finds the Epicurean theory improbable, even though he contrasts the clear and weighty exposition of Velleius with the unpolished language of Epicurus. In this way he keeps up the role of one who refutes without offering another set of certainties or even probable beliefs. Yet Cotta is a Romanized sceptic in more ways than one. In the first place he is admired because he is not only an Academic but also an orator and binds the two disciplines into one cogent 'rhetorical philosophy'. Secondly Cotta is portrayed as a solid Roman, with loyalties to the state religion (he is a pontiff) that may override his loyalty to the sceptical argument against Stoicism. At the end of the work he says expressly that he wishes to be refuted by Balbus and adds that he knows for certain that he can easily be defeated in argument. This would be surprising if he were a sceptic committed equally against both the schools. It is more accurate to think of Cicero (through Cotta) as asserting that Epicureanism is false whereas the Stoic theory of providence, while not certain, is less improbable and, at any rate, more welcome to a Roman official. The last sentence of the work is a delicate reminder of Cicero's professed Academicism —he says that Balbus' speech seemed to him to be closer to a resemblance to the truth—and shows that this kind of doubt is in the end partial and eclectic. Though neither theory is certain (for such matters are obscure), the Stoic is likely to be more acceptable to Cotta and Cicero for reasons of state rather than argument. Cicero affirms this view of his Cotta in another work, where he says that 'Cotta argues in such a way as to refute the proofs of the Stoics; he does not set out to destroy religion'.[70]

This passage is typical. Cicero uses a form of doubt, it is true. But his spokesmen are orators as much as they are critics, and Roman customs are often invoked as the decisive criterion to which argument is referred. The case of Claudius Pulcher illustrates this very clearly. Claudius ignored the auspices, set sail and lost his fleet in a naval battle. Cicero denies that this should be read as a proof of divination, but he also says that one should obey ancestral custom and that a man like Claudius deserved to be punished for his offence.[71] Yet if there is no good cause for divination, why blame a man for acting against the auspices as though they did not matter? Such action is held to be wrong, not because it issues from false logic or sheer unreason, but merely because it is contrary to Roman custom.

In the light of the above we can now consider whether Cicero's version of Socratic method corresponds with the techniques actually employed by Socrates. Superficially, it appears tha tsome statements are reasonably accurate. Socrates, in Plato, often declares that he himself does not know and is delighted to question those who claim to have knowledge; especially in the early dialogues, he is engaged in refuting others without always making any positive statement of his own, and in that respect is not unlike Cicero's Cotta. However, there are certain distinctions which Cicero does not make or which he overlooks in practice. There is, for instance, an obvious difference between the Socrates of the early dialogues and the other Socrates (as in the *Phaedo*) who asserts views of his own which he seeks to defend. Even though Cicero could not have been aware of the chronology of the dialogues, he might still have noticed the changes in Socrates' role. Secondly, Socrates' whole approach is bent on discovery (to which refutation is incidental) with a view to basing action on the results of the enquiry; but Cotta and Cicero may still act according to custom. As for the technique of question and answer, Cicero certainly admits to a liking for this method but tends on the whole to use the longer speech which suits his taste for oratory. (Perhaps we should add that he speaks of Socrates as a good orator[72] and he would probably have felt that the oratory used by his Roman characters was akin to the lengthier speeches of Socrates.) But the most important difference may be the following: most of tho who dispute with Plato's Socrates and who at first give confident answers to his questions are not members of a philosophical school. They are ordinary citizens, politicians, sophists, and they typify such classes rather than a sect with articulated doctrines.[73] In Cicero, on the other hand, the spokesmen do usually represent a school, and Socratic doubt is used partly to show inconsistencies but also partly to make a probable choice among existing theories. Thus Cicero sometimes follows the Stoics (as in the *de officiis*) and sometimes rejects their theories.

These recognizable differences suggest that Cicero was not as philosophically attentive to the Socrates of Plato as he might have been. Cicero's main debt was to Carneades, the second-century Academic who used a form of sceptical enquiry to combat the dogmatism of the Stoics, such as the view that certain knowledge is possible. Instead, Carneades and his predecessor Arcesilaus put forward the view that an action should be performed, not because it is known to be good, but because it is probable or reasonable. It is obvious to us that this kind of scepticism differs from Socratic enquiry, which may question the validity of a definition (of justice, say) but does still presuppose that justice is knowable. Why, then, does Cicero claim that all three thinkers are proponents of the Academic method he favours? He says in one place that what Arcesilaus derived from the Socratic dialogues was the idea that 'neither the senses nor the mind can perceive anything certain.'[74] It might be surprising if this was Arcesilaus' own view of his debt to Plato's dialogues—they do not suggest that conclusion—but such was Cicero's belief. He assimilated Socratic method to the kind of scepticism practised by the later thinkers. The targets were different but all three Academics would have agreed that admission of ignorance or uncertainty is better than the presumption of knowledge. This family resemblance is the reason why Professor Long writes: 'Arcesilaus' philosophical method is the Socratic procedure updated to take account of the state of philosophy in the third century B.C.' We can say that Cicero modelled his Socrates on the sceptical tradition rather than on a close reading of the dialogues.

Before we leave this subject it is important to discuss the Roman conception of Socratic irony, a quality for which the Greek philosopher was famous in antiquity and which has since been evaluated in many different ways. When Thrasymachus describes Socrates as ironical he means nothing complimentary; he is referring to Socrates as one who perpetually asks questions without giving his own opinions in an outspoken manly way. This pejorative definition of irony was common in Greek from the time of Socrates to the portrait of the ironical man in Theophrastus. Modern analysis, however, has rightly concentrated on other aspects of irony which throw light on the whole nature of Socrates' thinking. Thus Friedländer[75] draws attention to 'erotic irony'; though Socrates describes himself as one who is always susceptible to handsome young men, it soon becomes clear that he does not look for ordinary homosexual indulgence but is in control of his appetites. Allied to this is 'pedagogic irony'; Socrates, the mature man, seeks the company of young men in order to investigate the truth, and yet leads the young on the path of ignorance, not knowledge. There is also a distinction between the more severe irony, directed at some of the incurable sophists, and the gentler irony which plays on the definitions offered by young hopefuls. A reader of the dialogues soon becomes used to these complexities and is pleased or instructed by the gradations in tone.

The Romans were not hostile to irony, as Thrasymachus was, yet they did not do justice to the full range of Socratic usage. They observed that Socrates 'made fun of the sophists', a point which the reader of the *Protagoras* or *Gorgias* cannot fail to notice. Cicero defines irony as a witty dissimulation, a kind of solemn play, that can pervade a whole speech 'when your feelings are different from your words'.[76] Both the definition and the context in which it occurs enlighten us about Roman ideas of irony. The definition is adequate as far as it goes but seems to overlook the purposes of irony, which are all-important in assessing its role in Socratic thought. The context is a discussion of wit and humour envisaged as a means whereby the orator can commend himself to an audience and display his *humanitas*. Cicero says that this form of wit is 'salted with *gravitas* and is well-adapted not only to oratorical speeches but also to urbane conversation'. The remark appears to allow irony scope both in the law-courts and in conversations like the Socratic dialogues. Yet the Roman theorists have in mind the orator above all; and while the orator uses irony to show that he is a serious man who can unbend, his ultimate aim is to win his case, not, like Socrates, to find the truth. Ciceronian practice, it has been said, is to make use of irony in order to prevail, not to convince or instruct.[77]

By seeing irony in the context of rhetoric, the Romans were following Greek theorists but nevertheless this view limited their grasp of Socratic irony. In the *Brutus* Atticus says that irony would be inappropriate to a work of history but he still commends it as a quality. Socrates and Scipio Aemilianus are here paired as the representative Greek and Roman. This comparison shows once more that the Roman conception was mainly oratorical. Though Scipio was praised for his *humanitas* when at leisure, the traditions suggest that he used irony as an orator or office-holder in order to score points off his adversaries.[78] He was an aristocrat, masking his arrogance with wit, whereas Socrates' irony was usually devoted to an educational purpose. The Roman feeling for the value of irony in politics and law perhaps made it difficult to appreciate the more delicate usage of Socrates or to understand Socrates as the midwife of other men's opinions.

It seems that Cicero's Socrates owes more to the later sceptical tradition, which he heard about from his Greek philosophy teachers, than to a *close* reading of Plato. Though much is uncertain about the historical Socrates, he certainly acted as the spokesman of philosophy against the claims of oratory; Cicero, however, who thought of Socrates as prevailing in argument by oratory, did not see any conflict here but found a precedent for his own version of rhetorical philosophy. It was probably because of rhetorical theory that he interpreted Socratic irony as a combative device; and one misses the Socratic habit of testing hypotheses by making analogies with the everyday arts. Perhaps the magnificent consular would have been as disturbed by this mode of enquiry as were some of the opponents of Socrates. Fidelity to this Academic tradition, as he understood it, was Cicero's way of making his name as a philosopher in Latin. It was a method, he says, which was difficult at any time and which was now without an heir even in Greece. For Cicero, then, originality lay in reviving the Socratic past; it was an achievement to make the method more widely known and to reassure Romans that scepticism could still offer probabilities as the bases for moral action.

Epicureanism and Stoicism, however, were well represented both in the Ciceronian age and later on; and these schools did attract more by way of comment from supporters and critics. The Roman treatment of Epicurus, for example, ranges from the enthusiasm of Lucretius to the pungent criticisms expressed by Cicero. Lucretius writes as the unreserved admirer of Epicurus, to whom he devotes four separate eulogies.[79] The Roman poet speaks of himself not as a rival but as one who wishes to imitate the 'father' and 'discoverer of the truth'. It is true, as we saw earlier, that Lucretius was very much aware of the language difficulties involved in creating philosophical Latin, but he does not dwell on the subject in order to urge that Latin is better or worse than Greek. He is concerned to remind the reader that it is difficult to write clearly on a subject so dark as 'nature'; though he is eager for poetic fame he does not contrast (as perhaps he might) his clarity and vigour with the crabbed prose of the Greek original. His Latin is designed to make Romans accept the message of the Greek philosopher because he thinks it is true.

Lucretius' dependence on his Greek teacher in part reflects the prevailing attitude among members of the school. The master was revered and his doctrines were hardly criticized; we are told that the school was not troubled with dissensions, and the Roman's lack of theoretical innovation is therefore no more than one would expect. Yet Lucretius never gives the impression that he is a second-rate imitator. This is largely because his Latin exposition is persuasive and energetic and seems all the time to be directed towards what is felt to be true. His pride in Latin is not an expression of anti-Greek feeling; he has a sense of achievement because he is doing in Latin what no one has done before. And even so, the verse is described as a mere sweetener for the doctrine. Lucretius may seem to be exceptional among the Romans in his devoted admiration for a Greek thinker who died many years before. Yet, on reflection, his regard for Epicurus is not all that different from Cicero's respect for Socrates. If the comparison is not at once obvious, there are, I think, two reasons. The Roman Epicurean is expounding doctrines which (by and large) are confirmed by the original, whereas Cicero's claim to be Socratic in method does not pass a similar scrutiny. Secondly, Cicero at times names certain Roman equals of Socrates (e.g. Cato and Scipio), while for Lucretius Epicurus is without a peer. Yet both Romans certainly believed themselves to be the latter-day followers of Greeks whose theory or method was not to be criticized.

Cicero's eclecticism did not make him tolerant of Epicurus and his theories. His various references to the subject amount to a complete rejection of Epicureanism, with the result that the Roman, whose theory would allow him to choose from all Greek thought, here excludes a Greek thinker from the Roman way of life. The criticisms of Epicureanism can be considered under three heads: charges of inconsistency, the dislike of particular doctrines and a sense of embarrassment about style. On the first point Cicero meant that the man was better than his words or that some Epicurean sayings, which were acceptable, were nonetheless in conflict with other Epicurean principles.[80] In attacking this inconsistency and some of the doctrines, Cicero is making use of criticisms which were levelled by Greek thinkers. He shows more awareness of the gap between this Greek theory and his ideal of Roman life when (as we saw above) Torquatus is reproached for holding a theory which could not possibly explain his ancestor's patriotic action. There is a similar allusion to the clash between Epicurean values and Cicero's idea of Roman values when he denies that he is partisan or zealous in his strictures on Epicureans.[81] Such zeal would be appropriate if he and they were competing for high office, but since no such competition can occur (because the Epicurean is a dedicated abstainer from politics) Cicero means us to infer that his account of the doctrine is disinterested. The question of style certainly brought out Cicero's aesthetic prejudices against Epicurus. Though he denies in one passage that he is a critic of the Greek's style (he is said to be clear and intelligible, and the absence of rhetorical grace is not damning) he disliked Epicurus for his (apparent) aversion to culture; furthermore he says that Epicurus is only read by his own sect, whereas Plato is read by men of all persuasions. But if there is still some uncertainty about Cicero's attitude to Epicurus' style, he leaves us in no doubt about the Latin Epicureans.[82] They are said to be at fault for neglecting the graces of exposition (even though Cicero says in the same passage that he has not read them); when Velleius is praised for his polished account of Epicurean theory, this is not just an idle Ciceronian self-compliment but also a reminder that Epicureans themselves neglected stylistic beauty. Cicero's objection to the moral theory was reinforced by his distaste for a school which was 'not suited for rhetoric' and would therefore fail to assist proof by rhetorical persuasion.[83]

We might expect that Seneca as a Stoic would be even more hostile to Epicureanism. But while it is true that the main doctrines (especially the moral theory) are not acceptable to him he borrows and adapts isolated sayings. This is a noticeable feature in the earlier letters addressed to Lucilius, several of which are rounded off with an Epicurean tag; this device is especially striking when the attribution is not given till after the actual words. There are probably many reasons why Seneca chose to vary his subject-matter in this way. He employs the fiction that his correspondent will not be satisfied with his letter unless Seneca pays him tribute, a final, memorable quotation; when a Stoic makes use of the funds of Epicurus for this purpose, he is settling his debt in borrowed goods which cost him nothing. But humorous surprise is not the only point. Seneca feels that witty or apposite remarks are public property; when Epicurus says 'you must be a slave to philosophy in order that you may receive true freedom' he is speaking to mankind, not just to his school. And borrowing from Epicurus in this way is said to be no different from using quotable passages from the poets. Finally, Seneca does make it clear that only some of Epicurus' remarks are transferable. They are the more significant because they occur seldom and unexpectedly. 'It is astonishing that the advocate of pleasure should say anything like a brave man.'[84] The quotability of Epicurus is therefore a paradox; in the end he is to be contrasted with the Stoics, whose books and sayings are pervaded by the truth which in others can only be found in parts.

In effect the Romans either swallowed Epicurus whole or rejected him entire (if we except Seneca's ingenious adaptations, which, after all, merely introduce or commend the simpler points of his own doctrine). Stoic theory, however, had been more varied and the Romans had a greater scope for those modifications which can at least look original.

It was relatively easy, on a popular level, to deride both Epicureans and Stoics. When Cicero vilified Piso, he made fun of him for misinterpreting the moral theory of Epicurus as a licence for hedonism; and in his defence of Murena he poked fun at Cato for his serious attachment to Stoic principles which are held to be incompatible with the realities of Roman public life.[85] It is tempting to suppose that many Romans would see Stoicism as a butt for humour, and the general oddity of the creed would then help to explain why Nero and Domitian were irritated by their Stoic opponents. But the prejudice is not specifically Roman; Gellius tells how a rich Greek from Asia made fun of a Stoic who showed his anxiety during a storm at sea.[86] The Stoic could easily be exposed as ridiculous in the eyes of philistines the world over.

In the philosophical works Cicero's negative criticisms are expressed in several ways. Stoic moral theory is attacked (as we saw earlier) on the grounds that it has merely changed the name of things without helping our conception of virtue; this is to fault Stoicism for denying the term good to the external 'goods' (such as health) commended by some other schools.[87] Again, the Stoics were famous for their syllogistic method. Yet Balbus, who expounds the Stoic theory of the gods, himself admits that the narrow compass of the syllogism leaves Stoicism exposed to the greater rhetoric of the Academy. The syllogistic method was criticized for playing with words, not things, and for failing to

provide helpful instruction for the moral life. Zeno's reasoning
on the subject 'death is not an evil' is alleged to do no more than
supply a definition; it does not remove the pain.[88] In some works
Cicero argues at length against particular doctrines, such as
Stoic ideas on divination and the practice of using allegory to
explain the names of the gods.

Even so, Cicero was able to accommodate parts of Stoicism and
in the *de officiis* freely admits that he has borrowed from Panaetius;
yet his borrowing is done with a critical eye and he draws attention
to his active improvements. Thus he begins by criticizing his
source for failing to define the term for which Cicero uses *officium*.
He then outlines the nature of the enquiry into 'duties' and says
that Panaetius treats the subject under three headings; deliberation about how to act can involve (1) questions of what is honourable or not (2) questions of what is expedient or not (3) questions
of conflict between the honourable and the expedient. Cicero's
criticism is that the subdivisions are inadequate since there can
also be conflict between degrees of what is honourable and degrees
of what is expedient. He supplies a short account of the former at
the end of Book 1, but it is so brief that one is led to think that
Panaetius' sin of omission was not so very grave. Thirdly,
Panaetius had not completed his work since he had not provided
the final, promised study on where the honourable conflicts with
the expedient; Cicero's third book is intended to fill this gap. In
general Cicero says that he has not translated Panaetius but has
followed him as his main source, with some corrections. The
acknowledgment is not entirely gracious since some of the
criticisms are rather petty; but nonetheless they show that Cicero
sought to improve what he took over.[89]

In considering Seneca's relationship with his Stoic predecessors
we have to remember that in general he is as a Stoic more favourably inclined towards them. He points out to Lucilius that truth,
commendably expressed, can be found among all the thinkers of
the school; there is no one Stoic king with a monopoly of admirable
thoughts.[90] The Stoics are often mentioned with praise and
seldom rebuked. The reproofs, however, are most informative
about Seneca's attitude.

In one respect he shares with Cicero a dislike of the Stoic
syllogism, considering it to be ineffective as a means of persuasion. Zeno's argument, designed to show that death is not an
evil, is held up as an example of Greek ineptitude. Seneca is
expressing the idea that this kind of reasoning will not help a man
to act; what is needed, according to him, is persistent meditation

on the subject, if you are prepared to discipline your mind. 'The man who tries to persuade you by quibbles that death is not an evil will do nothing to exhort you or elevate you to face death.'[91] Seneca, in spite of his protestations that the truth should be kept plain, is of the opinion that it needs to be coloured by more than dialectic.

A passage in the *de beneficiis* is rather similar, for it shows Seneca's urgent wish to deal only in thoughts that are relevant to the moral life. He asks the reader's permission to pass over the question why there are three Graces, a scene which philosophers had interpreted in different ways. One theory, for example, suggested that the first Grace was in the act of offering a benefit; the second was accepting it while the third portrayed the act of return, thereby completing the circle. 'Whichever explanation you judge to be true, how does that knowledge help?' Similarly, he pursues with ridicule the various allegorical accounts of the Graces' names and the attempts to give them a significant family-tree: poets and painters do what they like, because the fancy takes them so. He is therefore calling Chrysippus to order because he has filled his whole book with this sort of nonsense. He concedes that Chrysippus was a great man, concerned with action not words, but he was 'nevertheless a Greek'; and if some people think (because they are so in thrall to Greeks) that accounts of the pictures are necessary, even they will discount the theories of the Graces' names.[92] As often, Seneca tries to have it both ways: he alludes to the theories and also states that they are irrelevant. There is a kind of knowing philistinism both in his carping at logic and in his scorn for theories about the Graces in art and literature.

In both passages Seneca puts great emphasis on exhortation, since it is the philosopher's role to improve mankind. The same point emerges when he discusses the view of Ariston, who maintained that only the principles of moral philosophy are necessary and that precepts are superfluous. Ariston meant that casuistic advice addressed to particular conditions (husbands, wives, office-holders and so on) is unnecessary provided that a person knows the general rules under which his case falls. Ariston asks, 'What gain is there in pointing out the obvious?'; Seneca's reply is that admonition (by means of precepts) does not instruct us but wakes us up and serves as a reminder. Precepts are therefore as useful as the persuasive prologues to Plato's laws. On the other hand, as the following letter makes clear, precepts alone are not sufficient; principles too must be expounded. To take a simple case, it is useless to hear and obey an exhortation to virtue unless you know what virtue is.[93]

Seneca disagrees more fundamentally with Poseidonius, over the way philosophy has developed. He follows his Greek predecessor in believing that there was a golden age ruled by 'wise men'; then vices crept in and legislation became necessary. He refers here to the laws passed by men like Solon, Lycurgus and Pythagoras, which were still the laws of moral sages, not lawyers' codes; the last are regarded as the fruit of a far more corrupt society. But Seneca parts company with Poseidonius over the relation between philosophy and the arts.[94] The Greek thinker had allocated philosophy a presiding role over the other arts. Seneca, however, sees the lesser arts as so many ways of satisfying corrupt taste; architecture has developed to the point where it erects huge edifices, not the basic means of shelter. The lesser arts owe their discovery to cunning, not to 'wisdom', which is the goal of moral perfection. This difference between the Roman and the Greek shows very clearly the moralizing tendency of Roman interest in philosophy. Poseidonius was not only a philosopher in Seneca's sense; his many interests included history and geography, and he attempted to relate the arts to the highest art of man, philosophy. But Seneca wishes to draw a contrast between philosophy, which is the way to perfection, and the degenerate present, which becomes worse as the arts progress and succeed in catering for man's appetites. The Roman moralist therefore draws himself aloof from the Greek polymath.

The criticisms made by Cicero and Seneca, when they are friendly to the doctrines of a Greek source, do not reveal much depth in philosophic thinking. They look like the minor adjustments of sympathizers who have borrowed ideas from others but feel they can also give some sign of critical independence. Though it is difficult to characterize the more positive side of their adaptations, some features stand out very clearly. Both Cicero and Seneca were literary stylists with a strong sense that philosophy in Latin should give aesthetic pleasure. Their objective here is not unconnected with their feeling that rhetorical persuasion is an essential part of moral philosophy; men are improved, not by proof, but by exhortation and homily. The insistence that things matter more than words led them to look askance at logic, and the demand for moral relevance led to some neglect of difficult subjects in philosophy. Finally, since they were creating for Greek thought a Roman habitation, they were conscious of the need to put on show their own wise men. Because wisdom was regarded as the goal of philosophy and the supreme test was felt to be action, not talk, they could and did feel that Rome had examples to offer which were worth any amount of theory. Latin philosophy repeated arguments which it coloured with rhetoric and made familiar by means of examples from Roman history.

CONCLUSION

Rome followed and imitated Greece in nearly all branches of literature and thought, though satire is perhaps an exception. I shall here attempt to summarize the main features of the Roman assimilation as they stand out from this study.

The period of Greek history and literature which had most to offer covered the fifth and fourth centuries B.C. In poetry, it is true, both Homer (whose date was placed before the founding of Rome) and the Alexandrian poets were important influences on Roman poets. But on the whole, the writers who were most admired were Athenians by birth or culture, men who had discovered and sometimes perfected new forms of intellectual expression. Herodotus and Thucydides set high standards of excellence in history; the theory of rhetoric was invented by Greeks, and Athenian orators developed the art; Socrates and Plato gave aesthetic form to moral philosophy. A fuller study of this subject, with wider chronological limits, would necessarily discuss the Greek tragedians and writers of comedy, who were also popular with Romans and were translated or adapted into Latin. But it is clear even from this limited survey that Homer, Demosthenes and Plato were read with enthusiasm.

The Romans were not much interested, if at all, in an objective or scholarly study of Greek thought. They misconceived the nature of the Greek argument between rhetoric and philosophy, because they wished to bring about an understanding between these subjects in their own time. Hence Cicero and Quintilian argued that Socrates and others had sundered an earlier unity of thought and action which should be restored. The Roman idea that Greek learning should be relevant to Roman needs was responsible for distorting the history of Greek thought. As a 'philosophical orator' himself, Cicero advanced an interpretation which imposed his own convictions and ideas on Greece.

There was even less curiosity about the events of Greek history, except perhaps for the brief reign of Alexander, which seemed like an earlier promise of the Roman empire. Men were not induced by stories of the Persian Wars to investigate the facts for themselves. They were, perhaps understandably, wearied by the reiteration of facts and legends from long ago; Greek diplomats and teachers did their own country something of a disservice by making use of material which struck their Roman audiences as so much fanciful boasting about the past. Romans had their own stories of earlier Rome, which confirmed their idea that they were morally superior, and they thought that their history would look more magnificent than that of Greece if only the style and literary technique of Greek historians could be adapted into a Latin form.

There are some indications that Romans drew a contrast between Greeks of the past and their unworthy descendants of the present. Cicero undoubtedly admired the great Athenians, Themistocles and Pericles, and the outstanding Theban, Epameinondas, whereas he spoke disapprovingly of contemporary Greeks, except for those to whom he was grateful as his intellectual teachers. But it would be going too far to say that Romans freely acknowledged the glorious past of Greece. They thought, as we have seen, that the past exploits of Greece had been exaggerated by Greek historians; in their view the political failure of Athens had been caused by the influence of oratory on public meetings and assemblies, a feature of Athenian politics which was already prominent in what might claim to be called the great period. The Greek present was therefore in a state of subjection to Rome because earlier Greeks had mismanaged themselves and their affairs. Romans of the empire admitted that their own late republic had been a time of anarchy, but most looked back on it as a temporary illness which had been cured by Augustus. The freedom valued by Romans with republican sentiments seemed different from the excessive liberty of Athens.

I do not mean to suggest that Romans were blameworthy for not attempting to see Greece as she had been, for adopting interpretations of Greek history and thought which suited Rome better than they fitted the facts. Rome was the victorious power, and regarded the possessions or creations of the defeated with the mentality of a conqueror. If the treasures of Greek art were a lawful ornament in Roman temples, the literary masterpieces of Greece could also be taken and even improved by a transformation into Latin; Roman historians had nobler deeds to record than their Greek predecessors, for all their style, and Roman orators had more important speeches to deliver than the manuals seemed able to conceive. Perhaps the surprising thing is that the Romans had some scruples about the acquisition of Greek art, scruples which could even look like generosity; they were also careful to make their literary imitations of Greek models as perfect as possible, so that success in Latin would imply a tribute to Greek.

Romans did not think the worse of themselves for 'imitating' Greek forms, whether their model was the epic poem or the philosophical dialogue. In one sense 'imitation' implies the superiority of a chosen model to which one can only approximate; the copy is destined to a half-life of inferiority. But this is not how the Romans conceived of their imitations of Greeks. It was true, in their view, that Greeks had discovered many ideas, and the inventors were honoured. The task of perfecting the discovery was thought to be even more difficult, a lengthy or unending process to which Romans could contribute quite as much as Greeks. We should notice too that in some ways the Greek inventors received less than their due. It was sometimes assumed or implied that the inventor merely gives a name to that which is already there. Thus wisdom was the goal long before Pythagoras gave the name philosophy to his activity, and orators made speeches long before the art of rhetoric was put on a formal basis. If one attends to the fact or idea rather than the discoverer, it is relatively easy for the latecomer to suppose that he too could have made the discovery if only it still needed to be made. Aristotle had thought far more of the discoverer than of the man who perfects and develops what he has been given. Cicero on the other hand expresses an idea which was more congenial to Romans when he admits that Romans have borrowed from Greece but says they have improved what they have taken.

We can be tempted to draw a simple, yet meaningful, distinction between Greece as the inventor and Rome as the transmitter. The idea makes good sense of the relationships between Roman and Greek rhetorics and between Latin and Greek philosophy. In intellectual vitality Roman culture is no more than a successor to the Hellenistic commentaries on what we would call the great age of Hellenism. But such value-judgments would have puzzled the Romans. They would have pointed with justifiable pride to their poetry and history as true monuments to their creativity. They would not have understood complaints about the inadequacy of their rhetoric and their philosophy, since they approached writing on these subjects not with a sense of exploration and adventure but with the spirit of imposing order and aesthetic form on an unnecessary Greek chaos of ideas. Very few Romans capitulated to the Greek mind as Lucretius bowed to the theories of Epicurus, or marvelled at their teachers as Plotinus did when he said of Ammonius: 'That is what I was looking for.'

The Roman pictured himself as a practical man, committed to tasks in public life that made it necessary for him to abbreviate the best that had been thought or said. His duty was to rule other peoples, in Virgil's phrase, leaving to them the lesser function of the arts, painting, sculpture and even literature. He wanted an account of his Greek subject's devices in a manner that would be relevant to his own needs. Except for Lucretius (and even he has doubts about the rightness of a poem on Epicureanism at an unhappy time in Roman history) Greek ideas had no ideological power; Romans did not appeal to Greek ideas as an authority for changing the world in the way that the *philosophes* of the eighteenth century invoked the pagan classics against Christian conservatism.

If we venture to define Hellenism in its modern form we may then ask whether the Romans would have recognized it or could have thought that Hellenism as an ideal had more to offer than ideals associated with the name of Rome and Rome's past. Hellenism can perhaps stand as a shorthand term for freedom of reasoning, the aim of which is to investigate the nature of the universe and the nature of man without fear of convention or government, and to use means of persuasion and statement that are beautiful to the imagination as well as to the understanding. The Romans would not have sympathized with this ideal as a complex, for they valued custom more than enquiry or explanation. But they were partial or limited Hellenists in that they welcomed Greek forms of expression—ranging from hexameters to philo-sophical dialogues—as a means of portraying Roman experience with style. They had more use for the beauty that appeals to the rhetorical imagination than for the aesthetic of rigorous argument. Rhetoric of this kind (we should remember) was itself a Greek invention, just as much as logic or dialectic.

NOTES

CHAPTER ONE: THE GREEK CHARACTER

1. Quint. *I.O.* 5.10.24
2. Pliny *N.H.* 4.9
3. Virgil *Georg.* 2. 136–76; Pliny *N.H.* 3. 39–42. cf. Pliny *ep.* 8.20
4. See H. C. Baldry in *Grecs et Barbares*, Geneva (1961) pp. 167–95
5. Herodotus 1.60 (but see the remarks in H. Lloyd-Jones, *The Justice of Zeus*, California (1973) p. 180 n. 45); Arist. *Pol.* 1327 b19; Vitruvius 6.1.11
6. Strabo 1.4.9
7. Livy 31.29. 12f
8. Pliny *N.H.* 29. 14; Aulus Gellius *N.A.* 13.9.4; Fronto, 1.70 (Haines)
9. On Philip V, Livy 31.34.8; on Flamininus see Livy 33.33 and E. Badian, *Cincinnati Classical Studies* (1971) ii p. 271f
10. Dion. Hal. *Ant. Rom.* 1.11. See also Cic. *rep.* 1.58
11. Tac. *Germ.* 39; Cic. *Flacc.* 67; Tac. *Hist.* 5.2 and 5
12. See A. N. Sherwin-White, *Racial Prejudice in Imperial Rome*, Cambridge (1967) esp. p. 21f
13. Livy 40.47
14. Velleius 2.107
15. Livy 39.1 (Ligurians); 30.14f (Masinissa); 5.28.3 (Timasitheus)
16. Tac. *Germ.* 45
17. Val. Max. 5.4. *Ext.* 5 (Scythians); 6.4. *Ext.* 1 and 2. Cic. *Arch.* 15. cf. *ep. Quint. fr.* 1.1.7
18. Cic. *leg.* 1.25
19. Cic. *de oratore* 3.135. cf. below p. 156
20. cf. Livy 38.46 on Gallograeci
21. Aulus Gellius *N.A.* 6.11
22. Cic. *rep.* 1.5; *Flacc.* 16 and 19
23. *Tusc.* 2.60 (Dionysius); *Flacc.* 24
24. Cic. *rep.* 1.5. Pliny *N.H.* 23.32; 29.17
25. Cic. *amic.* 4. Aulus Gellius *N.A.* 4.14. cf. Gordon Williams, *Tradition and Originality in Roman Poetry*, Oxford (1968) pp. 264, 382, 770
26. On *otium* cf. below p. 140f. See Cic. *Verr.* 2.2.7; *Flacc.* 90
27. cf. Cic. *leg. agr.* 2.95
28. Juv. 10.174. Virg. *Aen.* 2 esp. 152 and 195. For a *Roman* deception see Livy 42.47

29. Cic. *de oratore* 2. 17–20 (cf. 1. 111f); *Brut.* 292; *Tusc.* 1.86. Sen. *Luc.* 82.8
30. Tac. *Dial.* 32.7
31. Sen. *ben.* 1.3–4. cf. below p. 171
32. Cic. *Tusc.* 3.81
33. Strabo 3.4.19
34. Tac. *Germ.* 15
35. Cic. *Tusc.* 2.65; cf. 5.113
36. Aulus Gellius *N.A.* 19.14
37. Cic. *sen.* 43. cf. Marius' attitude at Sallust *Jugurtha* 85.32 and Plut. *Mar.* 2
38. *Tusc.* 2.27
39. cf. below p. 91
40. Tac. *Ann.* 15.45
41. *Flacc.* 10; 14; 62f (Athens); 42 (Heracleides)
42. See e.g. *Verr.* 2.4.5 and 16 (*religio*); 2.1.66f (Philodamus)
43. Juv. 3.60–1
44. Cic. *ep. Quint. fr.* 1.1.35
45. See e.g. *Verr.* 2.2.15f and 166
46. *Att.* 5.21.10
47. For Cic.'s attitude see *Att.* 5.10.2; 5.11.5; 5.21.5
48. *Att.* 5.21.5; *fam.* 2.11.2; 8.4.5
49. Tac. *Ann.* 15.20–2; Pliny, *Pan.* 70.9
50. *Att.* 5.2.3
51. *Verr.* 2.4.30
52. *Verr.* 2.5.18
53. *Verr.* 2.1.63f
54. *Att.* 6.1.15. See J. A. O. Larsen, *Class. Phil.* 43 (1948) p. 187f
55. *ep. Quint. fr.* 1.1.18–20; 1.2.4
56. *ep. Quint. fr.* 1.1.27; 1.2.6f
57. *Att.* 6.1.2; *fam.* 3.9–12
58. *ep. Quint. fr.* 1.1.32–5. On Greek misconduct see *Att.* 6.2.5
59. *ep. Quint. fr.* 1.1.22f; *Tusc.* 2.62. Cic. *Brut.* 112 is less complimentary to the *Cyropaedeia*; on the alleged rivalry between Xenophon and Plato see Aulus Gellius *N.A.* 14.3. On Cicero's *Republic* see *Att.* 6.1.8
60. Juv. 3.61
61. *Verr.* 2.1.44f and 154
62. Pliny *ep.* 8.24
63. For Trajan's attitude see Pliny, *ep.* 10.40.2; and B. Levick, *Roman Colonies in Southern Asia Minor*, Oxford (1967) p. 109
64. Nepos, *Atticus*, 2–4 anu 6; for Appius see Cic. *Att.* 6.1.26
65. Suet. *Tib.* 11
66. *de oratore*, 2.77
67. Cic. *Brutus* 313–16
68. Plut. *Cato ii* 10 and 16.1. For Taurus see Aulus Gellius *N.A.* 7.13; 8.6; 2.2
69. See E. L. Bowie in *Past and Present* 46 (1970) pp. 1–43
70. See S. Treggiari, *Roman Freedmen during the Late Republic*, Oxford (1969) pp. 1–11 and Appendix 3
71. Plut. *Cato ii* 13

72. Cic. *ep. Quint. fr.* 1.1.13 and 1.2.1 (Statius); Tac. *Ann.* 13.2 and 23
73. Cic. *Att.* 4.15.1; 7.4.1; 7.18.3
74. See J. Scarborough, *Roman Medicine*, London (1969) chs. vii and viii
75. For the influence of these Roman views of Greeks in the Renaissance see Terence Spencer, *Fair Greece, Sad Relic*, London (1954) p. 33f

CHAPTER TWO: PHILHELLENISM

1. See G. W. Bowersock, *Augustus and the Greek World*, Oxford (1965) esp. ch. iii
2. Plut. *Sulla* 12.5f. For Caesar's attitude to Athens after Pharsalus see Appian *Bell. Civ.* 2.88
3. Plut. *Sulla* 14–15; *Lucullus* 19.5f. Velleius 2.23.4
4. Plut. *Sulla* 26.6–9
5. Appian, *Mithr.* 211f and 259
6. Plut. *Lucullus* 19.8; 29.3–5
7. See Memnon *F. Gr. Hist.* 434.34f
8. Plut. *Lucullus* 42; *Cimon* 1–2 (Chaeronea). See also Cic. *Acad.* 2.4–6
9. Appian *Bell. Civ.* 4.65f
10. Dio Cassius 47.33; Plut. *Brut.* 30; Val. Max. 1.5.8
11. Plut. *Brut.* 35
12. Plut. *Ant.* 24.4; 33.7; Dio Cassius 48.39; Sen. *Suas.* 1.6–7
13. See *de oratore* 3.75; *leg.* 2.36
14. Tac. *Ann.* 3.60–3. cf. *Ann.* 4.14
15. Tac. *Ann.* 2.53 and 55
16. Tac. *Ann.* 4.15 and 55–6
17. Tac. *Ann.* 12.61–3. On Cos see I. Edelstein, *Asclepius*, Baltimore (1945) ii p. 254
18. Tac. *Ann.* 4.37–8
19. Tac. *Ann.* 14.15 and 20–1. Suet. *Nero* 21f
20. See I. Lana *Riv. Fil.* 29 (1951) 145f
21. Pliny *ep.* 4.22. On athletes see E. N. Gardiner, *Greek Athletic Sports and Festivals*, London (1910) p. 161f. Panaetius' analogy with athletes (Aulus Gellius *N.A.* 13.28) was not used by Cic. in *de officiis*
22. Cic. *Tusc.* 4.70; Sen. *Luc.* 123.15; Val. Max. 2.1.7. cf. Livy 29.19; Pliny *ep.* 1.22; Lucan 7.270f. See Gordon Williams, *Tradition and Originality in Roman Poetry*, Oxford (1968) p. 551f
23. Suet. *Nero* 21.3
24. Tac. *Ann.* 15.45
25. Dittenberger *SIG*³814; Pausanias 7.17.4. See B. H. Warmington, *Nero*, London (1969) p. 109f
26. On Hadrian see P. Graindor, *Athènes sous Hadrien* (1934) p. 118; W. den Boer, *Mnemosyne* 8 (1955) p. 123f. On Polemon see Philostratus, *Vit. Soph.* 1.25
27. (Panhellenia) Pausanias 1.18.9; Dio Cassius 69.16
28. Tac. *Ann.* 2.88; cf. below p. 78
29. Cic. *Tusc.* 1.1

30. Cic. *de natura deorum* 1.8; on translation see below pp. 63–5 and 140f
31. Sen. *Luc.* 40. 11–14; Val. Max. 2.2.2.; Pliny *ep.* 5.20.4
32. Quint. *I.O.* 12.10.27f; see R. G. Austin, *Quintilian xii*, Oxford (1948) p. 173f
33. Quint. *I.O.* 12.2.7
34. Aulus Gellius *N.A.* 11.8. Polybius 39.1 (on Cato i); Cic. *fin.* 1.9; *Tusc.* 5.108; *Brut.* 131; *prov. cons.* 15f (Albucius). cf. Cic. *off.* 1.111
35. Val. Max. 2.2.2 and 3
36. Cic. *fin.* 5.89; see also *div.* 2.131
37. Suet. *Tib.* 71; *Claudius* 42. On the Greek in Suetonius see G. B. Townend, *Hermes* 88 (1960) pp. 98–120
38. Val. Max. 8.7.6; Aulus Gellius *N.A.* 1.13.9f; Quint. *I.O.* 11.2.50
39. Cic. *Verr.* 2.4.147f. cf. Plut. *Cato i* 12.5..On the language question in Sicily see M. I. Finley, *Ancient Sicily*, London (1968) p. 165f
40. Suet. *Nero* 7.2; Tac. *Hist.* 2.80
41. Polybius 38.22; Diodorus 32.24; see A. E. Astin, *Scipio Aemilianus*, Oxford (1967) pp. 282–7
42. Appian *Bell. Civ.* 3.13
43. Suet. *Cal.* 22.1; Homer, *Iliad* 2.204
44. Several Homeric names were humorously applied; see L. Friedländer, *Roman Life and Manners*, London (1965) iv p. 131
45. Cic. *Att.* 1.16.5; Plut. *Brut.* 34; *Iliad* 1.259
46. Cic. *fam.* 13.15
47. Cic. *Att.* 6.4.3; 6.5.2; 6.7.1
48. Suet. *Tib.* 53
49. Suet. *Claudius* 4; *Jul.* 30.5. Cic. *off.* 3.82
50. Quint. *I.O.* 1.5.32; cf. 4.1.1; 5.10.1; 6.1.2; 6.2.8
51. Cic. *Att.* 5.17.2; Suet. *Cal.* 47 and 29.1; Quint *I.O.* 1.5.70
52. On Cicero's Greek see H. J. Rose *JHS* 41 (1921) p. 91f
53. Sen. *Luc.* 107. 10–12
54. Dio Cassius 55.9.6 (Vesta); Pliny *N.H.* 34.84
55. Pliny *N.H.* 34.93; cf. Platner-Ashby, *A Topographical Dictionary of Rome*, Oxford (1929) p. 450
56. Plut. *Marc.* 20; Polybius 9.10
57. Livy 25.40; 39.6 (Vulso); Pliny *N.H.* 34.14
58. Velleius 1.13.4
59. See e.g. Pliny *N.H.* 33.5, 148 and 153
60. Cic. *Verr.* 2.4.124 and 134; *fam.* 7.23.2. Cic. is more enthusiastic in *Att.* 1.4–9. On Cic.'s attitude see E. Rawson, *Cicero*, London (1975) p. 48
61. Pliny *ep.* 3.1.9; 3.6; 3.7.7
62. Cic. *Verr.* 2.4.54–55; cf. *Tusc.* 1.4 and Pliny *N.H.* 35.19
63. Pliny *N.H.* 37.14f
64. Cic. *rep.* 1.21
65. See e.g. Pliny *N.H.* 33.149 and 34.36; Cic. *off.* 2.76f; Strabo 8.6.23; *RE* xvi. 1.1200
66. See J. J. Pollitt, *The Art of Rome*, New Jersey (1966) p. xiii
67. Sen. *Luc.* 86.11f

68. Livy 26.30; Plut. *Marc.* 23
69. Livy 27.16; Pliny *N.H.* 34.40
70. Livy 26.34.12; Plut. *Cato i* 19.5
71. Livy 43.4 and 7 (Lucretius); 42.3 (Flaccus)
72. Cic. *Verr.* 2.4.72 and 97f
73. *Res Gestae Divi Augusti* 24.1; Pliny *N.H.* 34.58
74. See P. A. Brunt and J. M. Moore, *Res Gestae*, Oxford (1967) p. 66
75. Dio Cassius 51.17; Strabo 14.1.14
76. Cic. *Tusc.* 5.102. cf. *leg.* 3.31
77. Pliny *N.H.* 35.26; Josephus *Bell. Jud.* 7.158f
78. Pliny *N.H.* 36.33 (Pollio); 34.6f (Verres)
79. Pliny *N.H.* 35.26; 34.62
80. Pliny *N.H.* 34.82 (Nero); Cic. *Verr.* 2.4.6f
81. Pliny *N.H.* 33.147; but see *N.H.* 17.2–4
82. Statius, *Silvae* 4.6. esp. 22f

CHAPTER THREE: GREEK POETRY

1. *de oratore* 2.60f
2. Cic. *Tusc.* 1.3
3. Cic. *fin.* 1.7; Horace *Ars.* 260–74
4. Aulus Gellius *N.A.* 19.9
5. Suet. *Vita Virgilii* 21
6. Prop. 1.7.3–4
7. Velleius 1.5; Pliny *N.H.* 7.107f; 17.37
8. Suet. *Cal.* 34; Dio Cassius 69.4.6
9. Sen. *ad Polyb.* 8.2; 11.5
10. Quint. *I.O.* 1.1.12; 1.8.5
11. Sen. *Luc.* 27. On reading at table cf. Juv. 11.180
12. Statius *Silvae* 2.1.117; 5.3.159f
13. Aulus Gellius *N.A.* 9.9
14. Horace *ep.* 1.2.1–26
15. Quint. *I.O.* 10.1.46f
16. See above ch. 2 p. 46f
17. *Att.* 2.5.1; 7.1.4; 7.12.3; 8.16.2; 13.13.2; 13.24. See *Iliad* 6.442f
18. Pliny *ep.* 4.11.12 (*Iliad* 18.20); Quint. *I.O.* 10.1.49
19. Suet. *Cal.* 22.1; *Dom.* 12.3; *Vesp.* 23.1
20. Sen. *Luc.* 108.30f
21. Suet. *Tib.* 70
22. Aulus Gellius *N.A.* 14.6; n.b. ref. to *Odyssey* 4.392
23. Aulus Gellius *N.A.* 9.9; 13.27
24. Quint. *I.O.* 10.1.46. On Quint.'s reading see A. Gwynn, *Roman Education*, Oxford (1926) p. 225f
25. See e.g. Cic. *Brut.* 40 and 50
26. Quint. *I.O.* 10.1. 48–50
27. Quint. *I.O.* 8.3.84; 8.4.21 (Helen)
28. Pliny *ep.* 3.9.28; Quint. *I.O.* 5.12.14

29. See F. Buffière, *Les Mythes d'Homère et la Pensée Grecque*, Paris (1956)
30. Cic. *Tusc.* 1.65; *fin.* 5.49
31. Sen. *Luc.* 56.15; 66.26; 88.7; 123.12
32. See W. B. Stanford, *The Ulysses Theme*, Oxford (1954), ch. x
33. Cic. *de natura deorum* 1.41f; Horace *ep.* 1.2.3–4; Sen. *Luc.* 88.5–8
34. Pliny *N.H.* 10.7; 19.25f; 18.33
35. Lucr. 1.921–47; Horace, *Ars*, 343
36. Martial 1. *praef.*
37. See e.g. Cic. *de natura deorum* 2.7; *Tusc.* 1.36
38. Quint. *I.O.* 10.1.27f; cf. 2.4.2
39. Tac. *dial.* 11–13
40. Prop. 1.9.11; 2.1.14. Ovid *Trist.* 1.5.79
41. Martial 4.49; 8.3; 10.4
42. Pliny *ep.* 3.21. See also 4.18; 5.3; 5.10; 7.9
43. Strabo 1.1.2f

CHAPTER FOUR: GREEK HISTORY AND HISTORIANS

1. Aulus Gellius *N.A.* 3.7. On Thermopylae see Livy 36.15
2. Cic. *rep.* 2.2f. See below p. 88
3. Sallust *Catiline* 2.2
4. Val. Max. 8.14 (glory); 3.2.22 (Acilius). Herodotus 6.114
5. Val. Max. 4.7.4
6. Tac. *Ann.* 2.88
7. See R. M. Ogilvie, *A Commentary on Livy 1–5*, Oxford (1965) e.g. pp. 315; 684; 720; 726 (Coriolanus; capture of Rome)
8. Cic. *Acad.* 1.8
9. Nepos *praef.* 4
10. Nepos *Epam.* 2.3. See also Cic. *rep.* 14f, for comparisons of peoples
11. Nepos *Pelop.* 1
12. Cic. *fam.* 5.12
13. Suet. *Claud.* 25.3. On Troy see M. Grant, *Roman Myths*, Penguin (1973) p. 67f, and H. Tudor, *Political Myth*, London (1972) esp. ch. 3
14. Quint. *I.O.* 1.9.18f. On 'Greek histories' see 2.4.19
15. Cic. *off.* 1.61f
16. Sen. *Suas.* 1; Sen. *ben.* 6.3 (Xerxes). On law see S. F. Bonner, *Roman Declamation*, Liverpool (1949) esp. pp. 93–7
17. Cic. *Sest.* 48 and 141; *Balb.* 12f. cf. *Scaur.* 4f
18. Cic. *Tusc.* 1.113; Herodotus 1.31
19. *fin.* 2.67
20. Aulus Gellius *N.A.* 2.1; 7.10
21. See L. Casson, *Travel in the Ancient World*, London (1974) esp. p. 262f
22. Appian *Bell. Civ.* 4.65f. cf. above p. 31
23. See e.g. Aulus Gellius *N.A.* 3.11.6
24. Tac. *Hist.* 2.2–4 (Venus); 4.83–4 (Serapis)

25. Cic. *Brut.* 28 and 49; *fam.* 9.16.6. On the term *annales* see R. Syme, *Tacitus*, Oxford (1958) i p. 253. On the opening of Tacitus' *Annals* see Peter Gay, *Style in History*, London (1975) p. 21f
26. Cic. *off.* 2.26f
27. Cic. *Brut.* 41f; *Tusc.* 4.3f
28. Cic. *rep.* 1.58; Florus *praef.* 1–8
29. Appian *praef.* 8
30. Lucr. 6.1f; Cic. *Flacc.* 62f; Velleius 1.18; Florus 1.40.9
31. Sen. *Suas.* 2.5
32. Florus 1.24.13
33. Cic. *rep.* 1.44; Tac. *dial.* 40.3–4
34. Sen. *dial.* 9.5.3
35. Val. Max. 5.3. *Ext.* 3. Legal redress; S. F. Bonner, *Roman Declamation*, Liverpool (1949) pp. 87–8
36. Cic. *rep.* 1.5f; 2.2f; *leg.* 2.36f
37. Cic. *rep.* 1.43
38. Livy 31.6, 14, 26, 44
39. Cic. *Brut.* 50; Thuc. 2.34f
40. *rep.* 2.50; 58; 24. On Sparta see E. Rawson, *The Spartan Tradition in European Thought*, Oxford (1969)
41. Val. Max. 4.5. *Ext.* 2. Cic. *sen.* 63. Aulus Gellius *N.A.* 2.15. Val. Max. 2.6.1
42. See K. M. Chrimes, *Ancient Sparta*, Manchester (1949) p. 27f and G. W. Bowersock, *Augustus and the Greek World*, Oxford (1965) pp. 59–60
43. Cic. *Tusc.* 2.34 and 46; 5.77. Sen. *dial.* 1.4.11
44. Sen. *Luc.* 94.62
45. See e.g. Cic. *off.* 1.155; *fin.* 2.97 (Leonidas); *de oratore* 3.139 (greatness); *Brut.* 50 (learned); *de oratore* 1.210 (as general)
46. See esp. Cic. *rep.* 1.25. On his 'speeches' see Cic. *Brut.* 27f; Quint. *I.O.* 12.2.22; see below p. 158
47. Val. Max. 5.3. *Ext.* 3; 6.5. *Ext.* 2 (Aristeides); 8.14. *Ext.* 1 (Miltiades). Quint. *I.O.* 11.2.50 (memory). Cic. *Brut.* 41f; *Att.* 9.10.3
48. See e.g. Cic. *rep.* 2.5f; cf. Livy 5.54.4. For Greek dislike of closeness to the sea see Plato, *Laws*, 704d
49. Cic. *leg.* 2.38f; Quint. *I.O.* 1.10.9–33. For other comments see Cic. *Rosc. Am.* 134; Athenaeus 14.615
50. Pliny *N.H.* 4.33
51. Diodorus 18.4.2–5; Pliny *N.H.* 3.57
52. Cic. *Att.* 5.20.3; 13.28.2
53. Curtius 8.5.7; 10.9.3f
54. Cic. *Brut.* 42. cf. Quint. *I.O.* 10.1.74
55. Pliny *N.H.* 8.154; Aulus Gellius *N.A.* 5.2
56. Pliny *N.H.* 8.149; 12.21
57. Aulus Gellius *N.A.* 6.1
58. Plut. *Pomp.* 2. Suet. *Jul.* 7
59. See B. H. Warmington, *Nero*, London (1969) pp. 98–9

60. Suet. *Aug.* 50 and 18.1. See also S. Weinstock *JRS* 50 (1960) p. 44f. For Trajan see Dio Cassius 68.30
61. See W. Hoffmann, *Das literarische Porträt Alexanders des Grossen,* Leipzig (1907)
62. Livy 9.17f. cf. Aulus Gellius *N.A.* 17.21.33
63. Cic. *leg. Man.* 36–48; *Font.* 42
64. Tac. *Ann.* 2.73
65. Aulus Gellius *N.A.* 7.8
66. Curtius 4.5.11f; 8.5.7; 8.10.12
67. Sen. *Luc.* 91.17; 94.62; 119.7f
68. Livy 31.1.6 and 16; 44.4 (Perseus). On Alexander cf. Plut. *Titus* 7
69. Livy 36.14; 32.13; 32.33f
70. Livy 45.4f
71. Livy 36.7
72. Livy 45.9
73. Juv. 10.175f
74. Pliny *N.H.* 7.8; 12.11; 10.136; 8.80f. cf. 19.86; 7.174
75. Cic. *Brut.* 42f
76. Pliny *N.H.* 8.6; 9.33; 12.9. On the dolphin *N.H.* 9.25
77. *de oratore* 2.51–62
78. Pliny *ep.* 7.9. But at 5.8.4 he says that history gives pleasure however it is written
79. Cic. *fam.* 5.12
80. cf. Pliny *ep.* 9.27
81. Cic. *leg.* 1.5f; *div.* 2.116. On Herodotus see A. D. Momigliano, *History* 43 (1958) pp. 1–13
82. Aulus Gellius *N.A.* 3.10.11; 8.4; 17.8.16; 16.19
83. Pliny *N.H.* 8.43
84. Aulus Gellius *N.A.* 16.11
85. Herodotus 7.152
86. Cic. *orator* 39f. Quint. *I.O.* 9.4.16; 10.1.73f
87. *Att.* 10.8.7; 7.1.6
88. Pliny *ep.* 5.8.11; 4.7.3
89. Cic. *orator* 30. See below p. 116
90. Quint. *I.O.* 10.1.73
91. See P. Perrochat, *Les Modèles Grecs de Salluste,* Paris (1949) p. 13f
92. Aulus Gellius *N.A.* 2.27
93. *rep.* 1.34; 2.27
94. See J. Briscoe, *Commentary on Livy 31–33,* Oxford (1973) p. 6f
95. Livy 33.10

CHAPTER FIVE: RHETORIC

1. Cic. *de oratore* 1.155; Pliny *ep.* 7.9.2; 9.36.3
2. Sen. *contr.* 10.4.21; 1.2.22; 1.4.10; 1.8.7; 10.4.18
3. Cic. *Brut.* 26–51. See *Tusc.* 1.5 for a somewhat different view of the orator at Rome

4. *de oratore* 2.92f
5. Cic. *Brut.* 37–8; cf. 285
6. Cic. *Brut.* 52; Quint. *I.O.* 12.10.16
7. Cic. *orator* 226 and 230 (Hegesias); 25 (Rhodes)
8. *de oratore* 3.43
9. Cic. *Brut.* 325f
10. See G. Kennedy, *The Art of Persuasion in Greece*, London (1963) p. 301f and Appendix
11. See A. E. Douglas, *Cicero, Brutus*, Oxford (1966) pp. xiv–xvii
12. Cic. *Brut.* 67f and 292f; *orator* 28f
13. Cic. *Att.* 15.1a.2. cf. *orator* 234
14. Quint. *I.O.* 12.10.14f
15. Pliny *ep.* 1.2; cf. 1.20; 3.18; 7.12; 9.26. See A. N. Sherwin-White, *The Letters of Pliny*, Oxford (1966) p. 86f
16. Cic. *orator* 105; 110. Quint. *I.O.* 10.1.105; 9.4.63. Cic. *orator* 23–4
17. Pliny *ep.* 9.26
18. Quint. *I.O.* 10.1.22
19. Quint. *I.O.* 11.3.97; 4.2.131; 4.1.32; 10.1.22
20. See esp. Quint. *I.O.* 12.10.24. Cic. *de oratore* 1.89
21. Quint. *I.O.* 11.3.168 (Marathon). Aulus Gellius *N.A.* 3.13
22. Cic. *Brut.* 141f; *de oratore* 3.213. On Lucius, *fin.* 5.5
23. Cic. *orator* 56f and 133f
24. Quint. *I.O.* 10.1.39 and 76f
25. Quint. *I.O.* 10.1.107. On wit, 6.3.1f
26. Aulus Gellius *N.A.* 8.9; 1.8; 11.9
27. *de oratore* 1.45f; cf. 3.122. On references to the *Gorgias* in antiquity see E. R. Dodds, *Plato, Gorgias*, Oxford (1959) index 1
28. Plato, *Gorgias* 464b 467a
29. Plato, *Gorgias* esp. 484c–488b
30. *Phaedrus* 266c–274b. On the probable see G. Kennedy, *The Art of Persuasion in Greece*, London (1963) pp. 60 and 89
31. See G. Kennedy, *The Art of Rhetoric in the Roman World*, Princeton (1972) p. 214f
32. *de oratore* 1.93 (views of Charmadas)
33. *orator* 10 compliments Plato's style as well as his understanding
34. *de oratore* 1.50
35. On definitions see Quint. *I.O.* 7.3.14f; on 'things not words' see below ch.6 n.16
36. For Cic.'s views see also *de inv.* 1.2–3 and *de oratore* 1.16f
37. See esp. *de oratore* 3.56f; Quint. *I.O.* 10.1.35; see below ch. 6 p. 159
38. Quint. *I.O.* 2.20.7 (Zeno's image); 2.15.38 (definition of rhetoric)
39. Quint. *I.O.* 2.15.24–32
40. cf. Val. Max. 6.4. *Ext.* 2 (n.b. *gravitas* of Socrates)
41. See R. J. Bonner, *Lawyers and Litigants in Ancient Athens*, Chicago (1927) p. 59f
42. See Quint. *I.O.* 12.7
43. Quint. *I.O.* 2.17. esp. 1–4

44. See G. Kennedy, *The Art of Rhetoric in the Roman World*, Princeton (1972) p. 103f
45. *de inv.* 2.6–10
46. cf. G. Kennedy, *op. cit.* p. 128f
47. *fam.* 1.9.23. cf. *Att.* 2.1.1
48. *de oratore* 2.152f
49. See O. Gigon, *Hermes* 87 (1959) pp. 143–62
50. Quint. *I.O.* 3.1.13f. See G. M. A. Grube, *The Greek and Roman Critics*, London (1968) pp. 272–4
51. *ad Her.* 1.1; *de oratore* 2.81f; Quint. *I.O.* 2.15.37
52. *de inv.* 1.8
53. *de oratore* 2.133f
54. Quint. *I.O.* 2.21.21. See also 3.6.59 and 3.11.22
55. *de oratore* 1.14; Tac. *dial.* 19.3
56. Quint. *I.O.* 5.14.32
57. *de oratore* 2.75 (Phormio); 2.28 (Antony's speech)
58. *de oratore* 1.122 and 163
59. *orator* 7–10. See Erwin Panofsky, *Idea*, New York (1968) p. 11f

CHAPTER SIX: PHILOSOPHY

1. Quint. *I.O.* 10.1.123f
2. Plut. *Cic.* 5.2–3; Plutarch mentions this pejorative nick-naming to explain popular neglect of Cic. at the start of his career. For remarks on *Graeculus* see N. K. Petrochilos, *Roman Attitudes to the Greeks* (1974) pp. 48–54
3. Sen. *Luc.* 108.22; *ad Helviam*, 17.4 (where his father is said to have been *maiorum consuetudini deditus*)
4. For Nero see Suet. *Nero* 52, and for Agricola Tac. *Agric.* 4.4–5
5. cf. A. Birley, *Marcus Aurelius*, London (1966) p. 121
6. Cic. *Tusc.* 2.1–2; see *rep.* 1.30; *de oratore*, 2.156; Apuleius, *Apol.* 13. Gellius Poplicola, in jest, called on philosophers to agree; Cic. *leg.* 1.53
7. Aulus Gellius *N.A.* 5.15 and 16; see H. D. Jocelyn, *The Tragedies of Ennius*, Cambridge (1970), fr. xxviii and note
8. Sen. *N.Q. praef.*
9. Quint. *I.O.* 7.3.14–15; Sen. *Luc.* 45.4–5
10. Cic. *amic.* 10. cf. *Verr.* 2.2.5. For the elder Cato's criticism of Socrates see Plut. *Cato* i. 23
11. Aulus Gellius *N.A.* 13.8. Eustathius makes a similar point about Nestor; see on *Iliad* 1.250
12. Cic. *orator* 51
13. cf. Sen. *Luc.* 108.3 for a striking formulation
14. Critics recognized that Epicurus was better than his doctrine and some of his followers (see Sen. *Luc.* 21.9) but distrusted the theory for placing man's good in the body, not in the soul. cf. too Val. Max. 4.3.6
15. Sen. *Luc.* 6.6 and 24.15

16. For the importance of *res* as opposed to *verba* see esp. Cic. *Tusc.* 5.32 and 120; *fin.* 3.5 and 10; 4.2 and 21; 5.22. Sen. *Luc.* 40.14; 45.4–6; 52.14; 83.27. Aulus Gellius *N.A.* 5.21.2; 13.8.5; 13.24.2; 17.19. The antithesis between *mores* and *verba* emphasizes still more the concern with ethics; Aulus Gellius *N.A.* 1.10.4 and Sen. *Luc.* 100.2

17. Cic. *off.* 3.2–4; see J. H. D'Arms, *Romans on the Bay of Naples*, Cambridge Mass. (1970) p. 72

18. Cic. *Tusc.* 1.1; for 'Greek *otium*' see *orator* 108. cf. *paradoxa Stoicorum* 3

19. Sen. *Luc.* 8.6 and 19.2–3

20. cf. Sen. *de otio* 4

21. See R. Poncelet, *Cicéron Traducteur de Platon*, Paris (1957.), esp. pp. 280–1 and pp. 196–205

22. See Lucr. 1.139 and cf. Pliny *ep.* 4.18.1

23. cf. Cic. *fin.* 3.5 which allows new-fashioned words in the discussion of unfamiliar things

24. Cic. *Acad.* 1.4f

25. cf. Cic. *fin.* 1.6f

26. Cic. *Tusc.* 2.35f. On Latin *inopia* see too Cic. *Caec.* 51

27. Cic. *Tusc.* 3.11; cf. *div.* 1.1

28. Cic. *sen.* 45

29. cf. Quint. *I.O.* 2.14.1–4

30. Sen. *dial.* 11.2.6 (on Latin and Greek); also 3.4 (on anger)

31. Sen. *Luc.* 58.1–7; but see Quint. *I.O.* 8.3.33

32. Sen. *Luc.* 111.1; cf. *Luc.* 45.8; Aulus Gellius *N.A.* 18.13; Cic. *Acad.* 2.75

33. *N.A.* 2.26

34. For Taurus see *N.A.* 17.20; on Plutarch, *N.A.* 11.16

35. For Sextius see *Luc.* 59.7; 64; 73.12

36. For reflections on style see esp. *Luc.* 75.4; 100; 114 (on Maecenas)

37. Cic. *fin.* 2.1 and 17

38. See *Att.* 4.16.3 and 13.19.4; *fam.* 1.9.23. cf. W. Jaeger, *Aristotle*, Oxford (1948) p. 27f

39. cf. Cic. *amic.* 3

40. cf. *Luc.* 70.20

41. See J. G. R. Wright in *Seneca* (ed. Costa) London (1974) p. 45

42. Aulus Gellius *N.A.* 2.2; 14.2; 1.13; 1.26; 12.5

43. Plut. *Brutus* 12. Cic. (49 B.C.) did Greek and Latin exercises on political themes, partly because they seemed relevant, partly as an escape; see *Att.* 9.4. For a subversive question see F. Millar *JRS* 55 (1965) p. 148

44. See G. R. Stanton, *Historia* 18 (1969) p. 570f

45. Cic. *Tusc.* 5.7–10; cf. Sen. *Luc.* 89.7

46. See A-M. Malingrey, *Philosophia*, Paris (1961) p. 29f

47. Cic. *Tusc.* 4.1–5; on Pythagorean song cf. Quint. *I.O.* 9.4.12

48. For equivalents cf. Pliny *N.H.* 7.118; see U. Klima, *Untersuchungen zu dem Begriff Sapientia*, Bonn (1971)

49. Cic. *Tusc.* 2.9 and 4.6. cf. *Acad.* 1.17; *div.* 1.5; *fin.* 4.5

50. Cic. *fin.* 4.21f

51. Quint. *I.O.* 10.1.123

52. *Tusc.* 1.1; *de natura deorum* 3.5–6 and 2.8
53. *div.* 1.54f; *de natura deorum* 2.7; *fin.* 2.60; *off.* 2.26; *Tusc.* 5.105
54. Sen. *Luc.* 86.4f (Scipio); 44.3; 70.20
55. Aulus Gellius *N.A.* 7.14; 1.9; 13.24
56. Cic. *Tusc.* 3.9–11; Aulus Gellius *N.A.* 11.18. On the Twelve Tables see H. F. Jolowicz and Barry Nicholas, *A Historical Introduction to Roman Law*,³ Cambridge (1972) pp. 108–13; R. M. Ogilvie, *A Commentary on Livy 1–5*, Oxford (1965) pp. 449–50
57. Cic. *de oratore* 1.195; Aulus Gellius *N.A.* 20.1.4
58. Cic. *amic.* 9, 13, 18; Plut. *Tib. Gracch.* 8.5
59. Cic. *de oratore* 3.135
60. The name has been given, with rather more truth to philosophy, to Musonius; cf. C. Lutz, *Yale Classical Studies* 10 (1947) p. 3f
61. Sen. *Luc.* 13.14; cf. 24.6f; 70.19; 71.16; 79.14
62. Sen. *Luc.* 6.5; on precepts and principles cf. *Luc.* 94 and 95 and see below p. 171
63. Cic. *de oratore* 3.55–61 and 137–41
64. cf. A. D. Leeman, *Orationis Ratio*, Amsterdam (1963) i. p. 123
65. A different view is implied in Cic. *Brut.* 292
66. Quint. *I.O.* 1. *praef.* 10–20
67. Cic. *Tusc.* 1.112–19. cf. *fin.* 2.17 on philosophical rhetoric
68. cf. *div.* 2.27 and 89
69. *de natura deorum* 1.11
70. On Cotta see *de natura deorum* 2.1; 3.94f; *div.* 1.8
71. *div.* 1.29 (comparison with Agamemnon); 2.20 and 71
72. *de oratore*, 3.129
73. cf. *Att.* 2.3.3 with its explicit reference to being Socratic in politics
74. See *de oratore* 3.67 and cf. A. A. Long, *Hellenistic Philosophy*, London (1974) p. 89
75. See P. Friedländer, *Plato*, London (1958) i. p. 138f; W. K. C. Guthrie, *A History of Greek Philosophy*, Cambridge (1969) iii. p. 446f
76. Cic. *de oratore* 2.269f; see also Quint. *I.O.* 6.2.15 and 3.68; 9.2.44f
77. A. Haury, *L'Ironie et l'Humour chez Cicéron*, Leiden (1955) p. 274
78. See *Brut.* 292f and *de oratore* 2.272
79. Lucr. 1.62–79; 3.1–30; 5.1–54; 6.1–42
80. See e.g. *Tusc.* 2.17 and 44; 3.46
81. *Tusc.* 3.50. On Epicureans in politics see A. D. Momigliano *JRS* 31 (1941) p. 151f
82. On style see esp. *Tusc.* 2.8; *fin.* 1.14; *de natura deorum* 1.58 and 2.74
83. *de oratore* 3.63
84. See esp. *Luc.* 8.8; 21.9; 26.8; 33.2–4
85. Cic. *in Pis.* 68f; *pro Mur.* 60f
86. *N.A.* 19.1
87. *fin.* 4.23
88. *de natura deorum*, 2.147f; *Tusc.* 2.29 (Zeno)

89. For explicit remarks about Panaetius see *off.* 1.7f; 152; 161; 2.16; 51; 60; 86; 3.7; 33. Poseidonius is acknowledged at *off.* 3.8, and more generously at *Att.* 16.11.4

90. Seneca asserts his independence at *Luc.* 45.4; cf. *ben.* 1.3.6. On his rhetorical and persuasive debt to Greeks see J. G. R. Wright in *Seneca* (ed. Costa) London (1974) p. 44

91. *Luc.* 82.9f

92. Sen. *ben.* 1.3.2—4.6. See Edgar Wind, *Pagan Mysteries in the Renaissance*, Penguin Books (1967) p. 26f

93. *Luc.* 94 and 95

94. *Luc.* 90. See D. A. Russell in *Seneca* (ed. Costa) London (1974) p. 92, on this letter

SELECT BIBLIOGRAPHY

GENERAL

G. Bloch–J. Carcopino, *La république romaine de 133 avant J.-C. à la mort de Sulla*, Paris (1940).

M. L. Clarke, *Higher Education in the Ancient World*, London (1971).

G. Colin, *Rome et la Grèce de 200 à 146*, Athens (1905).

B. Forte, *Rome and the Romans as the Greeks saw them*, Rome (1972).

E. Fraenkel, *Rome and Greek Culture:* Inaugural Lecture, Oxford (1935).

L. Friedländer, *Roman Life and Manners*, London (1965).

T. J. Haarhoff, *The Stranger at the Gate*,[2] Oxford (1948).

L. Hahn, *Rom und Romanismus im griechisch-römischen Osten*, Leipzig (1906).

R. MacMullen, *Enemies of the Roman Order*, Harvard (1967).

A. D. Momigliano, *Alien Wisdom*, Cambridge (1975).

H.-I. Marrou, *Histoire de l'Education dans l'Antiquité*,[6] Paris (1965).

N. K. Petrochilos, *Roman Attitudes to the Greeks*, Athens (1974).

R. Pfeiffer, *History of Classical Scholarship*, Oxford (1969).

H. H. Scullard, *A History of the Roman World from 753 to 146 B.C.*, London (1964).

A. J. Toynbee, *Hannibal's Legacy* ii ch. xiii, Oxford (1965).

L. P. Wilkinson, *The Roman Experience*, London (1975).

CHAPTER ONE

E. Badian, 'Philhellenism and *Realpolitik*', Cincinnati Classical Studies ii (1973) pp. 271–328.

H. C. Baldry, *The Unity of Mankind in Greek Thought*, Cambridge (1965).

—— 'The Idea of the Unity of Mankind', *Grecs et Barbares*, Fondations Hardt viii, Geneva (1961) pp. 167–95.

G. Bowersock, *Augustus and the Greek World*, Oxford (1965).

—— *Greek Sophists in the Roman Empire*, Oxford (1969).

E. L. Bowie, 'Greeks and their Past in the Second Sophistic', *Past and Present* 46 (1970) pp. 1–43.

H. Guite, 'Cicero's Attitude to the Greeks', *Greece and Rome* 9 (1962) pp. 143–59.

J. Hatzfeld, *Les trafiquants Italiens*, Paris (1919).

W. Kroll, *Die Kultur der Ciceronischen Zeit*, Leipzig (1933).

J. A. O. Larsen, 'Foreign Judges etc.', *Class. Phil.* 43 (1948) pp. 187–96.

B. Levick, *Roman Colonies in Southern Asia Minor*, Oxford (1967).

R. Lonis, *Les usages de la guerre entre Grecs et barbares*, Paris (1969).

Terence Spencer, *Fair Greece, Sad Relic*, London (1954).
G. H. Stevenson, *Roman Provincial Administration*, Oxford (1949).
S. Treggiari, *Roman Freedmen during the Late Republic*, Oxford (1969).
G. Walser, *Rom, das Reich und die fremden Völker*, Baden-Baden (1951).
A. N. Sherwin-White, *Racial Prejudice in Imperial Rome*, Cambridge (1967).
A. J. N. Wilson, *Emigration from Italy*, Manchester (1966).

CHAPTER TWO

J. H. D'Arms, *Romans on the Bay of Naples*, Cambridge Mass. (1970).
R. G. Austin, 'Quintilian on Painting and Statuary', *Classical Quarterly* 38 (1944) pp. 17–26.
G. Becatti, *Arte e Gusto negli scrittori latini*, Florence (1951).
K. Jex-Blake and E. Sellers, *The Elder Pliny's Chapters on the History of Art*, Chicago (1968).
W. den Boer, 'Religion and Literature in Hadrian's Policy', *Mnemosyne* 8 (1955) pp. 123–44.
P. Boyancé, 'La connaissance du grec à Rome', *Revue des Etudes Latines* 34 (1956) pp. 111–31.
G. Cuendet, 'Cicéron et saint Jérôme traducteurs', *Revue des Etudes Latines* 11 (1933) pp. 380–400.
M. I. Finley, *Ancient Sicily*, London (1968).
P. Graindor, *Athènes sous Hadrien*, Cairo (1934).
P. Grimal, *Les jardins romains*, Paris (1943).
I. Lana, 'I ludi capitolini di Domiziano', *Rivista di Filologia*, 29 (1951) pp. 145–60.
D. Magie, *Roman Rule in Asia Minor*, Princeton (1950).
C. Mossé, *Athens in Decline*, London (1973).
J. van Ooteghem, *L. Licinius Lucullus*, Brussels (1959).
J. J. Pollitt, *The Art of Rome*, New Jersey (1966).
—— *The Ancient View of Greek Art*, New Haven (1974).
E. Rawson, *Cicero*, London (1975).
T. Reinach, *Mithridate Eupator*, Paris (1890).
H. J. Rose, 'The Greek of Cicero', *JHS* 41 (1921) pp. 91–116.
E. Smallwood, 'Jews and Romans in the early Empire', *History Today* (1965) pp. 232–39 and 313–20.
G. B. Townend, 'The Sources of the Greek in Suetonius', *Hermes* 88 (1960) pp. 98–120.
B. H. Warmington, *Nero*, London (1969).

CHAPTER THREE

F. Buffière, *Les Mythes d'Homère et la Pensée Grecque*, Paris (1956).
G. K. Galinsky, *Aeneas, Sicily and Rome*, Princeton (1969).
A. Gwynn, *Roman Education*, Oxford (1926).
J. Perret, *Les origines de la légende troyenne de Rome*, Paris (1942).

E. D. Phillips, 'Odysseus in Italy', *JHS* 73 (1953) pp. 53–67.
W. B. Stanford, *The Ulysses Theme*, Oxford (1954).
Gordon Williams, *Tradition and Originality in Roman Poetry*, Oxford (1968).

CHAPTER FOUR

S. F. Bonner, *Roman Declamation*, Liverpool (1949).
P. Burke, *The Renaissance*, London (1964).
L. Casson, *Travel in the Ancient World*, London (1974).
K. M. Chrimes, *Ancient Sparta*, Manchester (1949).
P. Gay, *Style in History*, London (1974).
M. Grant, *Roman Myths*, Penguin (1973).
W. Hoffmann, *Das literarische Porträt Alexanders des Grossen*, Leipzig (1907).
A. D. Momigliano, 'Herodotus in the History of Historiography', *History* 43 (1958) pp. 1–13.
R. M. Ogilvie, *A Commentary on Livy 1–5*, Oxford (1965).
P. Perrochat, *Les modèles Grecs de Salluste*, Paris (1949).
E. Rawson, *The Spartan Tradition in European Thought*, Oxford (1969).
R. Syme, *Tacitus*, Oxford (1958).
—— *Sallust*, Oxford (1964).
H. Tudor, *Political Myth*, London (1972).
P. G. Walsh, *Livy*, Cambridge (1961).

CHAPTER FIVE

M. L. Clarke, *Rhetoric at Rome*, London (1953).
E. R. Dodds, *Plato, Gorgias*, Oxford (1959).
A. E. Douglas, *Cicero, Brutus*, Oxford (1966).
—— *Cicero*, Oxford (1968).
O. Gigon, 'Cicero und Aristoteles', *Hermes* 87 (1959) pp. 143–62.
G. M. A. Grube, *The Greek and Roman Critics*, London (1968).
G. Kennedy, *The Art of Persuasion in Greece*, London (1963).
—— *The Art of Rhetoric in the Roman World*, Princeton (1972).
A. D. Leeman, *Orationis Ratio*, Amsterdam (1963).
D. A. Russell and M. Winterbottom, *Ancient Literary Criticism*, Oxford (1972).
B. Vickers, *Classical Rhetoric in English Poetry*, London (1970).
A. N. Sherwin-White, *The Letters of Pliny*, Oxford (1966).

CHAPTER SIX

A. Birley, *Marcus Aurelius*, London (1966).
P. Brunt, 'Marcus Aurelius in his Meditations', *JRS* 64 (1974) pp. 1–20.
C. D. N. Costa (editor), *Seneca*, London (1974).
T. Degraff, 'Plato in Cicero', *Class. Phil.* 35 (1940) pp. 142–53.
D. Furley, 'Translations from Greek Philosophy', in *Aspects of Translation*, London (1958) pp. 52–64.

U. Klima, *Untersuchungen zu dem Begriff Sapientia*, Bonn (1971).

A. A. Long, *Hellenistic Philosophy*, London (1974).

C. Lutz, 'Musonius Rufus, the Roman Socrates', *Yale Classical Studies* 10 (1947).

A-M. Malingrey, *Philosophia*, Paris (1961).

F. Millar, 'Epictetus and the Imperial Court', *JRS* 55 (1965) pp. 141–60.

R. Poncelet, *Cicéron Traducteur de Platon*, Paris (1957).

E. Wind, *Pagan Mysteries in the Renaissance*, Penguin (1967).

INDEX